Praise for Fix

C000067652

"From the first page, Jackie Van Dyke captivated me with her precious story. Her journey through her past heartaches, painful setbacks and true vulnerability brought me to tears. *Fixin' to Get Nekkid* explores life through the eyes of truth and challenges us all to question how much our past should define our future. In true Jackie form, she authentically shares her beautiful transformation found through God's love, and I, for one, am so grateful she did."

    —KELEN E. OWENS, M,Ed., NCC, Professional Counselor,
      Executive Director of Elevate Counseling Center

"Exposing one's heart is risky business, and Jackie Van Dyke takes on this challenge and so much more in her memoir *Fixin' to Get Nekkid*. In the tradition of solid southern writers, Jackie gives voice to love and pain, fear and ambition, family and self-discovery. Her guiding light? God. Her humorous and surprising exploits? All Jackie. *Fixin' to Get Nekkid* is Jackie's invitation to be authentic, to strip down and dive in to story, faith, and surprising transformation."

    —VIVIAN I. BIKULEGE, MBA, MFA, poet, essayist, and writing mentor

"Our stories share certain commonalities … suffering, survival, and, hopefully, salvation. Author Jackie Brewer Van Dyke delves into these themes with humor and honesty. She courageously drops the MASK in search of the MEANING and is rewarded with healing for her soul. *Fixin' to Get Nekkid* issues the challenge to embrace vulnerability and willingly expose our true-and too often hidden-selves. You will be inspired reading about her journey, but better yet let this book precipitate your own journey toward a greater sense of personal insight."

    —SUSAN RUTHERFORD, Teacher and Trauma Counselor

Fixin' to Get Nekkid

Stripping Down My Journey of **Freedom** and **Recovery** from Codependency

JACKIE BREWER VAN DYKE

HIGH BRIDGE BOOKS
HOUSTON

Fixin' to Get Nekkid
by Jackie Brewer Van Dyke

Copyright © 2023 by Jackie Brewer Van Dyke

All rights reserved.

Printed in the United States of America
ISBN: 978-1-954943-84-1

This work depicts actual events in the life of the author as truthfully as recollection permits and/or can be verified by research. Occasionally, dialogue consistent with the character or nature of the person speaking has been supplemented. All persons within are actual individuals; there are no composite characters. The names of some individuals have been changed to respect their privacy.

High Bridge Books titles may be purchased in bulk for educational, business, fundraising, or sales promotional use. For information, please contact High Bridge Books via www.HighBridgeBooks.com/contact.

Published in Houston, Texas by High Bridge Books.

Cover and author bio photos by April Elizabeth Photography

Lovingly dedicated to my husband, my sons and my DILs who have put up with and still managed to love, support, encourage and pray for me through the long, arduous process of writing my story. Also, without whom I might have finished this book several years ago. (wink)

Seriously though, thank you all for the last few years of graduations, weddings, out of state moves, ordinations, vacations, holiday dinners, many nights of playing STRIFEagories (our family version of Scattergories), but mostly for the greatest gifts of all ...

Jesse
Jude
Kyler
Barrett
John

You boys are truly MJ's ♥
I love you ALL more than words could say
(and y'all know I'm never lacking words to say)

Contents

Foreword

When I was seven years old, I remember having a beautiful teacher that I really wanted to impress with my newfound second-grade coolness. Simultaneously, I had a mom that wanted me to give her a kiss every morning when she dropped me off at school in front of this same teacher. Though I loved my mom dearly, I knew that giving *her* a kiss would totally ruin my chances of ever landing one on the cheek from the lovely Ms. P. So, I told my mom the smooches were on pause.

"What's the matter, don't want to kiss your mom!?"

"Nope. Sorry Mom. I'm too big for all that."

"Well, alright then, Son. Have you ever heard of the "Funky Chicken"?

"Um. No.... what is it?"

"It's a dance, Son. A goofy dance that will require me to get out of the car and flap my arms like a chicken all the way around the car while clucking. Really loudly. Would you like to see it?"

"No. NO Mom...please don't. You wouldn't...would you? I was mortified.

She leaned across to the passenger seat, closed her eyes and puckered up. Sensing that I was temporarily frozen, unsure of what to do, she winked one eye open and busted out laughing.

"Just kidding, Suhn...on ya go!" She drawled. I leaned in and gave her a quick air kiss, all the while looking over my shoulder, certain she would still deliver on her promise to demonstrate this "Funky Chicken" thing right in front of all my arriving classmates and Ms. Cutie, who I was convinced were just waiting for my mom's performance. I flung my backpack over my shoulder and bolted in, head down. That was it. The end of my short-lived swagger.

Looking back on this episode 25 years later, I recognize three truths that I was hardly conscious of at the time. One, I wholeheartedly trusted my mom, even when she was joking. Two, she loved me immensely and three, she was fearless. Ok, so I guess there are four truths...she certainly didn't mind getting naked, or "nekkid" as she always says.

Let me tell you about my first experience getting "nekkid" with my mom. Now we're definitely getting weird. To be fair, however, I did climb out of my mom's womb some thirty-plus years ago now, so it doesn't have to be *that* weird. As a result, my story is inextricably linked with hers. Isn't that the case for most people, though? Whenever we tell our own story, it almost always starts with some explanation of our parents' stories. It's a well-known fact that the people we *are* depends on the people our parents *were* – geneticists, behavioral psychologists, and just about every parent or grandparent would testify to this. The setting we are born into and grow up in sets the direction for our lives. The overlap between our parents' stories and our own is significant, even in those unfortunate cases of absent mothers or fathers. We come into this world utterly dependent. Not that I consciously remember it, but once I was unfolded from my dark, warm little sac and thrust into my mother's arms, I *needed* her. The need precedes the love, perhaps, but the most natural love is that between a mother and her child. Babies have a need, and, under normal, healthy circumstances, that need is met by the mother. What my mom might not have known then, but certainly recognizes now, is that she also needed me. She tells me that I was the first person in her life that she felt loved her without condition and who needed her, not to fix or change, but to just love her, as she was. It's hard to say with confidence that there is such a thing as unconditional love between humans, but we get darn close with our kids.

And my mom certainly has a knack for getting others to bare their soul with her. The forum for such dialogues has varied wildly over the years – from car rides to and from school to our worn-out leather couches in the living room, from over a glass of wine in my twenties, to sipping coffee on Saturday evenings now – but the nature of the conversation has remained relatively consistent. Even at seven, when she wasn't funky-chickening around the car, we'd often sit together and discuss deeper subjects than most moms and sons ever broach. As a young boy, I trusted my mom with everything in me. Many of the things she told me, even rather boldly promised me, have changed my faith—in people and in God. From the time the first love of my life dumped me, when Mom came in to pick up the pieces of my broken heart, until today, with a wife and three kids of my own, I seek out her wisdom on a regular basis. She speaks the truth in love in a way that hardly anyone else can. Why? Well for one, it's therapy. But two, I have seen that woman go through so many trials in her own life and I've heard countless stories about her childhood and life before I came around. Time and again I've seen her lean on her faith and the love she has for her family. She may not always have the perfect, or unbiased answer, but at the center of it all, is a woman who loves first and learns from her mistakes. Her journey that you have the privilege to explore on the following pages shares so much of that learning and may inspire some course corrections on your part. I know that's my mom's hope. But more than that, I believe her story is one that ultimately points to the greatest story ever told.

I am certainly no expert on codependency, though I have certainly learned a ton about it since my mom started sharing her theme for her memoir. What I do know is my mom's story: that of a woman who eventually comes to grips with the freeing, true message that *we cannot fix ourselves, and we cannot fix each other*. When she set out to write this book a few years ago, I don't think any of us knew the direction it would take, but I was certain of two things: one, exploring the catacombs of her memories and opening those long-abandoned rooms in her mind would offer healing and refreshment to her spirit; and, two, she could alter the trajectory for so many other lives on a similar path and point them to the ultimate truth. If even one person reads this book and is able to release the chains that bind them the way she did, it was all worth it. Spoiler alert: Even as her son, it changed my life, even though I thought I already knew the story!

—**Hayden Van Dyke,**
LCDR, US Navy
MBA

Introduction

Strippers, Addicts, and Fixers ... Oh My!

Nothing anonymous about this ... no twelve-step program to follow ... no meetings to attend. Just an opportunity to get real. Take it off. Strip down. Be vulnerable. That is what I am willing to do, and trust me, it did not come easy for me, nor might it for you.

Let's start with a few of my own personal definitions/explanations/ metaphors. You won't see official sources given because these are straight out of my head and based upon my experiences.

- NEKKID— vulnerable; uncovered; exposed; undisguised; raw; bare-butt; unadorned.

- STRIPPER—one who is willing to be all the above—emotionally, relationally, and spiritually; definitely NOT PHYSICALLY (lest anyone get the wrong idea)—especially while viewing themselves through the "proverbial mirror"; One who wishes to stop hiding behind a mask of attempted perfection. One who will expose their true self—pain, scars, and all—in an effort to heal.

- ADDICTION—a thing, activity, substance, or proclivity that a person finds themselves thinking about or doing an exorbitant amount of time. A thing one believes will bring them peace, relaxation, enjoyment, or respite. Often called "coping skills" by certain people who don't like to use the word addiction. A word/condition that is OFTEN argued; justified; rationalized—depending on who you are.

- FIXER—helper; problem-solver; approval addict; white knight syndrome; control freak. One who might find themselves often correcting others; offering a "better way" to do things; believe they are born to "assist others" in everything, to the point that they take on a personal responsibility and often feel like a failure if they are not accepted into that role. Those who are always thinking to themselves, "why wouldn't that person do it the way I would do it?" Fixer personality disorder can be an emotional need that can lead to feelings of uselessness if their attempts are ignored or unsuccessful.

- CODEPENDENT—another often misunderstood word/ term and based upon who defines it. An unhealthy pattern of thinking and coping in relationships. Often rooted in childhood, it is where one begins to think that their worth depends upon whether they are able to help, control, or fix problems in their family. This can lead into adulthood where they begin to believe that they are not worthy enough to be loved unless they are needed. I define it as simply a "need to be needed in order to be loved." A relationship addiction of sorts, and not in a healthy way. It may or may NOT have anything to do with alcohol or substance abuse but is often associated with both.

Okay, so here's my disclaimer: as I explained initially, these are my definitions, insights, and opinions based upon my personal experiences in life. I am not an expert, a mental health professional, or otherwise educated authority on any of these things. But my "school of hard knocks" approach, while a bit cliché', has brought me to where I am today. I am only here to share and tell my story.

I have been ALL the abovementioned titles, but I never thought I would be willing to admit it. I have tried to live securely tucked in the middle of conservative safety and extreme boundaries. I have attempted to appear all "buttoned up," keep my "church face" on, smile, and act like all is right in my world. I always thought, *I'm not going to expose myself or let anyone get too close to me. Keep your distance, please.* I never wanted anyone to see my brokenness.

I don't feel that way now and have been finally set free from trying to pretend and hope that people would love and respect me anyway. I've adopted the attitude of *I'll show you mine if you show me yours.* No more hiding. I've made my choice; I'll live naked and squeeze my eyes shut tightly as I do so. I might occasionally wink one open—just to sneak a peek of who's looking and what they might be thinking. But mostly, I'll enjoy the freedom of taking it all off: the burdens, the masks, the coveted persona of what I have tried to achieve, impossibly. No longer trying to cover up the unsightly, dangly bits that I've been ashamed of. This is the buck-nekkid version of who I really am. Sure, it's easier to keep those ugly parts hidden, right? No respectable southern lady should be willing to just strip down and show all her hidden stuff, should she? Yeah, well … I am willing. Besides that, I've never been accused of being overly respectable.

Ultimately, it's a story of recovery, redemption, and learning to love myself. If you catch a recognizable glimpse of yourself in these stories, know that you, too, can be free to love and be loved.

> Therefore, since we are surrounded by such a huge crowd of witnesses to our life of faith, let us *strip off* every weight that slows us down, especially the sin that so easily trips us up. (Heb. 12:1 NLT, emphasis added)

Y'all ready to strip down and get naked? I am.

Part One

Mama said things will get easier. Things will be brighter. Some-day, we'll walk in the beautiful sun. She couldn't tell me when, but she promised. I believed her.

—paraphrased from "Ooh-ooh Child,"
a song by The Five Stairsteps

1

Rainy Night in Georgia

December 2015

I was tired of being drunk. And angry. I'd had enough, and this was the night I would finally do something about it. What I didn't know was that this would end up being the worst, and the best, night of my life.

I sank to the floor, holding a half-empty bottle of chardonnay in one hand and my cell phone in the other. My head was spinning. I had a decision to make. I felt my body stiffen as my thoughts raced. *I'm doing it. I'm so tired of this. I can't take it anymore.* I punched in the numbers.

"9-1-1 ... what is your emergency?"

Suddenly I couldn't breathe. *Am I having a heart attack?* I couldn't think clearly, and my heart was pounding out of my chest. I didn't answer.

"Hello ... this is 911. I repeat, what is your emergency?"

"Help..." It came out as a broken whisper.

"What is your location?"

I clicked my phone off. *Oh my God, what have I done? Why am I so stupid?*

I dropped both the wine bottle and my phone onto the floor and instinctively wrapped my arms around my knees, dropped my head and rocked back and forth. I'm not even sure what time it was, but it was dark. Really dark. The inky blackness surrounded me, so thick and heavy, that I could almost feel it pressing down on my skin. But despite its suffocating presence, I couldn't shake the feeling that this night held something even darker. Hearing the sirens blare in the distance, my hands instinctively shot up to cover my ears, as if cupping them, my shaking hands would drown out the nightmarish sounds that assailed me from all sides. But even as I did so, the voices in my head continued to scream and clamor for my attention.

Loser!

You're an idiot!

Have you lost your freakin' mind?

I was startled when I heard the sound of an open palm banging on my front door, not bothering to ring the doorbell; this was not a social call. Forcing myself to stand up, I managed to stumble to the front door. I switched on the porch light and peered through the side panes. The officer's countenance that met my gaze was solemn and serious. I also saw the ambulance lights flashing just adjacent to the police car. *Oh my God.* The last time one of our local police officers had knocked on that same door had been just a few months prior, telling me that my next-door neighbor and dear friend, Denise, needed me to come over immediately. Her husband had passed away suddenly. I knew that a police officer standing at my front door was never a good thing. I swallowed hard, clicked the deadbolt, and opened the door.

"Ma'am, are you okay?"

"Um ... yes. I mean, no. I don't know ... I didn't mean to call! I shouldn't have called..."

"Do you need an ambulance? Are you injured?" he persisted.

"No ... I'm okay..." My voice trailed off.

"Ma'am ... someone from this house dialed 911. What is the emergency?" His voice was angry, demanding. I could only stare at him; I didn't have an answer.

"Are you alone in the house?"

"No. My husband is upstairs." He motioned for the EMT to hold off, as he pushed past me and bounded up the stairs. I could no longer stand so I collapsed into the chair beside the door, my breathing quick and shallow. My eyes were darting from the stairs back to just outside my front door, where the emergency vehicles were parked askew, waiting for further instructions from the officer. I could barely hear their voices from upstairs. I wasn't worried. I knew no one was hurt, just drunk. I allowed my eyes to close as I passed out.

Minutes later, I was awakened to realize I was being lifted up by one arm.

"Get up, Mrs. Van Dyke. C'mon ... I need you to stand up and walk." Again, the voice was gruff and irritated.

I wasn't wearing a coat as I began to stumble out the door and across my front yard, quickly realizing how frigid the air was outside. And it was pouring down rain, the wind blowing the rain in slanting sheets. I closed my eyes and tucked my head down but could still feel the relentless slap, slap, slap of the rain against my face. It stung. I instinctively wrapped my arms tightly around my body, dropped my chin down even further, and began what felt like a slow-motion jog toward my destination, which was the unwelcome car parked in front of my house. The man who was holding my arm leading me forward, opened the door to the back seat, and pushed me inside. I jumped, startled, as I felt the heavy door slam against me. I sat there, numb and motionless.

Once inside the car, the night sky appeared to become even blacker, and the heavy rain continued and began to sound like it was pounding on the roof of that car. That is when I realized just how extremely cold it was on that December night. Not just the temperature, but also inside my heart, colder than anything I could ever remember. Like the darkness–it was all encompassing, wrapping itself around me like a burial shroud. I felt myself shaking uncontrollably and was only vaguely aware of the flood of hot tears streaming down my cheeks.

I finally lifted my head and attempted to peer through the foggy window from the back seat of the car. I could barely see my house. I tried, unsuccessfully, to reach up and wipe the glass so I could see it better. I pressed my face up against the window and squinted, desperate to see it. Of course, I knew it well: this house, our home, that my husband and I had built and where we had raised our family for so many years. I thought about the old saying, "If walls could talk." Well, these walls would tell of laughter and love, and plenty of both. The walls would say that this home was filled with mostly good—why, they might even use the adjective "great" —memories. My head dropped again. I had to look away. Walls don't talk. And that night, I was thankful; I didn't want to hear them.

As my head hung on my shoulders, I felt the tears dropping from my cheeks onto my lap. I closed my eyes tightly and shook my head, as if trying to shake away, even unsee, what was going through my head. I thought to myself, as I had a million times through the years,

C'mon, Girl! Be strong. Don't give in to your emotions! Toughen up ... you can fix this!

But I couldn't, not this time. I felt helpless.

I looked back up. The window was even foggier now. And mixed with the burning tears, everything was just a blur. But I squinted, desperate to see the house we had just decorated a few days prior. It was all aglow with Christmas lights and wreaths. I managed a smile as I remembered past Christmases there, in such a beautiful neighborhood. I glanced down our street at all the other pretty homes, all perfectly decorated with colorful Christmas lights. They looked a bit like little twinkling islands of bright and cheery shades of green, red, and gold, despite the surrounding darkness and the freezing rain. Our happy, little street was lined with other happy, little houses, filled with happy, little families with 2.5 kids, puppies, and fenced-in yards. The sardonic thought occurred to me that perhaps the fences had been erected in our efforts to contain, inside our properties, the illusions we had created of perfect bliss. Perhaps we had put those fences up to keep out anything or anyone that might disrupt the perfect lives we imagined we had. Or pretended to have. Funny, isn't it, how easily we can "decorate" any facade, and no one ever needs to know what's inside?

I attempted to push those cynical thoughts away as I continued to peer down the street. I then imagined that all the twinkling lights were dancing, as if to the beat of the faint Christmas music I could barely hear playing in the background on the car radio. The happy holiday tunes in stark contrast to what that car otherwise represented. I became mesmerized. My mind wanted to transport my body outside of the reality of where I was, so I did what I had always done as a little girl—dove into my imagination. Create a happy story, the fairy tale that I had dreamed about but never thought I could attain.

I continued to stare blankly at this wonderful, magical array of flashing lights. But the truth was at that very moment, through my eyes blurred from tears and straining to look through the rain and fog, the only lights that were prominent to me were from a blue light rotating around from somewhere overhead. It was throwing intermittent bright blue beams across the facade of my home. I then realized that, even louder than the Christmas music playing faintly on the car radio, there was the hateful, crackling sound of another radio—the two-way device that was interrupting the fairy-tale video I had playing in my head. The reality was those random, bright blue flashing lights did not bring me joy at all. I was also acutely aware of the cold, metal device that was pinching my wrists.

I could see my husband who, by this time, was standing on the front porch, devastated, but helpless to do anything for me. I had to close my eyes; it was too difficult to look at him. I couldn't help myself, so I glanced up one more time, hoping this wasn't really happening. I closed my eyes again, this time tighter. Like somehow, if I looked away and squeezed my eyes as hard as I could, this might all go away.

I can't believe this is happening. Dear Lord, please help me ... I didn't mean to do this!

The man slid into the front seat of the car and began to slowly pull away from the curb and drive down the street. As we drove away from my home, I wanted to turn around and still see my house, but I was unable to twist my body around far enough to get a good look back. This would become a metaphor in my life ... looking back with regret and wondering what I could have done to fix this, but realizing I couldn't.

I returned my gaze toward the front of the car, attempting to look through the front windshield, but all I could see was a black grid in front of me, separating the back seat from the front. I caught a glimpse, in the rearview mirror, of the man's eyes looking back at me. I had to look away, as I could no longer stifle the cries that were rising from deep within my soul—my gut was wrenching. The cries came out in short gasps, and the burning tears felt hot on my cheeks. The feeling felt the same as the pain I remembered from so many years ago, from a life and memories I thought I had buried. A life of sadness and fears that I thought I had overcome and had hoped to never experience again.

The metal was pinching now. I began to writhe around, hoping to loosen its awful grip, even if only slightly. I wondered how much longer I could take it. The man driving me away was ignoring my sobs and all my desperate questions.

"Wait ... please! Is this for real? Am I dreaming? Where are you taking me? What did I do wrong?" I was asking myself, more than him. Of course, I knew the answer.

"You're getting exactly what you deserve," he snapped. His voice was flat and emotionless. As I continued to maintain eye contact with his reflection in the rearview mirror, all I could see were his unforgiving, judgmental eyes looking back at mine. I shook my head, tucked my chin back into my chest, and asked myself the same questions over and over again.

"What have I done … Dear Lord, what have I done?"

Of course, I knew. I had always been a strong-willed, impetuous girl—often reacting impulsively whenever anything scared me. And I also knew my tendency was to react in anger anytime I feared anything. Tonight, I was in shock and disbelief. And I didn't have answers to all the questions swirling through my head. Answers I had convinced myself I would always have. I had *willed* myself to have.

Then, the realization that I couldn't fix this. Not this time.

I was so sad, uncharacteristically scared, and profoundly aware that I was not nearly as strong as I'd always proclaimed to be.

2

Pickin' Scabs

That rainy night taught me a lot about choices. And about shame, which is a horrible thing. When I was growing up, my mama used to tell us, "Shame on you for thirty minutes!" whenever we did something wrong. She always said it laughingly but never wanted us to feel real shame. I always knew when I had been disobedient, and it always mattered to me if I disappointed her because I never liked to break rules. I always felt judged and thought if I always followed rules and never broke them, I would be accepted. Back then, I would do almost anything to be accepted.

Mama would always tell me what a good girl I was and how she trusted me to always make the right choice. But back then, I didn't understand how important my choices would be. How much they would matter. I know this now. I always told my own kids that everything that happened to them in this life would come as a result of the choices they would be faced with. I told them, "Disobedience brings consequences, so that makes it your choice. Obedience brings blessings. Again, your choice. So, what did you choose today? Consequences or blessings?" It was important for my kids to understand that there is a difference in just being a bad kid versus one who will invariably make poor choices and break the rules on occasion, like we all do. I wanted them to understand there was power in their choices. And I would hope that they would never feel they were less than anyone else, as I often had. However, this time the consequences of my rule-breaking would be life-changing.

Six weeks after that horrible December night, the aftermath of my poor choices continued. I was required to attend court-ordered family reconciliation group sessions.

I remained mortified, hating myself for being so stupid, but was determined to put on a brave face. I resigned myself to go but was never going to let them see me sweat.

The small, red brick county government building was unassuming, and the façade was typical with only a few visible windows. I intentionally parked around on the side of it just in case there might be someone in another department of the building who might recognize me or my car. I didn't believe I belonged there.

All heads turned when I walked in. The little bell chimed loudly, indicating another poor sap had entered the premises. I was not happy to be there and from the looks on their faces, neither were any of the others. I smiled, shot a cursory glance across the sea of faces, then lifted my chin confidently as I strode up to the front desk. There was an old clipboard dangling from a chain in front of a sliding glass window that had a sheet with one simple word typed at the top—ARRIVAL. I obediently signed my name on the next available dotted line. The girl behind the glass never looked up. I turned back to the open room to take a seat.

I was surprised to see how large the waiting room was. There were rows of armchairs: some connected, others single. Most were occupied. It hadn't occurred to me how many people might be there when I had made my required appointment. Clearly, there were plenty of other people who were being forced to obtain "assistance" with their attitudes. Counseling, they called it. Getting "help," whether you think you need it or not. I sure didn't. I was only here because I was told I must, and I most certainly didn't want to discuss it with any of the other folks in that room. I chose an empty chair that wasn't near anyone else. Not in the mood to chit-chat.

I looked around and checked to see if there was a place to sit my purse. The old red carpet appeared to have seen better days and was quite frayed, well-worn. I decided to just hold the purse in my lap. I felt myself clutching it tightly, wondering why I had brought it inside. When I looked down, I noticed my knuckles were white. My heart was racing. I took a deep breath, exhaling slowly. As I raised my head back up, I was determined to look confident. Self-assured. Not nervous at all. I had lots of practice doing that.

The room was well lit by fluorescent lights, and, despite that, there were lamps on all the tables located between the chairs. I couldn't help but notice the shades were still covered in the plastic wrapping. The chairs were navy blue with thin wooden arms, which were not big enough for anyone to rest their arms on. I waited, trying not to be so obvious in looking around but I couldn't help myself. I didn't expect there to be so many people. But then again, I had no idea what to expect. I had never been in a place like this, nor a situation. Unfamiliar territory.

I found an old issue of *Reader's Digest* mixed in with copies of *Family Circle* and the kid's *Highlights* coloring books and Bible stories. *Well, they sure have something for everyone here.* I rolled my eyes inwardly before picking up the *Reader's Digest*, pretending to read. I even forced a smile and intentionally let out a fake chuckle as I read the section "Laughter, The Best Medicine." If the other waiting "patients" happened to be assessing me, they would see that I'm not worried. Or sad. I didn't want to appear uncomfortable or awkward. But I felt both.

I occasionally tilted my gaze upward to check out what all the others who were waiting were doing. I mentally assessed them. Why were the women with young children there? They appeared frazzled and eager to get whatever it was over and done with. And there were also a few men who I decided might also be there because they were forced to be. There seemed to only be a handful of older folks. *Ha,* I thought to myself, *older people know better.* They have long ago learned what to do and what situations to avoid. I thought I had too. I was certainly no spring chicken, for goodness' sake. Yet here I was.

When the inside door that led from the waiting room to the inner sanctum of the place opened, all the faces looked up, questioning if it might finally be their turn to be called back. I watched as one name after another was called from that opened door. Finally.

"Mrs. Van Dyke?" The lady appeared to be about my age, maybe a couple years older. I really couldn't tell. But I was thankful she wasn't a kid, which, at that time, in my mid-fifties, was anyone under thirty-five. She was wearing a calf-length khaki skirt and a tucked-in blue Oxford. Her hair was mousey brown with greying temples and pulled back by a barrette. Brown clogs. Comfortable.

"Yes, Ma'am," I answered cheerfully, as I returned the *Reader's Digest* to the little table, gathered my purse, stood, smoothed my slacks, and began to walk toward the open door. Head held high and with feigned confidence, I met her eyes and smiled. She did too. She had a sweet face. Good start.

As the door closed, I made sure to pause so that I could fall into step behind her. Keeping my happy, unfazed face on, I commented, "Lead the way!" *Keep the smile on, Girl.*

"Yes, right this way," she spoke while walking down the long hall, with her back facing me. I tried not to but couldn't help but sneak a glance or two into some of the other little rooms lining the hallway. Finally, at the end of the hallway, she ushered me into a rather large office with lots of windows overlooking the parking lot. At least it wasn't a small, dark, windowless office. I needed to see a ray of sunshine.

She quietly shut the door behind us and gestured toward the chair that was angled strategically in front of where she would be sitting. As she walked around a large desk and took a seat in her leather winged office chair, I was assessing her. I couldn't help myself. I imagined that she must be one of the "big wigs" here. Or, as we used to say, one of the "head honchos." Part of me was impressed while the other part of me wondered why I needed her. Why had I been escorted all the way back to this large, corner office and why her? All kinds of thoughts occurred to me. *Maybe they think I need the "big guns" pulled out for me.* That's another one of my old southern expressions. *They must think I'm a hard case.*

I sat down in a burgundy swivel chair across from her. After shuffling some papers around on her desk, stopping to study one form in particular, she finally looked up at me. I was still staring directly at her, waiting. *Who goes first here?* I sure didn't know, but I was ready. Poised to defend myself, but not sure why I had set myself to do that. Old habits die hard, I suppose.

"So, why are you here?"

"Because I was instructed to come." Again, the feigned smile.

"Do you think you need to be here?"

"Frankly, no." I forced a sarcastic laugh. "But I have been raised to follow the rules, and this is what they told me I had to do." I realized the irony of that statement. *Follow the rules?*

"Okay." Her only response through a tight-lipped smile. Her facial expression seemed to be saying, *"Bless your heart."*

I looked down and noticed my folded arms and rigid bent legs, knees touching as I bounced my legs up and down. This was what I always did anytime I felt nervous or apprehensive, and I was feeling a combination of both. And a twinge of defiance. *Who does she think she is? Trying to get in my head...*

"How's your marriage?"

"Fine." Curt, short, and sweet. I stared directly at her. I was determined to maintain calm confidence.

"How long?"

"Almost thirty years." I was proud of that. I bet not many people who came to see her could boast about this fact.

"So, what does your husband think about all this?"

"He's *fine* too." I almost hissed and could feel my gritted teeth. *What difference does that make, you nosy bitch?* I didn't like that my vocabulary still automatically deferred to "bad words," as Mama always called them, the words I had grown up hearing my entire life. I felt a bit like a feral animal backed into a corner, ready to bite. Fear most always manifests as anger with me.

"Ok, good. That sure helps. You'll need his support." She looked back down and shuffled some more papers. I never took my eyes off her, knees still rigid and bouncing.

"Do you have a good marriage?" she asked without looking up.

"Yes, of course!" I answered, waving her off with a pish. "I mean, like all couples, we have occasional issues ... doesn't everyone?" I glanced down, still shaking my head and smiling uncomfortably.

"Really?" She looked at me with her left brow raised and chin tucked.

"Yes ... REALLY! Look, we both know why I'm here, so clearly there have been some problems. You know that—you've got all the details right there in front of you." I gestured toward her desk and the pile of papers she kept looking down to read. She continued to look at me. Silent. "No need to sit there all pompous and ask me questions about what you OBVIOUSLY already know. Can we just get to whatever we need to do here? What happened is over and done with. I've accepted my punishment, done my time, and I'm sorry about it, and I'm moving on. No need for the interrogation, Ma'am." By now, I felt myself shaking, and my bottom lip had begun to quiver; I hated that about myself. I had always had difficulty talking about anything painful without crying. She was picking at old wounds that I thought had healed. I guess they hadn't completely healed, just scabbed over. And I could feel the scab coming off and the blood beginning to trickle. Damn it!

She appeared to slightly soften. Or was it pity?

"What's wrong, Jackie? Why are you so angry?"

"I'm NOT angry!" I laughed incredulously, this time throwing my head back while shaking it back and forth to indicate *no, no NO! You are NOT going there, lady!* I felt a single tear slip out and trail down one cheek, which I quickly swiped away. Then I leaned down and considered gathering my purse to prepare to leave. Before I could do it, I noticed she had reached across her desk and was offering a tissue in her extended hand. I took it and gently wiped my eye, sniffed demonstratively and self-assuredly.

"Does he abuse you?"

"NO!" I snapped. "NEVER!"

"Then what happened? Why are you here?"

Initially, I just stared at her wide-eyed, attempting to come up with some sort of reason that might make sense. I leaned forward a bit, trying to think of something to say. A good answer. I didn't have one.

"I'm not sure..." I could hear my voice trailing, and I finally had to look away. My confidence had ebbed, I couldn't maintain the façade of confident eye contact, and I could feel myself sinking back into the chair. My head dropped, and I could no longer hold back the tears. "I've been asking myself the same question."

She looked back down at the papers on her desk, began to straighten and stack them up and return them to a folder. As she slid the folder off to the side, it became apparent that she was no longer looking at the reports. She folded her arms and leaned over the closed file, looking directly at me. Her voice was not accusatory this time.

"Tell me about your childhood. What was it like in your home growing up?"

Silently, I returned her gaze. I had no words. Her eyes were soft, caring.

I looked down and allowed mine to close, as I felt one last tear escape and slide down to my chin.

3

Talladega Nights

Taking a journey back into days I've tried my best to forget is difficult. All these years later, just when I think I've conquered the pain of the past, moved on, healed ... I realize I haven't. There is that old wound, being ripped right back open, feeling as fresh and as painful as it had forty years earlier. Sometimes, worse. At least when an injury initially happens, it's a new pain, new blood. I can deal with it while it's fresh, maybe even be able to stop the bleeding quickly and prevent it from scarring. But sometimes it's the old wounds, with scars so thick around them that I think they can't possibly be re-opened. Then suddenly, I feel a dagger so sharp that it easily slices the wound open again, and my heartbeat stops for a few seconds. I feel that familiar, painful tightness in my throat. My lungs constrict, making it hard to breathe. My lips tremble, as the visions from my past return.

I'm glad that I have now forced myself to look back, to discover why I have struggled with so much anger and insecurity as an adult. Why I had become so determined to control my destiny, and everything and everyone in my life. In realizing I was so wounded that I unwittingly masked it with what I perceived as grit, steadfastness, and determination, I promised I would never ever live a life like the one my mother had.

So, when that court-ordered counselor asked me why I was so angry, I immediately experienced self-loathing, blaming myself for allowing the anger to surface in the first place. I had promised myself I never would. Then when she asked me to tell her about my childhood, I stiffened, not wanting to remember. But I knew I had to.

With veins beating a visible pulse beneath my skin, elbows pressed into my sides, and collapsing into myself, I felt very small. And scared. I thought those old fears were gone, but they weren't. My thoughts wandered back to when I was a little girl. I closed my eyes and swallowed hard as I remembered.

Talladega, Alabama 1960s and early 1970s

A typical Saturday in our small, rural Alabama town consisted of ... well ... a whole lot of nothing. My older sister, Jean, and I had a routine, though. We never failed to tune in to our favorite TV show, *American Bandstand*. It was the only television show back then that she and I watched regularly. Come to think of it, we never sat down as a family to watch television together; it was mostly for Daddy to watch his sports. Even though we could barely afford our tiny rental house with ripped linoleum floors and no air conditioning, Daddy always made sure he had a big ol' console television set. I remember it never looked like it "fit" in that tiny, little room with yellowed walls—evidence of a decade of my parents' smoking unfiltered cigarettes—the second or thirdhand couch and chairs, and those plastic curtains on the window that Mama would buy at Elmore's Five and Dime. We didn't have window blinds, but I do remember the old, brown, crusty roll-up shades. Daddy always wanted them down so no one could see inside. He would say it was to keep the sunlight out because he worked third shift and slept during the day, but we knew he just didn't want any of our neighbors to accidentally see inside the house.

This particular Saturday, Jean and I would scoot up to that big, fancy television set and plant ourselves, cross-legged, on the floor right in front of it. It was our favorite part of the week. We could always count on Dick Clark to entertain us with the latest pop star, and he never disappointed. We especially loved The Jackson Five, and I'd always act out the song "ABC," complete with a hairbrush as a pretend microphone and spreading my fingers demonstratively as I danced and belted out "easy as one, two, three... simple as do-re-mi...ABC!"

Jean and I loved music. When we weren't watching *American Bandstand*, we'd turn on the old radio that was also in that room. It sat on top of Daddy's fancy TV, right beside Mama's ceramic Siamese cat lamp that she got by saving up a few books of S & H green stamps. Just above it hung a crooked brass frame surrounding a picture of a mountain, maybe trees, clouds ... I don't exactly remember. It was some cheap print probably also picked up at a thrift store. Mama told us to never move that picture because she liked it; it made her feel peaceful, so we didn't touch it.

Yep, Jean and I liked our Saturday mornings, but never knew what to expect on Saturday nights.

One random Saturday evening, Mama and Daddy were in the living room after having been out most of the day. When they went "out," Jean and I never asked where they were going or what they were doing. Quite honestly, we were just happy to be left home alone sometimes, as we always found something fun to do together. Jean was five years older than me, so most Saturday nights she went to spend the night with her friend Regina, or one of her other friends from the little school we attended. Back then, it never occurred to me why none of Jean's friends were ever allowed to come to spend the night at our house. Most of our classmates' parents didn't allow their kids to even come over to play with us. I was only six years old at the time and was too little to understand why. I didn't understand a lot of the things I see clearly now as an adult.

After supper, I had taken my bath and had settled into my brand-new pink pajamas, still creased and stiff from the plastic packaging they had been in when Mama brought them home that morning from the dollar store. I headed into the kitchen for a quick snack and after grabbing a Honey bun® and a bottle of RC Cola®, I skipped back into the living room. Maybe we would watch *The Carol Burnett Show* because she always made us laugh. My eyes immediately fell to Daddy asleep on the couch; that was typical for him, particularly after a day of him and Mama being out at the American Legion binge drinking. I can still see that old, lumpy Naugahyde couch where he would take his "naps."

My daddy was a large man: tattooed arms, hairy chest, and balding head. He always slept on that same, old couch, right in the middle of our living room in the already too-small house. I always wondered why he didn't just go sleep in his bedroom. It sure would've made life a little easier for us, because as it was, we always had to be really quiet, tiptoeing around the house and whispering anytime we wanted to speak. Honestly, we usually just didn't speak at all. If we happened to slip up, speak too loudly, and wake him up—well, we didn't like to even think about that possibility, so we just didn't risk it.

Mama was sitting in her usual spot, the old floral armchair with an orange crocheted blanket covering the worn spots on the upholstery. As soon as she saw me walk into the room, she immediately "shushed" me. I stopped short and noticed she was holding her drink in her hand in a mock protective way, covering her glass and gesturing with her head toward, what I thought, was my sleeping father, as if to say, "Don't wake him and he'll never know..." I knew immediately what she was referring to. I had seen it so many times in my young life. Mama would secretly pour herself alcoholic drinks and try to disguise them in coke, orange juice, but mostly in sweet tea from that pitcher that was always in the fridge. I had been smiling as I had come in, hoping this might be a good Saturday night, not like most of the ones in the past I had come to dread.

I walked up to her, leaned in, and whispered, "Mama, why are you still drinking? You know it makes Daddy so mad." I could feel my legs quivering and my heart pounding. Daddy always accused Mama of drinking too much. He never thought he did, only her. She was never, ever supposed to drink by herself—only when he was there to supervise. That night, they had both already had too much. Daddy was passed out, yet Mama was still drinking. And hiding it.

"Oh, it's okay, baby—he's passed out, so he'll never know," she replied. Then she did what I had not only seen her do so many times but had come to recognize as her face of escape—she closed her eyes, took a long swallow, and I saw the faintest attempt at a smile. She had that look on her face that always spoke much louder than her words ever could. The worn expression that read *I'm just so weary, and this is what I need right now.* I knew her face very well. I remember my body tightening up as I watched her, praying that Daddy really was asleep, but I saw him stir. He wasn't.

I can still see this, as if it's a video playing in my head. Daddy shot straight up from lying on the couch and within seconds, he snatched up the saucer that was on the coffee table with smears of Blue-Plate mayonnaise on the edge of it, evidence that he had eaten his usual bologna sandwich a few minutes before. He flung it across the room at my mother, and I saw it strike the side of her head. As the bright red blood began to pour down her face, she dropped her drink. Her hands flew up to her face in a protective reaction. I stood there— frozen and unable to move. Daddy jumped up off the couch and ran over to Mama, punching her in the face. They were both screaming—she was crying, and he was cussing. I couldn't move. Mama began kicking her legs, with both arms raised and crossed, trying to cover her head and face. My thoughts were racing, but I remained paralyzed, wanting to run but frozen in that space and time.

Why is he always so angry?? Why won't he stop? What do I do now?
I felt a rush of adrenaline as suddenly my legs began to move, and I turned and ran as fast as I could into the small bedroom I shared with Jean. I clambered over the twin bed that was up against the one small window in the room; it was my only way out. I frantically tried to open that window. My hands were shaking as I fumbled with the cracked wooden frames that surrounded each pane. I pushed and pushed, crying but determined not to make any noise so Daddy wouldn't hear me. The window wouldn't budge. Heart pounding, I began to tug and pull as hard as my little arms would allow until finally it began to move. Only slightly at first, then I heaved as hard as I could, and I felt the window begin to slide up. One last final shove, and I could begin the scramble to get out.

I vaguely heard Mama run into the room, calling my name, and then felt the mattress sink in as she climbed across the bed and grabbed the hem of my pajama top, desperately trying to pull me away from the windowsill. She was crying and screaming, "No, baby, No! Don't leave—it'll be okay!" Shaking uncontrollably and blinded by tears, I continued to kick at the window screen in my attempt to flee. Out of the corner of my eye, I saw him—Daddy came bounding into the room, his face red and contorted with so much rage. In full panic mode, I pulled away from Mama as I struggled even more. It was then that I felt the warm liquid begin to run down my legs, soaking my new pink pajamas. I don't remember ever being so terrified, more afraid of what Daddy might do to Mama than to me. I just knew I had to get out that window. With one final, guttural scream, I kicked the screen as hard as I could and saw it fall outward. I immediately climbed upon the sill and jumped the six feet down to the ground. Picking myself up quickly, I ran as fast as I could into the darkness, crying and wiping my tear-streaked, dirty face but still trying to be very quiet because I was so afraid my daddy would hear me. I could just imagine that he was running right behind me. He never wanted any of us to go outside the walls of our house and tell anybody anything that went on behind closed doors.

Uncle Grady lived just a block away, so all I could think of was, *If I can just get to Uncle Grady—He'll make Daddy stop!* Uncle Grady was Daddy's uncle, my great uncle, and one of the only men that I loved and trusted. He was a big man, a sweet, gentle soul. Daddy respected him, and he was one of the only people in the world who could talk sense into my daddy. I ran as fast as my legs could carry me down the dark street until I could see his porch light in the distance. Out of breath but still running hard, I stumbled up the stairs to the front porch and began pounding my tiny fists on the door.

When the door opened, I ran in, unaware that I was soaking wet from my own urine and my tear-stained face was dirty and streaked from the windowsill and screen that I had encountered in my escape. I was heaving, crying, and breathless as I ran straight into the arms of my sweet uncle.

"What's wrong, Jackie?" he asked, as he wrapped his gentle, bear-like arms around me.

"Daddy's hurting Mama again!" I cried.

All I remember after that was him kissing the top of my head and, without a word, passing me over to Aunt Berry before he walked out the front door into the night. I knew where he was going. I could finally stop sobbing and gasping, as I relaxed into my aunt's arms and easily fell asleep. I knew Uncle Grady would make sure Mama would be okay.

As years passed, not much had changed in our family. Most of what happened in the dark places at home was kept secret. People just didn't talk about these things, but, of course, everyone really did. The "do-gooders" would never refer to it as gossip though; it was always called "prayer requests," and Sister Sally at the church led the charge.

"Y'all need to be praying for the Brewer family. Somebody said they think they heard a gun go off over there the other night. Them poor ol' young-uns. They need our prayers. And their mama, well, bless her heart ... y'all just keep 'em in your prayers, okay?" Every small town has its own version of "Sister Sally." Sally gets around; she's everywhere.

By the time I had reached the age of eleven or so, I was at a point in my life where I had certainly developed strong opinions and was not afraid to declare them to anyone who dared to disagree with me. I had grown sick and tired of seeing my daddy's violent outbursts and his tyrannical behavior. That scared, little girl had morphed into a pre-teen woman-child who just wanted to be in control and fix everyone and everything wrong in her house. God knows nobody else in the family seemed to even try. And even if they did make the effort, they couldn't do it. But I was determined to. I had become very tired of being so scared of what might happen next, what my daddy might do, and I had made up my mind that I would stand up and be strong. I had become defiant.

Daddy had started calling me a "little shit," and that was fine with me. It was better than him looking down at me cowering in a puddle of tears, then melting away and hiding in the nearest hole I could find. And the nickname he gave me was fitting because I didn't mind causing a stink.

Supper time at our house was always a roll of the dice. We just never knew what might happen. Our kitchen table was a small linoleum rectangle with little yellow flecks on its shiny top. It was covered with a large, crocheted doily that my Aunt Clara had made for my mother years before. In the center of the table was a ceramic bowl with fake ceramic fruit in it. I remember there was a little nick on the end of the banana where one of us kids had dropped it. Mama always worked a full-time clerical job but dutifully came home every day and cooked supper. That was until Jean and I were old enough to cook. Daddy slept most days because of his job, so supper was the only time we all ever sat down together. Most families in the seventies were stereotyped as being like *the Brady Bunch* or the Cunninghams on *Happy Days*. They would talk about their day, share stories, laugh, etc. Not the Brewers. Quite the contrary.

When we all sat down together, Jean and I were always nervous. *Will Daddy like the dinner tonight? Will he be mad or happy?* We would always wake him up at six p.m. to eat supper. Sweet Jean would always sit down quietly and surreptitiously look around the table ... just hoping we could eat our meals without incident. On the contrary, I sat down most days with an attitude—raring to go—just waiting to see what kind of mood Daddy would be in. I was scared also, but I dared not show it. I'd put on my fake "brave face," one of the many masks I had begun to wear, and sit there bracing myself, prepared, just in case.

Some days were quiet. No one really spoke during dinner, which was fine with us. No words were certainly better than angry words. We always ate our meals very tentatively because we just never knew. However, one night stands out in my mind, maybe because I remember this specific meal as the night I "came out of the timid closet," so to speak. I was done putting up with Daddy's moods. We had just sat down at that little, yellow table and Mama, as always, had the food arranged on the table in order of importance. Daddy sat on the end, at the head of the table, so he always went first. She had gingerly placed the entrée in front of his plate. Jean and Mama sat to the right, on one side of the table, and me to Daddy's left on the other side. This arrangement was strategic so that I was facing Mama, and Jean and I could see each other. We did this so that we could look at each other and perhaps be able to gauge Daddy's mood.

Jean and I preferred sitting across from each other just in case we needed to make eye contact to check on the other. Not sure why it mattered, except that we could at least look at each other's faces. Made us feel more secure, I suppose, but we mostly kept our heads down as we served our food out of the big bowls Mama would place in the middle of the table.

That night, Daddy seemed agitated. He sat down and scanned the spread on the table before us. In a flash, he picked up a chicken casserole and just dumped it on top of Mama's head. "What the hell is this?" he screamed. I remember looking across the table, watching my mother reach up and begin to wipe the food out of her hair, off her face, and away from her eyes. She was shaking. My eyes darted over to my sixteen-year-old sister, who immediately had a look of terror on her face but decided to hang her head, chin to chest, and cry. Quietly though, as she dared not make him any madder. I remember looking at her, then back to my mother, still trembling with fear, and I lost it. What felt like an unseen force came over me, and before I even realized it, I bolted upright, slammed both my fists onto that table, and found myself leaning in toward Daddy, shaking.

"What is WRONG with you?!?" I literally screamed the words. I was tired of always being scared of him.

My big, angry daddy snapped his head around and was facing me directly. Determined not to show him my fear, I continued to lean in, staring directly into his eyes. OK, so this was not what he expected—at all. He was used to everyone cowering in fear and withdrawing whenever he did something like this. So, when he saw his eleven-year-old daughter get all up on her "hind legs," as Daddy used to say, reminiscent of a dog preparing for a fight, he looked shocked. I had never seen that expression on his face before. But it only lasted seconds. He stood up immediately, and as soon as he did, it was clear to me how big he was and how very little I was.

What are you thinking? My thoughts raced, and my once "bowed up" frame sunk into fear. I closed my eyes very tightly, braced myself, and waited. But he didn't hit me.

Oh, God—now what? I continued to try to come up with my next move, but just couldn't bring myself to do anything but stand there, never taking my eyes off him.

"GET IN YOUR DAMN ROOM ... RIGHT NOW!!" He roared at Jean and I simultaneously but continued to stare at me. Jean scooted away immediately, but I, suddenly with a newfound sense of courage, hesitated. I just stood there, unmoving. *Defiant, little shit. Yep.* His eyes were like fire as he turned all his attention onto me. Even Mama just sat there, mouth agape, not believing what was happening.

"Who do you think you are, little girl? You think I won't whoop your ass?!" (That was Daddy's "go to" threat). I knew he meant it, and Lord knows I was used to it. Back then that wasn't considered abuse. It was discipline. Daddy would never hit us in the face or anywhere else on our bodies. He just whooped our butts. With a belt. Or a curtain rod. He saved all the other stuff for Mama.

Rather than answering, I dashed out of the kitchen. As I ran into our bedroom to join my already curled up sister on the bed, weeping, in my little defiant mind I felt I had shown him that I did not approve. But would it matter?

That night and over the next couple of years, I began to feel like I was responsible for the whole family. Like perhaps it must be up to me to fix things. To make things okay—mostly for Mama and Jean. I was angry at Mama too; why did she allow him to beat her, degrade her verbally, and treat her like she was worthless? I felt she needed fixing. Maybe I could help her not to be so afraid of him, to help her stand up to him.

And my sister, whom I loved so much, I felt needed me to protect her also. She had protected and comforted me so many times when I was younger, I owed it to her. So maybe I could fix her too. Help her not be so timid. I hated to see her cry. And she cried a lot. And, oh dear Lord, what about Daddy? Was he beyond fixing?   Most of Daddy's tirades and the fights between he and Mama were when they were either drunk or at least had been drinking. I had begun to think that all the problems in our house were because of alcohol. Nothing good ever came from it. All I knew was that whenever Daddy was drunk, he was angry. Our family was so dysfunctional, and I felt as though they all needed me to take care of them. I had begun to get my self-worth from being needed by them, having not yet recognized my own dysfunction. I didn't know how to process it because I was too young. However, it would begin to unfold and slowly become clearer as the years passed.

I remember when I finally got up the nerve to move that old picture Mama had hanging over Daddy's TV, the one she told us never to touch. I found a hole that had been roughly covered with some Scotch tape that was yellowed and peeling off. When I had asked Mama what it was, she reluctantly told me; it was a bullet hole.

"He wasn't really trying to hurt me though, Jackie ... you know your daddy, just trying to scare me..." She shook her head and wouldn't make eye contact with me as she spoke.

Oh. My. God. I closed my eyes and shook my head. *Never, EVER, would I allow this to happen to me. Oh, hell, no.*

4

Beer Joints and Church People

All throughout our childhood, Mama was faithful to take Jean and I to church every Sunday morning, but she never joined us. Daddy sure didn't. He didn't like God and never mentioned Him unless it was during one of his tirades. He talked about God a lot then, but never in a good way. Pretty much the only time I ever heard him say God's name at all was when it was followed by "damn," and it was only when he was mad. And he was mad most of the time. But finally, at almost thirteen years of age, I had stopped living every day fearing him. I had begun dreaming about and imagining how, one of these days, I would get the hell out of that house and away from that town: away from my angry daddy, my abused mama, and my sad sister. What I didn't recognize back then was that I was an insecure, messed-up, little girl who just wanted all the bad stuff to go away. How, for the rest of my life, I believed it would be up to me to fix things, people, and situations. Be in control, and never let anyone know the fear I was battling.

Steele, Alabama

We had moved from Talladega to a little town called Steele, because it was closer to Daddy's job in Gadsden. The little Baptist church in our small town was right across the railroad tracks that ran parallel to our house, and it was also directly across the street from Smith's country store. There were a couple of other little family-owned stores in the town, a couple more little churches, a post office, and one school. No red light. It truly was the proverbial "one horse town" out in the country where everybody knew everybody, as well as their "business." There were no secrets in our little town. Nope. And even if there were secrets, we could always count on the town gossipers to make sure they didn't remain such. Yep, back to good ol' Sister Sally ... she was always snooping around somewhere. Another typical thing in a small, rural southern town were the haves and the have-nots. And we all knew who was who and into which category we fell.

Most of my school friends were in the "have" category. They wore bows in their hair and had neat white socks and shiny new shoes that matched their crisp, cotton dresses. I always envied them. Yes, their pretty clothes and houses, but mostly, I wanted to have a family like theirs. Ironically, our little cinder block rental house was on a street that ran parallel to the railroad tracks, side by side with several other small rental homes. Some were neatly kept, but mostly our little street was known as the "tenants" ... and we just so happened to be on that side of the railroad tracks. The wrong side of the tracks.

Smith's was the only store we ever did business with. They sold beer there, and Mr. Smith let Daddy keep an account open. None of the other little stores did either of the two; that was also kind of a "thing" back then—respectable stores didn't sell beer. And even though Smith's did, most of the other people in our town who did drink alcohol would do it in secret, so they'd drive across the county line to buy their stash. Either that or go to one of the tucked-away beer joints a few counties over, which made it easier to hide it from the church deacons.

Daddy would always send me to the store to buy him a pack of Camels and a six pack of Schlitz. It's so odd to think back to that now ... As a twelve-year-old girl, I was able to just walk right in and Mr. Smith would immediately know what I was there for. He also knew I was just the errand girl for my daddy. He knew our family well.

"Hey there, Jackie! You here for the usual?"

"Yes!" I smiled as I answered. He was always such a nice, old man.

He would bag up the beer and cigarettes, throw in a sucker or a piece of gum for me, wink, and say, "Tell your daddy to just pay me when he can." With that, I'd take the heavy paper bag, politely say "thank you," then turn and walk out of the store. But I always hesitated when I first walked out. I'd take a cursory glance outside, tuck my head down, then make a hard left to head back over the railroad tracks and hopefully out of sight. The town Baptist church happened to be right across the street from Smith's. I feared someone inside the church might be watching me.

They might think I was a bad, little girl and might not want me to come back inside their church.

I was a little scared of church people back then, and I was even more afraid of God. He was surely also watching me, and I felt pretty confident He wouldn't be happy with me either. I don't know why I had such a fear that there was always someone inside that church, looking out the window, as if their only job was to watch the door of the store across the street that sold beer and to take notes of who was hiding what. How they would probably judge me, our family, anyone in our little town that didn't attend every time the doors were opened. All the Bible stories I heard in Sunday school talked about how Jesus loved us, especially us kids, and how we were all supposed to love each other and take care of people. However, I never felt like that was true. I was pretty sure those church people talked about my family, and not in a good way. Why would they? I would run home, clutching the paper bag filled with beer and cigarettes, hoping no one would notice me. There was always a part of me who wanted to fit in at that church, who wanted to really know God, and who hoped one day that I would.

One Sunday, the youth pastor came into our Sunday school class and announced the plans for the annual Summer Youth Camp. As he walked around the classroom, handing out registration forms, I kept my head down.

"Jackie, do you want to sign up?"

"*Oh, no* ... I can't go. But thank you for asking."

"Oh, I'm sorry to hear that. I know you'd enjoy it. And most of your friends are going."

I just sat there, looking at him and saying nothing. I didn't know what else to say. I knew that it cost $40.00, and Daddy would never give me the money to go. I was also certain he wouldn't let me go anywhere for a whole week.

"I don't have any money." The words just fell out of my mouth before I even realized it. I knew I wasn't supposed to ever tell anyone that; Daddy was too proud to ever discuss such things.

"We have some scholarships available. Maybe you'd be interested in that?" *Why is he being so insistent?*

"No, Sir. I'm fine. Maybe I'll go next year." I smiled just before dropping my head back down.

"Ok. Well, you'll be missed."

A couple of weeks later, and for reasons I couldn't fathom at the time, the youth pastor showed up at my house and was standing on our porch, knocking on the front door. I was mortified when I peered through the curtain and saw his smiling face looking back at me through the glass pane. My mind was racing frantically. It was the middle of the day, and Daddy was asleep. We KNEW to never disturb him or wake him up, unless one of us was dying. And even then, I probably wouldn't. So, as I was standing there with my heart beating out of my chest, eyes darting around as if I might figure a way out of this one, I heard my daddy stirring from his bedroom, which is where he slept only in the summertime because I was out of school. It was just off the living room and the front door where my uninvited youth pastor stood waiting. Then I heard his feet hit the floor and his steps headed my way and thought, *What now?* Daddy entered the room in his normal daytime sleeping attire—no shirt and only a pair of baggy underwear boxer shorts.

"Who the hell is knocking on the door?!" he yelled.

"It's Mr. G. From the church," I said. I closed my eyes and swallowed hard. Oddly, he didn't appear as angry as he did confused.

"Why is he here?"

"I don't know." I had a pretty good idea it was probably about the church camp, but I didn't want to say.

After telling me to open the door to see what he wanted, Daddy disappeared back into his room to put a shirt on. I did as he said, and as I faced our youth pastor, Mr. G, he must have been able to tell I was scared and confused, because before I even said a word to him, he said, "Hi Jackie, are your parents home?"

"Mama's at work, but Daddy's home. He sleeps during the day. He's not asleep now, though. Because you knocked on the door." I just spat out the words without thinking. The only reason I felt the need to add that last part was just in case Daddy acted mad toward him for waking him up. I had never seen my daddy talk to any church people, so I had no idea what to expect. And, in my head, I was questioning both myself as well as Mr. G. I opened the door just wide enough so that he could step inside. I stood right up against him, unsure if I should ask him to come sit down. This was new territory for me. We weren't accustomed to having guests.

"Do I need to stay in here, or should I go into another room?" I guess he could tell what I was thinking.

"Can you just ask your daddy if I might speak with him for a few minutes? And, if so, why don't you just give us a little privacy? If that's okay with you."

I'm pretty sure he saw the relief flood over my face as I answered, "Yes, Sir—I'll go get him."

Before I even got the words out of my mouth, I quickly turned around and bumped right into my daddy. He had been standing behind me. At that moment, he looked even bigger and taller than normal. I looked up into his face and swallowed hard.

"Daddy ... he wants to talk to you." It came out as a raspy, broken whisper.

"Ok, git in your room then. Right now." He wasn't shouting this time, which confused me.

I scurried away into the bedroom I shared with Jean and didn't even bother to look back, introduce them, or anything else. They'd have to figure that out for themselves. But, not gonna lie, as soon as I closed my bedroom door, I kept my ear pressed hard up against it so I could eavesdrop. I couldn't really hear the conversation, but I did notice that it was Mr. G doing all the talking. I couldn't decide whether I believed Daddy was listening to him, or if he was just waiting to jump in and cut him off. I just said a silent prayer that he wouldn't drop the "GD" bomb. When I heard Daddy finally begin to speak, I was shocked that he was using a normal tone, not shouting.

What are they saying? And where is my big sister when I need her? I felt myself start to panic for a minute.

Because Jean was seventeen now, she was often gone during the day. She and her friends could drive now, so they were always out running up and down the roads, doing one thing or another. And I didn't blame them. I always thought that as soon as I was old enough to drive, I would be doing the exact same thing. So, I just continued to listen.

After about five minutes of indiscernible conversation, I heard Daddy's voice get a little louder, and all I heard him say was "No. We don't need no charity. I got my own money."

He didn't sound mad. I remember thinking how I couldn't tell what mood he was in. His tone was ... different than usual. Was it embarrassment or pridefulness that I heard? I heard a few more bits and pieces of random conversation between them, but I knew when I heard the creaking of the front door, followed by the sound of Daddy locking it back, that Mr. G had left.

Do I stay here in my room? Should I run over to my bed, grab a book, and pretend I was lying in here just reading all this time? Is Daddy going to come in here and fuss at me? Will he think I knew about this, and that I had perhaps even asked Mr. G to come over? All these questions were running through my mind.

I decided to just sit down at my dresser and stare into the mirror, as I waited to see what would happen next. As I was looking absentmindedly at my reflection in the mirror, I didn't even recognize my own face. I just saw, in that mirror's reflection, my bedroom door opening. I guess I had expected to hear the front door slam and loud footsteps pounding down the hall, then see my door flying open. But that didn't happen. I continued to gaze into that mirror, because somehow seeing everything in the reflection felt safer and easier than turning around to look at the actual scene. When I saw Daddy's reflection appear behind me, I didn't say a word; he didn't either.

I continued to look into the mirror, seeing his face looking back at mine. He wasn't angry. He kind of just stood there a few seconds looking at me. I wasn't sure if I recognized his facial expression. I still didn't move. The mirror was easier. And felt safer.

"Jackie. Turn around. Look at me when I'm talking to you."

I did. And when I looked into his eyes, I saw a sadness that I didn't recognize. It was an expression I didn't remember ever seeing on his face.

"Yes, Sir?" I asked.

"Do you want to go to that church camp?"

I didn't know how to answer him. Yes, I wanted to go, but I honestly had never thought that it might happen. I had already prepared myself, as well as told my Sunday school friends, that I would not be allowed to go. In my mind, it just had never been a possibility. It would cost money—which we didn't have a lot of—nor did I think Daddy would let me go anywhere for a whole week, since I was only twelve years old. But I was almost thirteen, and Jean was allowed to go to band camp that summer. She was already in high school and was in the marching band. I had rationalized that those were good enough reasons to allow her to go, but I thought that church youth camp was not a requirement for me so why would I even ask? Daddy had let me go to Six Flags with the youth group before, but only for one day. We always had discount tickets, and we never had to pay anything because the church took care of all that. So how do I answer him now?

"Yes. But only if you say I can go." I was careful not to imply that I might ever want to do anything that wasn't allowed. He just kept looking at me, letting me talk.

"Jackie…" He finally sighed and shook his head.

"But I don't have to go. I know it's too much money. I don't even really want to go that bad." I said all that to somehow make him see that I was old enough to understand I could not do everything I wanted to do. That I was responsible. He continued to look at me without speaking. It was only a few seconds, but it felt like an eternity.

"Do you know what that man from the church wanted?"

"No, Sir. I know it was about the camp, but not exactly. And I promise you that I didn't know he was going to stop by here." The last thing I wanted was for Daddy to think I was in on it somehow.

"Did you know that he said you could go for free? That the church would pay your way?"

"NO, SIR! I didn't know that!" I went along, continuing to babble about how I would never ask the church anything like that, would never want Mr. G to come to our house, blah blah blah. Anytime I was nervous, I had the tendency to talk fast, not really knowing the next thing I would say. He held his hand up and stopped me. I still was in shock that he didn't appear angry but seemed to be deeply thinking about this. I honestly didn't know how I was supposed to respond. I think this might have been the very first time in my life I remember having an actual conversation with my daddy where he wasn't yelling, and I wasn't crying or being defiant.

"Jackie, I don't take no charity from NOBODY. You know that. We ain't poor. Do you tell people we're poor?"

"No, SIR! I mean, I sometimes tell Angie that I can't go into town with them when her mama takes them to Elmore's or Woolworth's. But I don't say it's because we're poor! Oh, no —I'd never say that. I just tell them it's coz we don't have any money."

I saw the faint hint of what appeared to be a smile, but he was still looking right at me. Directly at my face and into my eyes, which made me uncomfortable. I looked back into his eyes too, but only for a second. Then I averted my eyes and turned around to look back into the mirror. I could still see him— his reflection—but I liked that better than looking right at him.

"I got money. If you really want to go to that camp, you can go."

"I can go? Really? I can?" I had to ask a few times to be sure.

"Yep, I reckon you can. I didn't know you wanted to."

I thought about answering back something like, *Heck yeah, of course I want to, but I am too scared to ask you,* but I dared not. I felt my mouth still agape, thought better of it, and shut it. Then, I smiled at him. He smiled back.

I began to slowly recognize that my daddy wasn't a mean man, not deep down in his heart. He had a tender side to him. We rarely saw it, but occasionally we did. I now understand that most of us are products of our upbringing. We do carry the emotions we felt back then into our adulthood, the good and the bad. Of course, for those of us who grew up in abusive, dysfunctional homes, the hope is that we can overcome and not repeat the same mistakes with our families. But Daddy had been unable to do that. He was born into a family that didn't show love and affection. And I suppose he could only give us kids what he knew growing up, which I now know was pain, confusion, and never being taught the concept of self-control.

His mama was a spitfire little Cherokee with a hot temper. My clearest memory of her is that she was always sitting in a perched position, with one of those little green glass bottles of coke in her hand and a cigarette dangling off her deeply lined lips, which were almost always in a frown. She had six boys and one girl who had given her a whole bunch of grandkids, and she was always hollering at one of us. I don't know what her childhood was like. Back then, in the country towns in Alabama, folks just did what they had to do to feed all the young'uns and survive. And, if we were lucky, every once in a while, we'd feel some love. It might not have been in the form of affection, but I could tell that day Daddy loved me. He was letting me go to church camp. I couldn't wait to tell Angie.

5

So ... I Met This Guy...

I had no idea how that church camp would change my
life. I just wanted to go with my friends, with the hope that maybe it
would be a first step toward being able to fit in at our little church. Jean
and I never liked that we were usually the only kids who went to church
every Sunday without our parents. After Mama would drop us off in the
church parking lot, she'd always holler out the window, as she pulled
away, "Y'all stayin' for preachin' or y'all want me to pick you up after
Sunday school?" We made that decision weekly, and it usually depended
upon what our friends were doing. Jean could always get a ride home,
since most of her friends had cars, but she wasn't always happy to have
her little sister tagging along.

We mostly told Mama to come after what we called "preaching" because that way, if Jean and her friends did decide to leave after Sunday
school, they could at least drop me off at home before they took off to ride
up and down the roads. Or I could walk home by myself, but I didn't like
to because I didn't want everyone to see me. I still worried about what
they all would think, how they would judge me. Silly girl. I really wanted
to understand this whole God thing, but I didn't know how. I thought
going to church every week was all I needed to do. I remember all the
Bible stories they taught us and all the little songs we'd memorize and
sing. My Sunday school teachers were always nice, most of them grand-
mas, and I remember being scared they might know what happened inside our house many Saturday nights and disapprove or judge.

The preacher was always asking everybody if they were saved, but I
didn't really know what that meant. Saved from what? I remember the
first time I tried to find out. It was a few years prior to my going to our

church youth camp, after Mr. G had talked Daddy into it. I was probably nine or ten years old.

Chandler Mountain was a little mountain located on the edge of the town of Steele. It was kind of up and away from the nosy people at "my" church. As I think back and tell the story now, I realize the "nosy" part is probably just the imaginations of a child who constantly felt scrutinized because of the family I was from. Family status was everything in our tiny town.

One of my friends had randomly invited me to go to a "revival" with her family one weeknight. Initially, I didn't know exactly what my friend had invited me to, but I was happy to be able to go somewhere. I would do almost anything to get out of the house on a Tuesday night.

"What's a 'revival'?" I asked her.

"It's a thing at church." She shrugged and looked at me like I was asking a dumb question.

"Oh, ok. What do we do there?"

"It's just church, Jackie. We don't do anything; we just go."

Satisfied with her answer, I simply shrugged back at her and nodded. So, we continued riding in the backseat of her daddy's big station wagon and as we wound around the big curves on the road up the mountain, we slid back and forth in that back seat that faced out the back of the car—no seatbelts back then—and giggled. I saw it as a bit of an adventure.

The church was small, much smaller than the big church I had been going to down in Steele. We walked in and sat down in the third row from the back. I sat on the inside of the hard, wooden pew while she sidled up beside me next to her parents and her big brother, on the edge of the aisle of the little church. We stood up to sing a couple of songs from the hymnals located on the back of the pew in front of us. Then, after the singing, it all became a blur.

The big man walked up to the stage with what looked like an encyclopedia tucked under his arm ... I assumed it was a Bible, but it was the biggest one I'd ever seen.

In a flash, he had whipped that book open and leaned into the people on the front row. The first thing out of his mouth was, "IF YOU DIED TONIGHT, WHERE ARE YOU GONNA END UP??? HEAVEN, OR HELLLLLLLLLL?!" He intentionally shouted and dragged out the last word. I felt myself jump a little because the shouting scared me. I looked at my friend, but she ignored me ... she seemed mesmerized, just staring at him. Or maybe she was scared too. Then I heard a cacophony of "Amen, Brother! Yeah, preach it!" mixed in with claps and whistling and a loud bang of the cymbal from the drummer, who was still sitting on the side of the stage. I dared not move again.

"Hell's HOT and you're—a' goin' if you don't get it straight tonight! You liable to drive off the side of this mountain tonight on your way home and wake up doing the backstroke in the lake of FIRRREEEEE! The devil is just rubbing his hands together, waitin' to catch you doin' somethin' wrong, and he's gonna drag you straight into HELLLLLLLLL with all the other bad people!! You better get up here to this altar RIGHT NOW so you can leave here knowing you don't have to BURRRRN THROUGHOUT ETERNITYYYYYYY!!!"

I don't remember much else after that. I saw a bunch of people slide out of that pew and head straight down to the front of that church, throwing themselves on the steps of the stage, crying and wailing.

"What are they doing?" I leaned over and whispered to my friend, neither of us taking our eyes off the scene playing out in front of us.

"They're repenting," she answered me, as if it was a normal occurrence and that I should've known.

"Repenting?"

"Saying they're sorry to God. Getting SAVED!" She looked at me incredulously. I just looked back at her, mouth hanging open. That's when her mama leaned past her and whispered in my ear.

"Jackie ... are you saved? If you die tonight, do you think you're going to heaven or to hell?" I didn't have an answer. Next thing I knew, my friend's dad had slipped out of the pew and joined the others at the altar, and I saw him whisper something into the preacher's ear while pointing at me. That's when the big man walked down the aisle and called me to come out of my seat.

"Come on, little lady ... come on down here and get saved. You don't want to go to hell, do you?" I just couldn't stop staring at the beads of sweat on his large forehead, and that he was unaware he had spittle coming out of the corner of his mouth. He was breathing heavily as he reached his large, meaty hand out toward me. I hesitated.

"C'mon ... your Father loves you and wants to meet you! I'll walk you down there!" he shouted as he grabbed my hand.

"Don't be scared, little girl ... Come on and meet your Father ... He's a-waitin' on you coz He loves you!" He grabbed a handkerchief and wiped his head and mouth all in one fell swoop. I stood up and we walked down that aisle and before I knew it, I was on my face on those carpeted steps. I felt people laying hands all over my little shaking body.

My FATHER? Who loves me?? What?!? I was so confused, as the big man's words raced through my mind.

Then he just told me to repeat after him ... he was very adamant that I say it out loud and it must be the exact words he said, or it wouldn't work.

"JESUS! I'm a dirty sinner!! I believe you love me, that you want to save me, that you want me to follow you all the days of my life! Say it ... SAY IT!" he shouted to me between sentences. What else could I do? I did it. Repeated his exact words, just as he had warned me I must.

"I don't want to burn in hell, Jesus. I want to spend eternity with you, not in hell with all the demons! Thank you for saving me, Father!!"

There was that word again: father. I guess they didn't know I already had one of those and if the one in heaven was anything like the one at my house, I knew I better do what he says. I didn't want to make him mad. But mostly, I really didn't want to burn in hell.

Fast forward to the Jesus I met that summer at church camp, Who was far different from the one I *thought* I'd met up on Chandler Mountain that night almost three years prior. He was kind, gentle. He didn't expect anything from me; instead, He just wanted me to know He loved me. At first, I didn't know how to act ... how to feel. I didn't know what unconditional love was and struggled with how I would come to believe it even existed. The youth pastor at camp described Him in a way that I understood. I used to think that going to church was all I needed to do. Like somehow, Mama dropping me off every Sunday was enough. I never imagined that it was about knowing and understanding it all. No one had ever mentioned anything about a relationship. I didn't have a lot of experiences with relationships, and the few I did have weren't very loving. Most everyone in my life just did whatever they had to do to get by. And, of course, the only "father" I had ever known was my daddy.

When preachers used to talk about God and use the word father in the same sentence, it confused me. I found out that God wasn't the big, scary guy who I pictured sitting up in heaven, holding a baseball bat, just waiting for me to mess up and do something wrong. He knew I would, many times, and He would still love me. I wish I could say that simply meeting Jesus at summer camp and inviting Him into my heart would mean that the rest of my life would be perfect. It would not be, far from it. Heck, I hadn't even wanted perfection—I just didn't want a life like the one I had. Like my mama had. I wanted a happy family. A good husband. Good kids. Was that too much to ask?

And did I really trust Jesus? I thought I did. I said I did. But how could I? How can someone trust an invisible God if they had never even learned what trust meant, even with real people that they could see, hear, and live with? So, I invited Him into my heart, asked Him to be my Lord and Savior, and I believed that time. As much as a young girl who grew up like I did could believe it. I remember Mama telling me that she knew Jesus, that she had invited Him into her heart when she used to go to Sunday school as a child. And I had seen how her life turned out. Jesus didn't fix it for her. And she hadn't, either. I was confused.

So, I made up my mind that even though I was "saved", that I'd just fix my own life. However, at such a young age, I didn't recognize that it would not be up to me to make things happen. To control, to fix my life and family. I was unable to foresee the fear that would follow me most of my adult life. A fear that would manifest itself as the need to control. I knew I had met the "real" Jesus, not the scary, angry one from that night on Chandler Mountain. The truth was that night at the revival, I had only said "yes" as a one-way ticket out of hell. No, this Jesus I met at camp was nothing like that. I wanted to know Him. I wanted Him in my life. They told me all I had to do was trust Him. Not trust Him to make my life perfect, but believe that He would be with me, guiding me through the good times and the really rough times that were to come.

But I didn't know how to trust Jesus, God, or anyone else, for that matter. There is one thing I did know ... that big, ol' southern gospel, spittin', fire-and-brimstone preacher scared the hell right out of me. But it was the Jesus I later met at camp who LOVED the hell out of me. I don't know really how else to explain it. It just felt different. Good. I wasn't afraid anymore. For now.

Part Two

I had dreams. Big ones. And I didn't want a parade to pass me by. I would learn to dance high upon the net, without a wire, and never look down.. I must fight through the fear. I would be strong. Mama told me to paint on a smile and learn how to hide my feelings. Never let 'em break you, Baby." I had made up my mind this baby would never be broken. Never.

—paraphrased from "Don't Cry Out Loud,"
a song by Melissa Manchester

6

Mama n' Em

The time had finally arrived—I was going to get my driver's license! Step one on my checklist of things to accomplish in my exit strategy. I was determined to get the heck out of dodge, or as Mama would say, "fixin' to blow this popsicle stand!" Mama had a bunch of funny things she would say ... we called them "Mama'isms." She used to always tell my sister and I, "You know cain't never could, don'tchee?" and "Never say never!" and "Whatever you do, don't git too big f'yer britches, either!" I can still hear the combination of southern Mississippi and central Alabama drawl, rattling off a string of words of wisdom to live by. I can also hear her telling us how to remember to spell Mississippi ... *M—I—crooked letter, crooked letter—I—crooked letter, crooked letter—I—humpback, humpback—I.* I still, to this very day, have to say that out loud in order to spell it. Funny how this stuff sticks with us.

Mama had so many regrets in her life, and the last thing she wanted was for us to repeat those same mistakes in our lives. She was raised in a good, loving Christian home with two gentle and sweet parents. She used to tell us that she had never heard anyone speak to another person in a raised voice until she met Daddy. She also recognized that her two daughters shared very few of the same personality traits. Even though Jean and I were very different people, we were both a little bit of Mama and a little bit of Daddy. She'd tell us, "None of that matters, girls, 'coz emotions don't care what yer personality is, they are what they are ... pain is pain, and it hurts." She knew that Jean and I both hurt a lot ... but while Jean would cry, I would get angry and scream. We didn't realize back then that insecurity is based on fear and makes one feel "less than." Jean would withdraw, while I would rare up and get in your face. But we both felt the exact, same emotion; it just looked different on me than it did on her. And as I grew into a young woman, I had some things to figure out. The first thing on my list was how to get out of this oppressive house and make my own life. A life that was happy, beautiful. Where the sun was shining, chasing the storm clouds away. Where love didn't have to hurt so much. Where I didn't have to be on guard all the time.

Steele, Alabama 1976

I was in the tenth grade, and it was my sixteenth birthday, so I had begged Mama to please take me to the DMV that very day.

"Why you in such a rush, Jackie? Where ya think yer goin'?" Mama always wanted to act silly and laughed almost every time she spoke to me. I think she did that inadvertently because she knew, in her heart, that our ability to have a little bit of fun together was rare and much needed. She was also aware that many times in our young lives, Jean and I had seen her cry, so as much as she could laugh and be silly with us, she did. We knew it was her way of dealing with the pain.

"Yes, and I'm also fixin' to ace this test ... can we go now?" I knew I never really needed to beg Mama. She would do almost anything for Jean and me.

"Well, you fixin' to get on my last nerve, girl!" Then she leaned over to give me a hug as she handed me the keys. "Go for it!"

As I climbed into the driver's seat of Mama's car, I couldn't help but think this could be my last time to be required to have an adult ride in the car with me every time I drove. To say I was giddy was an understatement. But I was also nervous, as Mama would say, "You feel like a long tail cat in a room full of rockin' chairs?" whereas Daddy asked me, "You as nervous as a whore in church?" And I was both. This would be my first step in getting out of this one-horse town. I was fixin' to get myself a driver's license!

As we walked into that little St. Clair County government office, I felt overwhelmed. I'm not sure what I had expected to see there but the fact had occurred to me that inside these dingy, gray walls were people who had power over me. Power to decide whether I was qualified to drive a car, or if I'm doomed to stay home forever. I was a dramatic sixteen-year-old.

I was struck by the amount of people—all waiting. My eyes scanned the old, dirty oversized linoleum tiles and the little metal chairs with split and cracking vinyl seats. I noticed that some were occupied by other pock-faced teenagers. Others by older folk who mostly looked tired and fed up. But the one thing they all had in common was that they were all waiting and, clearly, not happy about it. Many young moms were carrying writhing toddlers with snotty noses and dirty feet, which Daddy always called "grocery store feet." The thought of it made me smile on the inside. Most thoughts of Daddy's expressions made me angry, but even I had to admit this was funny. He'd say, "Damn, Jackie! Y'all's feet are filthy! What y'all been doin'... runnin' around the grocery store barefooted?" He said it to make fun of my friends and me because we almost always walked around town, even on the railroad tracks, barefooted. We never wore shoes in the summertime. Shoot ... I could run a 50-yard dash all day long on the sharpest of gravel driveways and dirt roads that we used to play on without shoes. That was life in small town Alabama ... not a lot of nicely paved asphalt surfaces in my neighborhood.

Now I was finally getting a chance to prove I could drive a car instead of my usual walking all over the county. Oh, I definitely did not stay home. The second I had turned fifteen, Daddy would let me go pretty much anywhere I wanted to go, as long as I was home before "dark thirty," as Mama called it. So, I knew just after it turned dark, I still had a little bit more time. I guess Daddy figured not much can happen, since I was mostly just walking around Steele. There was not a lot of trouble we could get into. I think by this time, he might have even trusted me a little bit. I had been going to church every single Sunday, and I didn't cuss, smoke, or drink. Mama used to tell me every day, "You're a good girl, Jackie. I don't worry about you getting into trouble."

Admittedly, while I was nothing like my dear sweet, "perfect" sister Jean, I was a good girl, and it did make me feel good when Mama told me that. I could hear her voice saying it anytime I even thought of doing anything against the rules. As much as I didn't really care if I made Daddy mad or not, I never wanted to disappoint Mama.

So, we sat ... quietly at the DMV. As we were waiting our turn, I was studying all the others around me. It was apparent to me that not everyone sitting in those chairs, holding their numbered tickets, was there to get their driver's license. Mama must have read my mind because she leaned in and whispered to me, side-mouthed, "Some of these people are here to sign up for their welfare checks and pick up their commodities." That's what we used to call the big blocks of cheese and the bags of dried beans that Mama would pick up occasionally if she didn't have enough money to get everything we needed at the Piggly Wiggly. She was also careful to add that while we did occasionally partake of these goods, "commodities," we did not have to rely on them. Thank goodness, she would say. "But these folk might," she would add, so she suggested I just keep smiling and be patient in case we had to wait on one of them to have their turn.

Mama always told Jean and I to "be nice." She didn't want either of us to turn out to be angry and impatient like Daddy. I'm pretty sure she knew Jean wouldn't; me, she wasn't so sure about. She continued the side-mouth whisper, "Looks like now there's more than one person working the lines, so maybe they'll call you up soon." I sat stone-faced, continuing to scan the room, tapping my right foot impatiently. I was studying the faces of the DMV workers. By then, I had become pretty adept at reading faces, and most of their expressions were saying, "*I hate my life, I hate this job, and all of you people in this room.*" No words were necessary. At last, one tired-looking lady with deep frown lines called out, "Number 38! You're next!"

I glanced down at my number, just to make sure. Yes! I jumped up so fast and, in my scurry to get up to that counter, grasping the now sweaty paper number I'd had held in my hand, I fumbled and dropped my purse. Its contents scattered around the feet of all the people I've been silently studying for the past hour and a half. As I lunged to receive my stuff, my eyes fell directly to the obvious, at least it was to me. The very large and very pink wrapped item, approximately 14 inches in length and as thick as a small mattress, landed perfectly in front of everyone and, notably, right between the feet of the little, old farmer man that had been sitting directly in front of me. I had only seen the back of his head until now.

As everyone around me sat and watched my mortified expression, the man slid one of his dirty, booted feet over, shot me a wink and a toothless smile, his thin lips framed with either Skoal or Copenhagen's Best. My little secret treasure had come within only an inch of landing right into his large, accompanying spit can. I literally snatched it up so fast that I almost toppled over onto him and another one of the discontented patrons. *Oh, dear Lord, have mercy.* I felt the flush creep across my cheeks and was unable to make eye contact with anyone. Except Mama, who, of course, was choking back laughing and pretty much just held her head down, shoulders bobbing up and down, and letting out the occasional snort from her covered mouth. *Gee, thanks, Mama.*

For the first time in my life, I couldn't wait to get into the testing room. I pretty much wanted to be anywhere, as long as I could slink away and free myself from the glaring eyes of all those I perceived as my judges. Looking back, no doubt my overactive, insecure mind exaggerated all of that, but at that time, I was quite upset with the designers of that product in my purse. What? Did the marketing team sit around a table in some boardroom and say, "Let's make this thing as huge and as blindingly pink as we can! That will be perfect ... it'll be just what every teenage girl will want to carry around in her purse!" I felt as though there was a big ol' spotlight shining right on it as it fell, in my mind, in super-slow motion. I also pictured myself diving, also in slo-mo, screaming the word, "Noooooooooo!" to no avail. How embarrassing. I finally regained composure, grabbed the Kotex and, keeping a death-grip on my purse, made it up to the counter to hand the lady number 38.

The good news is I passed the driving test. I also left promising myself I would write a letter to that personal hygiene company, explaining my horror and giving them advice on how to do things better. As I was telling all this to Mama as we exited the parking lot—me behind the wheel—she shook her head and snickered. Then she looked at me, as she had many times, with mourning yet hopeful eyes, and said, "Jackie, you can do anything you want in life. So, do it right."

"I will, Mama. I promise."

Within the first month of getting my license, I had driven over to Angie's almost every day, and I even volunteered to take all our dirty clothes to the laundromat for Mama, too. Anything I could do to be able to drive by myself, I did it. It gave me a sense of control that I hadn't experienced before. I remember feeling so grown-up, pulling into whatever driveway or parking lot and taking the keys out of the ignition. I'd make sure to be as conspicuous as possible anytime I would walk into wherever I was going, just so everyone could see me holding the car keys. I bought a few, huge, gawdy keychains—the bigger the better. I felt if people noticed the keys and even heard them rattling around in my purse, they might recognize that I was grown-up enough to have a car. Of course, I did not own a car; I could only drive Mama's when she wasn't at work. Daddy would never let me drive his.

By this time, Jean had an old green Chevrolet that she had bought after graduating from high school and technical school, which she would occasionally let me drive. I wanted to get myself a job as soon as I was old enough to buy a car, and I didn't want it to be in this gossipy, little town. I wasn't sure how I was going to do this, but I was determined to succeed. I didn't want to have to ask Daddy and Mama for anything. I wanted to grow up AND out as fast as I could without their help.

One day, later in the summer after getting my license, Daddy wanted something from the store. By this time, I had proven to him that I was a responsible driver, and the only "real" grocery store was in the next county over. We called it "going to town," which was kind of a big deal in my little, country bumpkin mind. Daddy was letting me drive *to town!* And we all knew that Daddy always wanted *what* he wanted and *when* he wanted it. It appeared that Mama had forgotten something vital in her only once weekly visits to the Piggly Wiggly in Attalla: his butter beans. Oh, my goodness, how dare she? Daddy loved him some butter beans, and we had them almost every single night with supper. Occasionally, he'd go a little wild and ask for some pintos or maybe navy beans, just enough to keep us all on our toes by proving he had a slightly more advanced palate. But God knows we would never consider eating a meal that did not include his dry beans. We always had a typical "meat and three" with homemade buttermilk cat head biscuits (as Mama called them).

By this time, either Jean or I would cook supper during the week because Mama never got off work until 5:30 p.m. I can remember each night, before she'd go to bed, she'd pour the bag of dried beans into a pot in the kitchen sink and start the process of picking out all the rocks, cleaning the remaining beans, and leaving them to soak all night in the pot full of salted water. The next morning, before work, she'd put the pot on the back burner of our old stove and set the heat on low so they could cook all day. It was Jean or my job to check on them throughout the day to add more water as needed. Dear sweet Lord, we knew we had better not burn those beans ... it had happened one time, and that was enough. I had learned to fry a lot of chicken and okra and make what we called "creamed potatoes." I became an expert in making homemade gravy by adding milk and flour to the leftover chicken grease and crispy bits of batter. Daddy also insisted upon some fresh red tomatoes and a big slice of raw white onion on the side. So, off I went to Piggly Wiggly by myself—and in Daddy's car, which was a miracle in itself. It was my first time ever driving outside the county line.

Just before arriving at The Pig, I had to drive past the local Omelet Shop (Alabama's answer to the Waffle House), which was located on the little town square in Attalla. I suddenly found myself noticing the tiny restaurant more than I ever had before, even though we had driven past it every Saturday morning when we went to buy groceries with Mama. I reckoned I hadn't paid near as much attention before because I had never been the one driving. But I was today. I suddenly had an adrenaline rush, as I whipped Daddy's big old Pontiac into the parking lot. I walked inside and marched right up to the counter where an older lady with bright blue eye shadow was popping her chewing gum and, through brightly, red-painted lips, asked, "What 'cha need, Darlin'?"

I found myself uncharacteristically nervous and just stood there watching her. She was standing with one hand on a cocked hip, looking directly at me, not smiling. I was also aware that I was standing at a long counter surrounded by older men drinking coffee and smoking cigarettes. I stifled a cough and almost choked out my answer.

"I need a job."

She looked at me for a second without answering. Instead, she eyed me up and down, continuing to pop her chewing gum, before turning around, walking toward the back, hand-cupping over one side of those red lips, and shouting, "Hey Chip ... get out here ... there's a little gal here wanting a job." Never looking back at me, she reached for the pot of coffee, poured the remaining drops into a patron's cup, then promptly put it back onto the coffee maker machine, and commenced making a new pot. I was watching her every move intently. I had already decided I needed to learn how to do this.

About this time, a skinny, little guy who looked to be only in his early twenties (if that), wearing a white paper Omelet Shop cap, walked out from the back, wiping his hands on his apron. He stopped at the counter in front of me, barely looking up.

"Hey ... what 'cha need?" Oddly, it occurred to me that both employees of this establishment had only spoken those same words to me. *What 'cha need?* So, in keeping with this, I decided to limit my words too.

"A job," I replied.

He looked at me the same way she did, eyes roaming, starting at the top of my head. *Were they assessing my legal age?*

"When can ya start, Sweetheart?" he asked, continuing to wipe his greasy hands on his apron.

"Um … I don't know." I hadn't expected this, nor had I thought it through.

"How 'bout right now?" He cocked one brow up. Still not smiling. I wondered if I should.

"Right now? Like, *today?*"

"Yep. You said you wanted a job."

"Um … oh…" I stammered before spitting out, "I've gotta go home and ask my daddy." Then suddenly, I decided I didn't. "Oh, never mind. I don't have to ask." I felt my face turning red initially, then took a deep breath before answering, "How about tomorrow? I can start tomorrow." I was proud of myself for making my own decision, and I could tell Mr. Chip was pretty pleased, too.

"Alrighty then!" He thrust that same, dirty, little, bony hand out to me that he had just wiped on his equally dirty, greasy apron seconds before.

My thoughts raced as I looked down at his extended hand. *What do I do now? Does this mean I have a job?* As a sixteen-year-old country girl from Steele, Alabama, it suddenly occurred to me that I had never shaken anyone's hand. Maybe once or twice the preacher at church, but never in a "professional" manner. I was pretty sure he had just offered me my first real job. I suddenly felt bold, did the full right arm extension right back at Chip, and we shook hands. I knew I was about to go rogue. I decided not to even ask Mama or Daddy; I'd find some way to get to that Omelet Shop the following day.

It was at least a week before Daddy even noticed I wasn't home for dinner most nights. School had just started back, and I'm assuming he just thought I was staying after school for cheerleading practice. But the truth was I had managed to talk Chip into letting me work the middle shift, which would allow me to leave school and come directly to work. When Jean couldn't take me, Angie gave me a ride. I desperately needed a car. Most of my friend's parents bought them their first cars for their sixteenth birthdays, but since I knew that wasn't going to happen, I would have to do it myself.

Many of the customers during my second shift hours at the Omelet Shop were older men who worked the third shift at one of the several local plants in Etowah County. One sweet man in particular "took a shine to me," another "Mama-ism." We had formed an odd friendship … he felt like a father figure to me, the good kind. Like Angie's daddy always made me feel. One night, as I was pouring him another cup of coffee, he asked me how I was getting to work every day. I told him either my sister or my best friend was driving me, but that I was looking for a car of my own. Of course, he asked me what my parents thought about that, and I proudly told him I didn't care what they thought. I was determined to buy myself a car; and I meant it. I was extremely proud that I had become independent enough to try to do everything without any help from my parents. I was especially proud of the fact that I had made a decision without my daddy's input, and I hadn't cared about the consequences.

So, when the kind gentleman offered to sell me a car, I was so excited I just said, "I'll take it!" The next day, he drove it over for me to see. He knew I didn't have a clue what to ask or do, but, for some reason, I trusted him. I didn't believe he would take advantage of me. It was a 1967 coppery, orange-colored Ford Fairlane, so it was almost ten years old. He had bought it for his son when it was new and had taken good care of it, and the miles weren't too high. The price was $400, and he let me pay him $20 a week. Sold.

Finally, I had accomplished a huge chunk of my plan of escape. I didn't know what would be next, but whatever it was, it'd be up to me to make it happen.

7

Little Girls Dream ...
Big Girls Plan

As I reflect on all these stories, I understand so much more now. We never see in the present as clearly as we do when we look back at the past. I see that I was in the process of becoming; and to become, I had to grow. All living things must go through a metamorphosis. They grow from seed and become, eventually, what they were designed to grow in to. Whether that living thing is a plant or a human being, we all start out as a seed. And the becoming is all about the root system and the nourishment received during the process. The seed will either grow to be healthy—producing flowers or fruit—or they wither and die— crackling, brown leaves falling all around. Some seeds that had so much potential when they were first planted end up dropping off into the cold, hard ground. The growth processes we all go through can teach us things if we're willing to be taught.

One of my favorite musical artists, Dan Fogelberg, wrote a song that I used to sing out loud to myself all the time when I was a teenager. I memorized each word. It was about the lessons we learn are usually like bridges that are burned—we can only cross them once. I didn't want to believe that. I wanted to believe that we could make similar mistakes more than one time, not learn the lesson, and go right back and have to do it all over again. I now know from experience that this idea is very true. When we make mistakes and the future seems unsure, we don't organically know how to do it differently the next time, assuming we get the chance. As a Christian, I always believed God had a plan for me, and that He, in His sovereignty, would keep me from making the same mistakes again. But I found out that the Creator of all living things allows us to make the decisions to plant ourselves and have the opportunity to establish a healthy root system, nourish ourselves, and grow strong. But God leaves that choice up to us. We must choose life—a strong and healthy one.

As a young girl, I didn't know then what I know now, so I just had to wing it and do the best I could. I wasn't sure exactly who, but I knew that it would be up to me to become whoever I wanted to be. I would have to make choices and knew I didn't want to stay the same person that I was, a messed-up, little girl—the seed from an unhealthy root system. I didn't want to wither and fall into hard ground, because I had always dreamed of more. I knew I would have to re-plant myself and create my own healthy root. Start out with good soil and work the ground around me, not relying on help from anyone to make it happen. I remained determined to be in control of my own destiny.

Of course, I didn't realize at the time that my efforts to do this would inadvertently lead me to becoming a person who felt that I would need to manage the people in my life. Manage always sounded so much better than control. I never intentionally set out to do that; it was just part of the osmosis of "controlling my destiny". Unless I thought my destiny involved just me—and, no, I hadn't considered becoming a Tibetan monk who is socially isolated. I wanted people, good people, in my life. So far, I had relied on my big sister to hold my hand. I loved my mama, but I saw how she handled adulthood, and I certainly didn't want to be a carbon copy of that. She wouldn't be with me during the most formative years of my becoming the adult I wanted to be. It was now up to me to set in motion a plan to make my little girl dreams come true. I felt that's what God wanted ... for me to be strong and make my own decisions. I had to figure out a plan that wouldn't fail. I was not willing to fail. Not ever.

As the years passed, my sister Jean and I grew into young women who had dreamed big. We knew we would both get married, have a gingerbread-clad house with a white picket fence, a few kids, and a dog. We knew that's what Mama had wanted. Had she simply dreamed but never planned?

Growing up, every year in October, we would get a copy of the Sears and Roebuck's Christmas "Wish Book" in the mail. Jean and I would lie on our stomachs, side by side, across one of our twin beds in the little room that we shared. As we turned every single page, we'd "dog-ear" the ones with the pictures of the things we wanted. I'd pick the beautiful, rosy-cheeked dolls with the long blonde curls. Jean wanted the fancy purple dress with the lace. I wanted shiny black patent leather buckle shoes, while my big sister preferred the white, knee-high go-go boots that laced up the front. Then there was the gorgeous white canopy bed with the pink ruffled bedspread and matching pillow shams. We both wanted one of those; we always wanted to be a little bit fancy, just like the highfalutin girls with their nice house and teenage girl-themed bedrooms.

We imagined we might have all our school friends over for "spend the night parties," which is what we called them back then. And even if Mama and Daddy could just afford one of those canopy beds, we decided we'd share it. We slept together many nights anyway, cramming ourselves into a single bed, especially if Daddy was drunk and mad. I always felt safer with my head on Jean's shoulder, and I could feel my sister's warm breath on my forehead as she whispered, "It's gonna be okay … we'll be all grown-up one day." *Yes. Everything IS going to be okay. I'll make sure of it.* Then we'd drift off to sleep and dream big-girl dreams.

In 1977, Jean met and married the love of her life when she was twenty-one years old. He was a young man that she worked with at Alpine Mills in Attalla. I remember the night he came to our little house to pick her up for their first date. Of course, Angie, our friend Cindy, and I were waiting with bated breath. *Jean had a boyfriend!* We were peeking out the window when he pulled into the driveway.

"He's here! Jean! He's here … he just pulled in!" Cindy was the first one to shriek with excitement. I ran back into our bedroom where Jean was still getting dressed and putting final touches on her makeup. "Are you ready? Do you want to stay in here until he comes to the door? You want us to go outside and greet him?" I paused my rambling sentences only for a second, reaching over to tuck a curl behind her right ear and straighten her necklace. Ever the fixer. She followed me into the living room where Cindy and Angie were still peeking out the window. We saw him walking up on the porch. I couldn't wait, so I opened the door and went outside. He was smiling and as soon as he saw me, he extended his right hand.

"Hello, I'm Steve!" Friendly AND good-looking. *Good job, Sister.*

"I'm Jackie. Nice to meet you." I continued to examine him, sussing him out. He looked past me to see Jean, who was standing behind me, just inside the door, looking pretty as a picture. I felt so proud and happy for her. Maybe a twinge of jealousy, dreaming of the day I'd meet my eventual husband.

Smiling from ear to ear, Jean invited him in. Mama was in the kitchen washing dishes but came into the living room as soon as she heard the commotion. She was grinning while drying her hands on the dish towel, and of course Cindy and Angie were giggling like little girls. I was trying to look like the mature one of the three of us. We introduced Mama, secretly thanking the Lord that Daddy wasn't home at the time, had a couple minutes of small talk, and away they went. This was the beginning of my knowing that soon it would just be Mama and me in the house with Daddy. My protective big sister had found her fairy tale, and her dreams were coming true.

And I was checking off my "big-girl plans" list, one at a time.

Driver's license – check.

First job – check.

First car – check.

Now, I just needed to find me a husband.

8

Eliza Doolittle
Meets the Higgins'

I love the story of *My Fair Lady*. The romance of it all, of course, but also the irony of a simple girl meeting an aristocratic man, and they end up falling in love despite their broad differences. If you know the storyline, it's all about the protagonist, Eliza, who is transformed by the elite socialite Professor Higgins, who takes on the challenge of making this street-smart, not formally educated young girl into a member of the upper-class elite. She rises to the challenge, undaunted by the many nay-sayers. I would like to say my story is almost the same, except I *was* daunted. Even though I had grown up wanting to appear confident and promising myself I would not settle for less, the truth was, inside, I was insecure and afraid of life on my own. I had also become even more sassy and mouthy in my effort to try to fit in with the other tough girls at my high school, but it was all a front. I just knew I wanted out of the family I had been born into, and while I wasn't sure how I would do it, I knew that I would.

January 1979

I was on the floor, on my knees, when I met him. I had become quite accustomed to this position over the last few months. I was an eighteen-year-old senior in high school from a poor family, so it had not taken me long to understand a girl's gotta do what a girl's gotta do to get ahead in life. *Keep it on the down low but always be looking up to any possibilities that might arise.* I heard his footsteps approaching but continued to keep my eyes fixed on the job at hand. When I saw his feet stop right beside me, I slowly looked up and saw he was looking down directly at me, smiling broadly with arms folded. I didn't even have to ask—I guess he could tell with one look that I would understand. His next words would change my life. "Hey, young lady ... I need a screw."

Ok, so now you can get your mind out of the gutter, and I'll tell you the story.

After my first job stint at the Omelet Shop, I grew tired of waiting tables and had taken a job at the F.W. Woolworth Company in Gadsden, which was a slightly bigger city in the next county over from my tiny town of Steele. It was the only big department store around, so many of the local high schoolers applied for the part-time jobs, sometimes if only to get the 5% employee discount they offered. For me, that 5% off meant my only chance to finally buy myself a pair of those fancy Jordache® jeans that Angie and all my other friends were wearing. I worked as a night shift hardware department clerk.

That night, I was stocking some new tools on the bottom shelf with that ridiculously bulky, poorly designed price sticker gun, and it had jammed. Again. I had almost completed putting the bright yellow $1.99 stickers on all the hammers when the machine decided to stop cooperating with me. As I struggled with it, I had begun sweating profusely and swearing under my breath. *Damn piece of junk!* I was on my knees working on the bottom display shelf, so I secretly prayed no customers would appear and expect me to get up and assist them in locating some random piece of hardware. Frustrated, I heard footsteps approaching me, so I had made the decision not to look up. If this was a customer and they needed me, they'd ask. Then I saw the feet. Planted. Whoever this was, they were clearly waiting on me to acknowledge them.

Annoyed, I looked up. With a deep sigh, I asked, "Can I help you, Sir?" He just stood there smiling. Shoulder-length brown hair, matching mustache, and beautiful brown eyes looked back at me. He had a dimple in his right cheek and a warm smile. I was immediately sorry that I had been annoyed. I didn't mind customers like him. As I pushed up from the floor, I clumsily toppled over onto the box of hammers that I had been unloading. To my surprise, he immediately reached down to steady my arms. "Oops ... are you ok?" he asked, never taking his eyes off mine. Mortified, I regained my footing, dusted my slacks off, and wiped my hands on a paper towel before finally looking at him. Face to face. Two feet away. He was handsome and taller than me by about four inches. I could tell he was older than me, but I couldn't tell how much. He definitely wasn't another high schooler.

By this time, I had noticed that he was wearing a Woolco name badge, so I knew he wasn't a customer. He had also obviously noticed mine, because as he was checking me out, he asked, "Miss Jackie, are you sure you're okay?" Still embarrassed for being such a klutz, I looked down, dusted off my pants again, and answered him, "Yes Sir, I am. Thank you."

"Did you just call me 'sir,' twice in a row?" He laughed out loud. He had a nice laugh too. Sounded genuine.

"Oh, sorry ... I didn't mean to imply you're..." I stopped short just before the word "older" slipped out. Awkward pause. "Anyway, I'm sorry if that offended you. Do you work here?" *Ugh, what a stupid question!* At this point, I was fumbling for words, still trying to recover. He pointed to his name tag, cocked his head slightly to the right, eyebrows up, and grinning from ear to ear. "Yes, MA'AM, I do." He intentionally emphasized "ma'am."

Touché. His name tag read "Woolco Furniture Department—Manager." As soon as I read that, I didn't even notice what his actual name was. Realizing what a goofball, little girl I must have looked like right then, I just stood there. He was one of the managers, and he had walked up to me. Since I assumed he was a customer, I had politely called him "sir." *Had this offended him? I mean, why would it have? Was he going to tell me what he needed? Or maybe fire me?* My mind raced. I continued to stand there silently, looking back at him.

"I actually came over here because I need some screws to assemble a new piece of furniture that just arrived."

"Yes Sir ... I mean, okay..." I was stammering. *Geesh*. "Do you need me to go get them for you?"

"You can call me David." Again, that gentle smile. Those brown eyes. "Can you just show me where the double-ended screws are?"

"Sure," I replied, as I attempted to regain some semblance of professionalism. He seems like a really nice guy.

Over the next few weeks, my part-time night job at Woolco had admittedly become more interesting. David would wander over to the hardware department often during my shifts. Our conversations were easy. He made me laugh, and I just felt that he treated me differently from the boys I had dated from high school. I had since found out that he had already graduated college a couple years ago. I really liked him, but I was sure he just saw me as a sweet, little girl who was fun to work with. And we had absolutely nothing in common, except working the night shift at Woolco, hardware and furniture.

When he finally asked me out, I was initially confused. And because I was basically an inexperienced teenager, I had to keep reminding myself David was not a boy, but it was obvious that he was a few years older than me. I'd never dated anyone who wasn't also a high schooler. But after we had talked and become friends, I had decided that didn't matter. And of course, Daddy wouldn't approve. Even better.

One night at work, he walked over to my department, smiling as usual, stopped, and just looked at me for a few seconds before speaking. I returned his gaze and the smile.

"Hey … so … you wanna go throw a frisbee Sunday afternoon?"

Not wanting to appear young and silly, I replied, "Sure. Where?"

"I don't know … where do you want to go?" he stood there smiling, waiting for my reply. He had such a sweet face, with those brown eyes and tousled, long hair. He was so confident too, another thing I wasn't accustomed to. While I liked the idea of that, it also made me a bit anxious.

"Do you mean like the park or something?" Ugh. I felt so insecure and foolish as I just stood there, twirling my hair around my fingers.

"Sure! What's your favorite park?"

Was this guy kidding me? The only park I knew of was the Steele Town Park, but it only had a couple of swing sets and a merry-go-round, and it was just for the elementary school kids. Suddenly, I had a thought.

"There's Chandler Mountain. And it's not far from my house."

I wasn't familiar with much outside the county. My first job at the Omelet Shop had been over in Attalla. I had honestly never spent much time in Gadsden, the next bigger city, where David lived, only driving there to and from my new job at Woolco, so I had zero ideas about parks around there. And I was very confused that he was asking me if I "wanted to go throw a frisbee." Was he asking me out on a date?

"Okay, sounds good. I can pick you up Sunday, and you can show me around your town."

"I go to church!" I spat out before I even thought about it. *Oh, Lord ... he's gonna think I'm a "Jesus Freak" just like my ex-boyfriend Donny Burton did a few years before. And Donny had broken up with me after that.*

"It'll have to be after Sunday school. I don't always stay for preaching, but I never miss Sunday school." *Oh, my goodness ... I sound like such a Bible-thumping KID. Geez Louise.*

"Ok sure ... what time?" He didn't skip a beat.

"Twelve?"

"See you then!"

I gave him directions to my house, then went about making plans for this "date" we were going on. Going to Chandler Mountain to "throw a frisbee" was different. I'd never been on a date like this before. All I'd ever done with my previous boyfriends was go out to eat at McDonald's and to the bowling alley or the skating rink, mostly on Friday or Saturday nights. On very rare special occasions, we'd go to Bonanza or The Western Sizzlin' and eat a steak, then to a movie. We'd end up sitting out in their cars in my driveway and smooch until Daddy started flashing the front porch lights, which was my signal to come in the house at ten o'clock. I wasn't sure how Daddy would enforce his curfew on a Sunday afternoon date; he'd be asleep, and it would still be light outside.

I knew the fact that I was dating a guy who'd already graduated from college would bother Daddy, but I decided not to care. I was eighteen and would be graduating high school in the spring. What could he do about it? I decided not to even tell him. I was far more concerned with what David would think of my house. It was so tiny and, well, ugly. It had a tiny porch, more like just a stoop, and there were no flowers or anything pretty outside. That poor, old azalea bush I had vowed to care for all those years ago had since been all choked up with weeds, and our grass was knee deep most of the time. Crazy fears began to run through my head ... *Will Mama be drunk?* She usually was when I got home from church. Daddy would be asleep. *Oh God, what if David wakes him up? What will I wear?* I closed my eyes and swallowed hard. I had three days to figure it all out.

As planned, I only went to Sunday school that day and left immediately after to come home and get ready for my date with David. The church was only a mile away, so I was home before eleven o'clock in the morning. Thankfully, I had already done my hair and put on my makeup before going to church, so all I had to do was change clothes. I settled on my new blue jean bell-bottoms, and a purple T-shirt. I pulled my long curls back in a ponytail, wrapped a bow around the rubber band, and put on lip gloss. I didn't want to overdo it. I stood peeking through the front window curtains starting at 11:50 until I saw a big, blue car pull into the driveway at exactly 12:03 p.m. The gravel crunched and the dog barked. I jumped about two feet in the air.

"Oh, shit!" The words that I had intended as just a thought in my head escaped out of my mouth before I even realized it. I had just left my Sunday school class at the Steele Baptist Church. *Sorry, Jesus. Please forgive me.* I was a Christian, but I inadvertently cussed a little bit ... repeating words of exclamation I had heard all my life, I suppose. As I continued to look, I saw David immediately get out of his car and head toward the front door. He was holding a daffodil. *What? Seriously?* I instantly turned and ran into the kitchen on my way to the back of the house. "Mama!! He's here! Get the door, and please don't wake Daddy up!"

My mama was so funny. She scurried into the living room and peeked through the crack in the curtains.

"Well, don't you think your loud mouth might wake him up? Where are you running off to?" She was still snickering.

"My room ... I don't want him to think I'm sitting here waiting on him!" I answered incredulously.

"But you are!" she reminded me, still laughing out loud.

"Shhh!" I disappeared around the corner.

I had already asked her to please not drink until after we left, and she had obliged. She continued to peer through the crack in the curtains, out the window, and even though I had left the room, I heard her saying, "Jackie, this boy looks older than you ... how old is he?" Mouth agape, she had just gone ahead and pulled the curtains all the way open, right as I peeked back into the living room. Her face was practically pressed up against the windowpane.

"Mama!" I hushed back at her. "He's barely twenty-four! And PLEASE don't say anything about his age. And don't ask him any questions. Just act normal."

I heard the front door open and Mama, in her usual fashion, said, "Hi, Guy," her standard greeting and another of the Mama-isms that Jean and I had always laughed about.

"Hello, you must be Mrs. Brewer. I'm David." He spoke very politely, and I deduced that he must've reached out to shake her hand after handing her that daffodil he had been carrying, because I heard my mama exaggeratingly say, "Awwwwww!" *How nice of him.*

"Well, well, well ... ain't you fancy! Nice to meet you! And you don't have to call me Mrs. Brewer ... I'm just Mama!" *Oh, my goodness,* I thought as I rolled my eyes. *Did she really just say that?* I wondered if she shook his hand or just stood there, looking at his extended hand, giggling. I continued to hold my breath, as I pulled myself away from the bedroom door I had plastered myself up against while eavesdropping. And I honestly was so nervous, I think I might've pranced a little bit like a show pony, as I entered the living room, putting on my biggest smile.

"Hey there! You found us! Steele's a bit out in the country, ain't it? I mean, isn't it?" I immediately corrected myself. *Oh, dear Lord.*

"Yes ... it's nice out here," he answered, then said, "Wow ... don't you look pretty?" I smiled. "I see you've met my mother, Sara?" I was trying to recover from saying "ain't" by calling her "Mother" instead of "Mama," as she had introduced herself to him. Inner eye roll, I did that a lot. Mama gave me a big ol' exaggerated wink and clicked her tongue. *Help me, God.*

"Yes, I sure did. My pleasure." He looked from me back to Mama, nodding his head to her as he spoke. He was so freaking polite. "Is your dad here? I'd like to meet him too."

"HE'S ASLEEP!" Mama and I said simultaneously, and a bit too quickly and high-pitched.

"Oh, alright then. Are you ready to go, Jackie?"

"Yes, let's go!" I spoke through a smile while glancing nervously at Mama, still standing there holding her single daffodil. My heart was racing, but at least my breathing was back to normal. Once outside, he walked behind me over to the passenger side of his car and opened the car door for me. *What the heck?* I didn't know how to act. *Will he close it too? Or do I?* As soon as I slid in the seat, he paused before closing the door for me. *Alrighty, then.*

After driving up the mountain, admiring the spring flowers, we found an open field and threw the frisbee he had brought. After a few minutes, we went for a walk along one of the trails. It was nice.

"I know I didn't mention this to you before, but my mother is performing in a play this afternoon at the Theater of Gadsden, and she suggested I ask you if you'd like to go. First performance is at four. Sound like something you might want to do?" To say I was caught off guard is an understatement. My mind raced. *A play? At the Theater of Gadsden? To-day? His mama is in it?* The questions in my brain swirled. I wasn't prepared to answer him.

"What do I wear?" was the first thing that fell out of my mouth. Ugh.

"It doesn't matter," he answered.

What the heck? Did he just say that it doesn't matter? Of course it matters! How I look and how I dress always matters. People judge each other based on these things! I knew this all too well. He must've read my mind, so he quickly said, "Just wear whatever you wore to church this morning. I'm sure that'll be perfect."

"Oh, okay." I was relieved. I had only worn the church dress for an hour this morning for Sunday school and had been careful to hang it back up as soon as I had come home. "When do we need to go?"

"We'll just hang out up here on the mountain a while longer, then I'll take you back to your house and wait while you get changed, then we can drive to my house, and you can meet my mother before we head over to the theater. Sound like a plan?"

Oh, hell's bells! I thought but would never say aloud. *I'm on a date with a twenty-four-year-old man that my daddy hasn't met and doesn't even know about—now he's taking me to the theater to meet a lady he calls Mother, who's acting in the play at a theater that obviously requires I wear a dress. Great.* I tried to keep smiling the entire time I had this one-sided conversation in my head.

"Sounds perfect!" I finally said aloud. "Looking forward to it!" I lied.

We drove back down the mountain to my house, and I went into my room to change into my church dress while he sat in the kitchen, talking to Mama. I took a quick look in the mirror and noticed my red face, and my hair all frizzed up around it, because I was still sweating from our excursion on the mountain. I washed my face and applied a little bit of blush and some mascara. I made the choice not to put my panty hose back on, thinking that would look too "churchy," so I put on a pair of flat, strappy sandals that looked nice with the mid-calf floral dress. I took the rubber band out of my hair, brushed it out, and left my hair hanging in curls around my face and past my shoulders. I decided to amp up the lips a bit by applying my brightest pink lipstick; it matched my dress too. I stared at my reflection in the mirror a couple of minutes before shrugging my shoulders and deciding this was as good as it was going to get.

When I walked into the kitchen, David looked up and gasped, "Wow. Gorgeous." I blushed and tucked my head in. "Thank you." *Why do I feel embarrassed*? That thought fled, however, as soon as Mama piped up and said, "Woo hooooo! You look fancy, baby! You clean up NIIIIICE!" she laughed out loud while leaning over to playfully punch David's arm. "You bringin' out my 'fancy pants' little girl! Y'all gonna have a gooooood time!" She always drew out her words when she was being emphatic and silly. And clearly, she had snuck a couple of drinks while we were out.

"Thanks, Mama! See ya later!" I said quickly, then started toward the door.

"What time y'all gonna be back? You know your daddy gets up to go to work at ten. You best be back before then. And tomorrow's a school day, remember?"

Oh, yeah. I had briefly forgotten about that. It reminded me that I was still a high school country girl going on a nice, mature date with a college graduate. Reality check.

David answered before I could. "No problem, Mrs. Brewer. I'll have her back before nine-thirty."

It was around three o'clock before we arrived at David's house. I had been so nervous the entire ride from Steele to Gadsden, and it only got worse when he turned down the road beside Pruitt's Barbeque that I happened to know led to the Country Club Estates. I had only ever seen that road but never had a reason to go down it beyond the barbecue joint. He pulled the car into a long driveway that led to a beautiful two-story house with a manicured lawn. I noticed a newer Cadillac sitting inside the open garage.

"Oh, I see Mother has already left. But Dad's still here. Let's go on in so you can meet him."

I noticed that David called his mom "Mother," but had said "Dad" when referring to his father. Interesting. He came around to open the car door for me but, not being accustomed to that, I had already opened it myself and jumped out. The hem of my dress got caught in the door. As soon as I started to take a step, I felt it tug me backward. I stopped short, mortified. *What if his dad is looking out the window like my family and I always did anytime a person would pull into our driveway? Maybe not*, I reasoned. Their driveway didn't make loud, crunching sounds because it was paved. Good. "I gotcha," David said, as he quickly re-opened the door I had just slammed, rescuing my snagged hem. "Thank you," I said, relieved he didn't laugh at me.

We started up the curved walkway toward the Tudor-styled home. I noticed the nice windows with diamond-shaped grids on the panes. The curtains weren't open at all; I wondered why they were closed on a sunny Sunday afternoon. It briefly reminded me of our little house. *Did rich socialites have secrets too?* David rang the doorbell while simultaneously opening the large, ornate front door. "Dad?" he called out. Sounded like more of an announcement than a request to enter.

"Back here, Son," I heard a voice call back from another room. I noticed there were no lights on in the entryway; it was quite dark inside. We wound around through the formal living room, past a formal dining room, and into the "library," as David had called it. His dad was sitting in the corner of the large dark room, lined with bookcases, in a green velvet high back chair with his slippered feet propped up on a brown leather ottoman. There was a dimly lit Tiffany-styled floor lamp beside his head. He looked over the top of his reading glasses as we walked into the room, and as soon as he noticed me walking behind David, he stood. I noticed he sat down a small glass with amber liquid, which rattled a bit from the ice cubes, before extending his right hand toward me. He had the same, warm smile as David. "Hello, young lady. I'm David's father, Jim." He didn't say he was David's dad. *Why do I notice these things so much?*

"Hi. I'm Jackie." I reached forward to accept his hand. He warmly, but gently, shook mine. David was already speaking. "Is Mom already at the theater?"

"Yes, she had to be there at two," Jim answered as he sat back down, retrieving his glass as he did. "Would you like a drink, Jackie? Dave?" he offered, gesturing toward a small oval glass table with several bottles sitting atop it. He waited for David to answer.

"No, thanks, Dad. We just wanted to stop by and see if you guys were already there. Are you going?"

"I'm going to the seven o'clock performance." He continued to sip until the glass was empty. He then got up and walked over to the oval table, picking up a glass decanter. There was also an ice bucket, filled with some ice but mostly water. The glass bucket was sweating, so I could tell it had been there a while. He poured more of the brown liquid into his glass, added an ice cube, then took a long swallow. I realized I had been staring, so as soon as he looked back at me, I averted my gaze. Looking around the room, I said, "Your house is really nice." Seemed like I needed to say something.

"Thank you, Jackie. We enjoy it." *What did that mean ..."we enjoy it"?* I'd never heard someone say they "enjoy" their house. I smiled at him; he returned my smile with a slight wink.

"So, Dave ... are you taking Jackie to see Mom's performance tonight? Should be a good one," he spoke while looking over the top of his glass as he took another sip. He never took his eyes off me though. Didn't look at David while they spoke. I thought I saw sadness in those eyes.

"Yes, Sir. We're going to the four o'clock performance. Then, I'll take Jackie to dinner, then back home. So, I'll see you guys back here tonight around ten."

"Where do you live, Jackie?" Jim asked, still looking at my face. Was he watching me? And why was I so uncomfortable?

"Steele. It's a little town over in St. Clair County."

"Ahhh. Okay, I've heard of it. So, do you work in Steele? Or are you still in college? What do you do?" *Now he is prying,* I thought. No wonder he was looking at me for so long. He was trying to figure out how old I was.

"Ummm, no Sir. I work at Woolco. That's where I met David."

"So, you're still in college then?"

"No, Sir. I'm still in high school. In Ashville. I'm a Senior though—I graduate in May." I didn't know whether to be proud of myself or a little ashamed. Was he thinking I was too young for his son?

"Oh, good. So, where are you going to college?" Since I didn't have any plans to go to college, I simply replied, "I'm not sure yet. Still thinking through my options." My smile and my answer were both awkward and, apparently, he could tell because he waved his hand and said, "Oh sure ... sure. You've still got time. You'll figure it out." He had class.

"Well, we should go. Want to get a good seat and see Mom hopefully before she goes onstage. Bye, Dad," David said, as he and his dad shook hands.

"Bye, Mr. Taylor. It was nice to meet you." I reached out to shake his hand. He returned the gesture but held onto my hand for a few seconds. I thought I saw pain in his eyes. Even though he smiled, his lips were tight. He nodded as he gave my hand a slight squeeze.

"You too, Jackie. It was my pleasure."

I thought about his face all the way to the theater.

She was beautiful: perfectly coifed platinum hair, pearl earrings, and a matching double strand pearl necklace. We walked backstage only minutes before opening curtain. Of course, she was in full stage makeup, but with one glance I could tell that she was perfectly gorgeous without it. Natural beauty. I was struck by her high cheekbones, bow-shaped lips, and pretty white teeth. She smiled broadly the minute she saw David enter her dressing room. It was evident she loved her son. Made me smile too. She hadn't noticed me until she and David were embracing, and she looked over his shoulder. I just stood there, hands clasped in front of me, studying her face, which was looking at me over David's back. *Could I read her face? Maybe I shouldn't even be thinking about that right now. Why am I always doing that?* I shook off the notion.

Her smile diminished slightly as David pulled away, turned toward me, and introduced us.

"Mother, this is Jackie."

I continued to smile, unclasping my hands, and reaching my right hand forward. I even felt myself slightly bow. It felt involuntary, but she didn't even notice. As soon as she left the embrace of her son, she immediately stepped toward me and held her arms open. Ignoring my extended hand, she leaned in and gave me a curt, little hug and a side-cheek air kiss. Well, this was new. I just went with it.

"Well, hell-ooooo, young lady. Jackie, is it?" Immediately following the hug, she leaned back slightly. Her face was only ten inches away, and her eyes were looking directly into mine. Her huge smile remained fixed and didn't appear genuine. *Well, she IS an actress,* I thought to myself. She's a professional when it comes to putting on the "right" face. So, I focused on her eyes. Eyes always tell the truth.

"Yes, Ma'am. Nice to meet you." This was awkward. I didn't remember ever meeting anyone for the first time and being only inches away from their face during the introductions. And I hadn't hugged her back because I had been so caught off guard by her immediate embrace. She leaned back, arm's length, with a hand on each of my shoulders. She looked from the top of my head down to my chin in a second, before immediately turning back to David.

"She's very pretty, Son." Again, the feigned smile. When she shot me a cursory glance, I returned it. I could do a curt, little smile too.

"Ok ... alright ... well, I best get prepared to go on stage. Curtain time is almost here!" she spoke gleefully as she kissed David on both cheeks before reaching a dainty hand, ring on every finger, to mine. "Lovely to meet you, my dear." I didn't believe her.

"Break a leg, Mother," David said as he kissed her forehead. I took a deep breath as she flittered out of the room and onto the stage, turning for one last blown kiss to her son.

I was relieved to finally sit down in that auditorium, lights dimmed, curtain rising. This would be a performance I would remember forever.

The play was *My Fair Lady*, and she was Mrs. Higgins.

9

All the King's Horses, and All the King's Men...

David and I began to regularly see each other after our date to the theater. Within a few months, I graduated from high school and Daddy declared that I was officially an adult.

"Alright, Girl ... your ass is done with school now so it's time for you to figure out what's next." He had such a way with words.

"I want to go to college. I can apply for scholarships?" I wasn't sure why I made what should have been a declarative statement into a question. I guess I was still a little afraid of him. Combined with the desire that I had carried from the time I was a little girl ... I wanted to do something that might make him approve of me. And I was determined to be a success in life.

"You already done that thing at the vocational school, Jackie ... that nursin' thing, or whatever you wanna call it ... that medical something. You ought to be able to find a good job ... ain't no sense in you trynna go to no college." He had always told Jean and I that as soon as we got out of school, we'd be on our own. I decided I'd follow the often-unspoken Alabama "rule" with girls like me: get married first, then figure the rest of it out. I felt like I might be in love with David—I certainly cared about him—but I was uncertain about it being forever, especially when I discovered the one thing he had been holding back from me, and why he hadn't told me sooner.

When David finally told me about his illness, I remember I wasn't exactly worried. I probably should have been; after all, I cared deeply about him. In fact, I saw it as maybe a sign from God ... he would be the man I was destined to marry because he needed me. I aspired to become a nurse, so I saw it as a challenge. I thought I could help him.

David was a brittle, juvenile onset diabetic and, since the age of five, had been in and out of hospitals. His parents had made sure that he always received top-notch medical care. However, back then, there wasn't a ton of information on how to treat his out-of-control blood sugar. He had been insulin dependent as long as he could remember, and no amount of insulin seemed to make a difference. He told me he had been sickly all his life, and how his mother was always an over-the-top protector of him, controlling every aspect of his life. All he wanted now was to enjoy living.

By now, he knew about my story, the dysfunctional upbringing I had, and he thought the two of us could together "escape" the rule of controlling parents. I couldn't disagree. We both wanted out of Alabama: he from an overprotective, doting mother, and me from an abusive, angry father. Surely, we'd be perfect together.

Everything began to happen so fast. Maybe even too fast. David had been offered an executive sales position at a company in Atlanta, so this was his chance.

"I'm taking that job in Atlanta, Jackie."

"That's good … I mean … for you." I wanted to be happy for him.

"Come with me!"

"What do you mean? I can't just come with you!"

"Marry me." There was that goofy smile of his. His dimpled chin.

"OK!"

My God, it was such a knee-jerk, immediate reply that both of us froze for a hot second, staring at each other. Then we grabbed each other and embraced, laughing. Looks like we were both getting what we wanted. And he had already told me that he loved me. I wasn't sure about love, but I was sure I wanted to move away. We decided not to ask our parents … we'd just tell them we were getting married. David didn't want to face his mother's possible disapproval with his choice of a wife, and I just didn't want to ask my daddy anything. I had waited for this day all my life. I also had no problem telling Daddy I was getting married, knowing there was nothing he could do about it. In true fashion, his response was, "Well, don't let the screen door hit you on your ass on the way out!"

When David's mother, Joy, invited me to meet her for lunch shortly after our decision, I didn't know what to expect.

"He's not well, Jackie. He needs you. If you go to the right school and get a good education, you could be the answer to our prayers. You can help me take care of him," she spoke through tears.

"Yes, I promise you I will help him." I'm still not sure if I was answering more from a desire to help him because I loved him, or if it was because I knew he needed me. And so did Joy. And by then, I had begun to recognize that I needed to be needed. I subconsciously navigated toward relationships, jobs, etc., where I could find some worth from being able to take care of things, fix things. I saw it as an attribute.

But, to marry David, I'd need to first begin the transformation.

"You'll need elocution classes, Dear. My son needs a wife who can hold her own in a business conversation." Joy was well-bred, formally educated, and a properly trained social "Delta Suth-uhn" lady. She would help me be the same. Truthfully, I was happy to learn. I hated my southern hick accent and had longed to be able to speak in a manner that was more ... well, elegant. She also scheduled a bridal tea at their country club and asked me to come early with my bridesmaids to help set up. The truth was, my bridesmaids and I had to be coached on some etiquette tips because none of us had ever seen the inside of a country club in our lives. She also insisted I enroll in more advanced nursing courses when David and I moved to Atlanta after the wedding. Get a real education. I promised her I would.

All this time I had considered myself to be the fixer, yet here I was submitting myself to being fixed. I was willing to let her make me into whomever she wanted me to be. I had to look right, talk right, and act right if I was going to marry her son and bear their family name. I must be transformed in order to become a proper young lady.

"We're going to have to take you shopping!" She lit up at the prospect. "I'll have you looking like a proper princess in your wedding dress!" I remember standing on that little, round pedestal in front of the large trifold mirrors and seeing her reflection behind me, hands clasped beneath her chin, smiling from ear to ear. She was downright giddy. Mama couldn't accompany us that day because, unlike David's mom, she worked a full time job. As I look back on it now, I think perhaps she chose not to come because she didn't want to play second fiddle to my future mother-in-law. And Mama knew me, inside and out. She knew it would never work, but she dared not say anything that she thought might hurt my feelings.

So, in the fall of 1979, only four months after I had graduated high school, we had the fancy wedding. Daddy even walked me down the aisle with a smile on his face. And another benefit from hindsight is, all these years later, I understand it. I was trying to build a life inside a palace made of glass. I fully intended to be a princess while David would be my Prince Charming. And together, we'd keep the glass shiny and clear—perfect and transparent. But glass breaks when anything hard is thrown at it, and before long, we were broken.

David's way of escape was to pour himself into his new job, only to come home, relax, and do whatever he wanted to do. His choice of relief from his sickness was to smoke pot. And a LOT of it. He was finally out from under the scrutiny of his mother, who demanded that he take care of himself in the manner she thought best. All his life, she hadn't really cared so much about how he felt emotionally or spiritually, just as long as he kept his diabetes under control and stayed alive. He had suppressed his true personality for years trying to please her. Now that he was married and away from her, all he cared about was relieving the stress of being the imperfect, sick little boy that she always treated him as. Of course, I had sort of morphed into doing the same thing. I cared about him, and as much as I understood love, that's what I was supposed to do. Keep him healthy; I had promised her. But we both realized we were broken.

All these years later, looking back on this time, I recognize there are many different definitions of that word. Broken. Separated into many pieces. Shattered. In need of repair. As a fixer, I thought I could locate the flaw and fix it. I could make it look almost like brand new again, and no one would be the wiser. On the contrary, I might conclude that the brokenness is irreparable. I can try to fix it but fail. I was frustrated with myself because I couldn't put all the pieces back together and I should have been able to. It's my own fault. Why can't I fix it?

I had learned a lot from meeting David. And his mother. He taught me that social status didn't really matter to him. He was looking for a simple girl who was genuine. Unpretentious. That was me. But even then, I recognized that I wanted more. I had always dreamed of being in a higher social class and I hated to admit, even to myself, that I secretly wouldn't mind being just a little pretentious. I wanted fancy clothes and a white house with columns and a big front porch with rocking chairs. Maybe even the stereotypical picket fence with roses and ivy curling around perfectly even slats, like those I had seen in the magazines and like the families of my fancy school friends. I wanted to cook big suppers where my family would all sit around the table, hold hands, and pray before eating. And I wanted my husband to need me, but I didn't really want to need him back. I didn't want to need anybody. I wanted to be the strong one. I wanted to have it all together and never show weakness. I wouldn't be like Mama, and the man I married would not be like Daddy.

However, I now realize that I was the one who had gone into the marriage for all the wrong reasons. It was a version of "love" based upon childhood dreams and fairy-tale wishes from a teenager who had painted an unrealistic image of what she wanted. I was a girl who was looking at her future adult life as a woman in control. One who could have it all, with a cherry on top. I didn't realize how ill-equipped I was to marry a young man who was so sick and who, in order to combat his pain, turned to drugs and alcohol for relief—both physically and mentally. He didn't need a wife who couldn't handle all that. A wife who kept insisting he shouldn't rely on booze or marijuana, but rather who preached at him all the time, trying to drag him to church with her, declaring, "If you just trust God, He will help you!" I was insistent, desperately pleading with him to go to church. It was the only way I believed he would ever get better.

I saw knowing Jesus as a cure-all for any problem he (or anyone) had, but I now recognize that I had a very unhealthy association with the idea of any type of external substance use. I honestly thought that if we all just lived right, while trusting God, all our problems would go away. Like having an imaginary genie or fairy who would just wave a wand, and all would be good. Anything that was broken would magically be put back together. For a period of my life, that's what I wanted to believe. However, David wasn't buying it, and I wasn't about to budge. I would remain in control and never, EVER compromise.

So, our relationship gradually began to fall apart into a million tiny pieces. I tried to put it back together, to fix everything. But I couldn't; this was out of my control. And all the king's horses and all the king's men couldn't put it back together again. I eventually left Atlanta and moved back to Alabama.

It was only a few years later that I received the news that David had died. It broke my heart. Still does, to this day. I have never spoken to his family again.

10

Which Is Better ...
One? Or Two?

I had no choice except to move back in with Mama and Daddy after leaving Atlanta. I had left David so suddenly that I didn't take time to plan any of it. I had no job, no money, and little to no self-respect. I felt like such a loser.

"Well, here you are," Daddy taunted when I returned to the house, "running right back to where you came from. I knew you would! Damn, Girl, when are you gonna stop bein' so hard-headed and start listening to me?" Daddy had told me again and again that I had made a mistake trying to "marry up" and fit in to that country club life, and I'd been desperate to prove him wrong. But the very thing I had determined I would accomplish, I hadn't. It had only been six months since the day David and I had made a promise before God that we'd stay together for better and for worse, in sickness and in health, but I hadn't kept my end of the bargain. I had turn-tailed right back into the hellhole I thought I had finally escaped. Daddy was happy with himself because he had warned me not to marry David. That we didn't match up. That I was just a poor, little girl from Steele, and I tried to fit in to a family that knew I would never be good enough.

I couldn't stand that he had been right, which is something I would never say aloud. So, I was determined not to remain single and continue living under my daddy's roof.

Almost immediately, I decided to just jump back into option number two. I'd get back together with my previous high school boyfriend, Alan. I knew I had broken his heart when I had abruptly broken up with him during our senior year right after I had met David. I hoped he still had feelings for me, and it turned out he did. He was from the same little high school as me, and his family was not unlike mine, at least not socioeconomically. They were a good family, salt-of-the-earth people. And he was sweet and handsome. He also had dreams of moving out of Alabama, and he said he loved me. That was all that mattered to me. I wanted to try again ... maybe this time I could get it right, be a good wife. I didn't even need time to think about it.

So, we did it ... within just a few months, we'd planned a small wedding at a little country church and tied the knot. Daddy had refused to attend. "I already gave you away once, and I ain't doin' it again!" he'd barked, shaking his head. "You don't know what the hell you want, Girl!" He wasn't wrong, but what I did know was that this time I was hell-bent and determined. This was a test I would pass.

I have never liked tests anyway. I don't enjoy being put on the spot and asked questions just to see if I will provide the correct answer. I need time to think about it, decide what I think the answer should be. And that would be dependent upon who was asking. Who was administering the test, and also what kind of test it might be. I really, REALLY don't like tests where the answers are objective—black or white. With only ONE correct answer. No wiggle room. It's too much pressure for me. That's why I always hated math. I prefer the subjective tests where I can form my own correct answer and organize as many words as I want to explain it. I want choices, not absolutes. Of course, now I understand that is part of being a control freak. A fixer. Those of us who struggle with this issue prefer to be able to analyze and decide for ourselves how to arrive at answers. Our answers, the ones we feel good about. I never wanted to be put on the spot, because what if I get it wrong? I had decided being wrong must never be an option. I had come too far to backslide now.

So, I promised myself that I would never do that, give people tests just so I could find pleasure in watching them fail. All because I secretly wanted to catch them not paying attention, but I did. Most of us do, even when we don't realize we're doing it. We both test and are tested by others. We set ourselves up, and those we love, with ridiculous expectations and find ourselves disappointed when they don't pass our unfair tests. When they fail, we subconsciously mark them with an oversized mental red "X," and up goes our guard.

I often wondered if this had been God testing me. I was certainly of the mind back in those days that He must've been. And I had made up my mind all those years ago that I would not fail a test God gave me. I needed to always pass His tests. Then maybe, He'd leave me alone; just love me and be glad I was a good Christian girl, trying my best to live right. I would push through and face the challenges along the way, knowing that at the end of this life, I would get to the pearly gates and He'd let me in, telling me what a good and faithful servant I had been. And He'll hopefully congratulate me for all the poor souls I had fixed along the way, those who were destined for hell had I not opened their eyes and made them see the light. I think I honestly *thought* that! Like God would just be happy with me because I had "got saved" and fixed some of the other "lost" people. Yeah, right.

One of these days, in the "sweet by and by," the first thing I think I'll do when I get to heaven is to give God a fist bump. Maybe a high-five. For many reasons. First, I made it in! Second, for the scripture He gave us in Romans 8:28: *And we know that in all things God works together for good to those who love him and who have been called according to his purpose.* Way to go, God. I really needed that scripture, more than a few times in my life. Then after I congratulate God on a job well done with that one, I'll have a few questions for Him too.

Before you start to go all sanctimonious on me, saying to yourselves, "Why, she's being downright disrespectful! Talking about saying that stuff to God," here's the thing ... I see God as a Father who is willing to answer the questions of His children. He made us, so He knows we're not perfect. We are far from it; that's why we need Him. Because even in the hard times, the tests, hopefully they are developing strength in us. Fortitude. The ability to go through the hardships of life and not only survive but thrive in them.

In making my own choices, I found out God has a sense of humor. For the next several years after my relationship with David ended, I decided not only would I rush into getting married AGAIN to Alan, but I'd also focus on my career. I became even more determined to become a part of the health care field. My dreams of getting my nursing degree withered, but I remained committed to some form of "nursing" ... defined in my mind as "taking care of and/or helping patients." I knew this was what I wanted to do. Help people. Ok, I didn't realize it at the time, but I do now—*fix* people. I wanted to fix people. Whatever their ailment might be, I wanted to be part of the healing. Control Freak 101. And of all the possible medical fields I could've landed in, it ended up being ophthalmology—the eye care field—where my main job all day, every day, was to give the eye tests. The ones where I force people to sit in a dark room, look at an eye chart twenty feet away, and make choices. My sole purpose was to dole out tests, demand answers, and, at the end of the test, hand them over a prescription that would help them see better. Yes, the test that so many people despise because they worry they won't get it right. Subjective. They choose.

So, I sat in front of patients, asking them, "Which is better? One? Or two?" as I was flipping different lens options in front of their eyes. They would invariably say, "Show me again; I can't choose!" Was this some sort of cruel joke God was playing on me? The career that would end up lasting thirty-seven years for me would be me testing people all day and forcing them to choose a lens that would help them see life clearly? I still smile at the irony of it all.

Many of my patients left my office so afraid they might've made the wrong choice and would end up unable to see clearly, and it would be all their fault. Like, they'd chosen their vision for the rest of their lives and whatever glasses they ended up with would be their life's vision. They'd re-live the exam, kicking themselves for not picking the right lens that day in that dark room, with dilated eyes, and that gal flipping so many lenses around they couldn't choose. They worried they'd failed the test. *Ok, again please ... can you show me again? Which lens should I pick? They look so close to the same, I can't choose. I don't want to choose the "wrong lens"; otherwise, I'll end up with the "wrong glasses" and the "wrong vision"! And it'll be my fault for making the "wrong choice" during the test...*

Now I understand that we don't just see with our eyes. We also see with our hearts. Life has a way of giving us increased wisdom, along with clarity of vision. I look at people, faces, circumstances through different lenses now. The old lenses have dulled and become foggy. Would I pick that same lens I chose all those years ago? Or would I have to ask the doctor to show me one more time? Sometimes, the lenses through which we view life can be distorted. We blink and squint, hoping that might help, but it's our worldview, or our circumstances at the time, that determine our vision.

Through the years, I have made choice after choice and what felt like mistake after mistake. I got a few things right, but more than a few things wrong. I hurt people. I hurt myself. Even disappointed God, no doubt. My marriage to Alan had started going downhill. I couldn't help but ask myself what I had done wrong this time, but I didn't have answers. I was in turmoil mentally and emotionally, asking myself, *Which husband is better? One? Or two?* Had I picked the "wrong lens" again? Did I need to check my own vision? I desperately wanted to see clearly. I wanted to get it right.

I needed to get naked with myself and do an "I" exam.

11

Braveheart

Birmingham, Alabama February 1987

Alan and I finally separated and admittedly, I was shattered. I had failed again and was disappointed in myself—my inability to
make it work. Of course, I had also never wanted to hurt him. After six
years, I believed I had finally got it right. Or, I guess I should say that I
had wanted to believe it. I was older ... and wiser ... so I thought I had
control of the situation. Yes, there were things that we disagreed upon,
but Alan was so easy-going that he just gave in to my demands most of
the time. He knew my family and was aware of the environment I had
grown up in. He was gentle and kind, never wanting me to feel taken for
granted or mistreated. And even though I was insecure, I pretended to be
confident. Self-assured, yet I was anything but, and I kind of hated myself
for it.

By this point, I decided I was just a failure. How had this happened?
We had gone to church, we didn't drink, we both had good jobs ... all the
things I believed could "fix" anything wrong in a marriage. They were all
the things that were not in my life growing up. I think we loved each other in a puppy-love kind of way, but I made sure I was strong and in control all the time. Making sure he needed me. But he didn't anymore. He
had done well for himself, starting his own business and had other wom-
en flirting with him all the time. Why not? He was a great guy. I knew he
was getting fed up with me, and I couldn't take the fear of rejection. So, I
left him. I dared not let him leave me first. Hell no, but I couldn't bring
myself to file for divorce. Not yet. Maybe there was a chance? I moved
into an apartment and decided to take a few months to think our marriage through.

I wasn't proud of the fact that I was alone again. At the age of twenty-six, I had already been married twice: the first one ended in divorce, and the second one wasn't looking good at this point. I certainly had no plans to jump back into another relationship with a man. I needed to prove to myself that I could make it on my own, and I was very determined. The first few months after we separated, I lived in my own apartment, had my own car, and thrived in my job. The physician I worked for at the time respected me professionally and had promoted me to a manager position. I felt like I had made it, not dependent on anyone but myself. And even better, the fixer in me, the control freak, had a gaggle of employees who were under my direction and leadership. I was finally accomplishing all my professional goals, and I lied to myself that I didn't need anyone to love me. I tried to make myself believe this was all I wanted. But, as much as I hated to admit it, I was wrong.

Jackson, Tennessee December 1987

After a few months of being separated from Alan, my friend Mary, from a previous job up in Tennessee, invited me to come up from Birmingham for a weekend getaway. "You *need* this, Jackie...it'll be *fun!*" I agreed. Why not? This would be out of my comfort zone ... it was Texas-Two Step night at the local country-western bar called The Waterhole.

I can't believe I'm doing this... I thought to myself as I stood there, leaning up against the rails surrounding a dance floor filled with people who were dancing, laughing, and having a good time. *This is supposed to be fun ... so, have fun ... have fun .... oh Lord.* I kept repeating this in my head, hoping that it would morph from a thought to an actual thing. The smell of alcohol and the cigarette smoke was stifling. There were far too many people crammed into that place, and every single one of them was moving. No one was still: they were either dancing or circling the dance floor, eyes darting to and fro, in search of a potential dance partner. Or someone to hook up with. I didn't know which—it was probably a little of both, but I had decided this was NOT my idea of a good night. But, as any good friend would do, I stood there silently, occasionally faking a smile if I made eye contact with anyone. There seemed to be an equal number of guys and gals, so, in turn, I was equally generous with my fake smile. Acknowledge everyone; it was the least I could do.

Then, I felt hot breath on my neck. "Hey Darlin'," I heard from behind, as I simultaneously felt an arm land on my back and hook around my neck. It immediately occurred to me that the hand at the other end of that heavy arm was precariously dangling over my right breast. Only an inch or two away. My immediate reaction was a big, demonstrative flinch. But because it was involuntary, I had no control of the lack of subtly. I looked right at his face, of course, not answering. *Who the heck are YOU? And what makes you think you can walk up to me and throw your arm around me?!* I had plenty to say in my head but couldn't manage to say it aloud. Not only had he startled me with such an abrupt gesture, but he was not my type at all. That was two strikes against him already. He was staring right at my face—eyes wandering from the top of my head, past my eyes, and to my lips, which were tightly closed, I might add. And I'm assuming my eyes were exactly the opposite. I could feel they were wide, nonplussed. Again, no words.

"Little lady. You. Are. GORGEOUS." He paused in between each word and left his jaw slack, as he continued to bobble his head around and lean in, his face almost touching mine. I moved away. Again, not subtly. "Thank you," I responded while backing away. Of course, I bumped right into another couple who happened to be standing up against the rails right behind me. I spun around, clumsily, toward them.

I felt my eyes widen as they tried to contact the female in the couple. "Oh, I'm so sorry. Please excuse me." I prayed she could read my pleading expression. However, the dude still hanging on my shoulder appeared to be unfazed by my disinterest. Persistent. "Hey, Baby, you wanna dance?" He slurred and when he opened his mouth a little wider, I noticed he barely had three teeth in his head, surrounded by a scraggly beard, and his breath reeked of a combination of Budweiser and Marlboro Lights. I began to frantically search for my friend as I answered, "Um, no … thank you. I'm holding onto my friend's purse for her right now." I gestured with my head toward the middle of the dance floor to Mary, who was right in the mix, dancing with everybody, having a blast and, honestly, quite oblivious to me and the toothless dude. *Oh, well…at least she's having fun.* Rolling my eyes—and this time I didn't mind if the eye roll was out loud or not—I just wanted that guy off me.

I bent my shoulder down slightly and ducked out from under his arm. "What'sa matter? Am I not good enough for ya?" He seemed perturbed now by my actions. "C'mon, Girl—let's dance! These people will watch the purses for you." He gestured toward the couple I had already almost knocked over. Thankfully, they read my face as I looked at them wide-eyed and attempted a discreet shake of my head in the negative. "No, sorry we can't. We're just about to leave," the female answered. They turned to walk away but not before she leaned in and whispered, "Good luck, Sister."

As I watched the back of their heads retreating, I turned back to face my new "friend," wondering if I was just going to have to bluntly tell him that I was not interested. That's when I noticed another guy had appeared and was standing right beside him. He was a big guy. Handsome. I only got a quick glance at him, so I was a bit confused at this point. My eyes were still seeking to make eye contact with Mary, who was having so much fun, she didn't notice what I was doing or what was happening. The big guy shot me a knowing glance before saying to Mr. Toothless Guy, "She's with me." Then he looked at me and said, "Are you ready for another drink?" Again, speechless, I just nodded. I noticed Mr. "T" throw both his hands up in a mock surrender and back away, mumbling, "Sure, okay, okay … I didn't know she was with anybody." I watched him disappear into the crowd, feeling relieved.

The big guy moved in closer. And as he did, I got a much better look at him. His face was handsome, eyes were kind, and he had a rather tousled mullet, which was endearing. But the main thing that stood out to me was that he was wearing a kilt! In Jackson, Tennessee, at a country-western bar surrounded by "good ol' boys." He held a bottle of beer in one hand and a lit cigarette in the other. "So, do you need another drink?" he asked me, as if the last couple minutes hadn't happened. He also offered no explanation as to why he had decided to walk up and get in the middle of it. He glanced down at my glass, raised his eyebrows, and said, "What are you drinking?" I noticed he had an accent. *Who IS this guy?* I thought before quickly answering, "Coke."

"Coke? You're drinking a coke?"

"Yes. I'm drinking a coke. Why?"

"No reason. Just not something you see often at a club. Ya know?" The accent sounded thicker. He smiled and walked away but not before reassuring me he'd be right back. Which I was hoping he'd do, since I didn't want Mr. Toothless to show up again. Mary, still tearing up the dance floor, remained clueless to my situation. I'm pretty sure she might've forgotten that I was even there.

The handsome, big guy reappeared after only a couple minutes with a fresh glass of coke in his hand. He extended it to me, and I happily accepted it. I hadn't realized how dry my mouth was, so I stood there and gulped it down. I was also careful not to make eye contact with him, lest he think I was staring. I mean, surely, he must KNOW that he did kind of stand out in the bar. He was wearing a skirt for goodness' sake! After swallowing the very much needed ice-cold liquid, I sighed, set the glass down on a nearby table, and looked at him. He was looking at me too, sipping his beer and had finally stubbed out his cigarette.

"Sorry if I did the wrong thing there … but it looked to me like you needed rescuing." He continued the stare and paused, waiting for my answer.

"Yes, thank you," I responded. "That guy caught me off guard."

"So, are you with anyone tonight?"

"Yes, my friend," I said, as I gestured toward Mary on the dance floor. "She's the one in the red dress who literally has not stopped dancing since we walked in the door."

"Yes, I saw you walk in with her. You don't like to dance?"

"Not really." *Is that the right answer? What if he shrugs, says "Ok," then walks away?* My thoughts were all over the place. If he'd noticed us walk in two hours ago, why hadn't I seen him? And honestly, how could I have missed him?! I laughed inwardly, still wondering what made him decide to come to The Waterhole wearing a kilt. *This guy's got a set of balls on him,* I said in my head as the thought occurred to me. *Does he realize where he IS?*

No sooner had that thought crossed my mind until I heard him throw a question to another guy a few yards away. Even though the music was loud, and the lights were low—not to mention the cloud of smoke hovering overhead—he didn't seem to be shy about shouting across the dance floor. "Hey, where can I buy some fags?" He didn't even TRY to say it quietly. He asked the question as if it were normal to be standing in Jackson—Podunk—Tennessee, inside a country bar, wearing a skirt, and asking where he could buy some fags?! *What's this guy's DEAL?* After asking his apparent friend the question, he looked back down at my face. Reading my expression, he said, "Oh, sorry. I should've said cigarettes. Fags are what we call cigarettes in Scotland; I'm from Scotland. Where are you from?" Again, this dude was just so chill and was talking to me like this situation was common for him. Well, it certainly wasn't for me.

"Alabama," I answered, still in awe.

"Yep, I could tell you have an accent," he smiled as he sipped.

"I have an accent?!? You think I have an accent?"

"You do to me," he answered and laughed. "C'mon, let's dance." He extended his right hand to me while gesturing toward the dance floor with the other. Without blinking, I placed my hand in his.

I really wasn't much of a dancer but when John Cougar's "Cherry Bomb" began to blare out of the speakers, I thought, *why not?* Since Mary had dragged me out to this bar, I might as well enjoy myself. The dance floor was crowded, and this dance was what we called a "fast dance" in Alabama. I had only ever been to the prom in high school, and all songs were classified as either "slow dance" or "fast dance." Mostly, my friends from school and I preferred slow dancing at the prom as it gave us a chance to be held close to our dates. Not shockingly, most of us country white kids had no rhythm whatsoever, so we rarely got on the prom dance floor when they played a fast song. I had a couple times, but it had been years. So, we danced. Awkwardly at first, then we seemed to connect, and I couldn't believe I was even having a little bit of fun.

"So, what brings you here?" He began the small talk.

"My friend insisted we come," I said, while gesturing with my head in Mary's direction.

"She had to convince you? So, you're not enjoying yourself?"

"It's ok. Just not really my 'thing.'" I shrugged but continued dancing. "You?"

"I'm here for work. There's a bunch of us engineers from Britain here working at Proctor and Gamble for six months."

"Six months? So how long have you been here?"

"In the United States four months and in Jackson, only a few weeks. Like I said, we'll be in the States for six months." He continued to look at me as he spoke. I was trying to read his face. Was he telling me this, wondering if maybe that was long enough to have more time to spend with me? "So, you live here now?" he asked.

"No. I still live in Alabama. I used to live in Jackson a few years ago, and that's how I met Mary. She and I worked together."

"Why'd you move back? Hate your job?" Now, he was digging a little deeper. I was already feeling a bit guilty for dancing with him because I was technically still married to Alan. I was not ready to talk to this guy on such a personal level.

"Long story," I answered, as I waved the question off. That was all I was going to say at this point. I didn't know anything about this guy, so I didn't trust him. We continued the dance until John Cougar belted out the last note of the song and exited the dance floor together. We stood at that same rail that ran along the side of the dance floor, and I still was holding both mine and Mary's purses. It hadn't even occurred to me that I danced with him holding those two bags, one draped over each shoulder.

We stood there a couple of hours talking, and it seemed time had stopped. Our conversation was easy and flowed well. He was interesting, regaling me with stories of his travels. He didn't ask a lot about me, which, honestly, was a relief.

A couple more hours passed before the overhead lights flashed a couple times. Being a novice to going out to bars on a Saturday night, I didn't realize it was the signal for "last call." He leaned in and asked, "Do you need another coke? And do you seriously not drink? At all?"

"No, thank you, and no, I don't drink. Seriously. Why are you so surprised?"

He shrugged. "I don't know ... I guess I'm just still confused that I've met a girl at a bar who doesn't drink."

"I dance," I shot back with a wink. He smiled.

I felt a tug at my elbow and spun around to see Mary standing behind me. She was sweating and had wiped most of her makeup off. Barefoot, she held her black high heels by the straps, one in each hand. "Who's that guy?" she asked, excitedly, eyes wide.

"Oh, my goodness, I'm not exactly sure. He told me when he first asked me to dance, but his accent is so thick and the music was so loud, I didn't catch his name and I didn't want to look dumb and ask again."

"Accent?"

"Yes!" I leaned into her giggling. I felt like a little schoolgirl again.

"Where's he from?"

"Gurllll, he definitely ain't from around here!" Again, giggling. *Why am I acting so silly?*

"So, do you LIKE him?" she winked, smiling broadly.

"Yeah, he seems like a good guy. He saved me from some random redneck who was hitting on me earlier. Which you, no doubt, never even noticed."

"What can I say, I was having fun! Looks like you are too, right?" Her eyes looked questioning; she wanted to ask me something else.

"Yeah, sure. But it's time to go, right? This place is closing?" By now all the lights were up, the music had stopped, and people had begun to file out. Then I felt someone behind me brush against my back. It was him, my mystery guy. He extended his right hand toward Mary. "How're ya doing? I'm Gordon," he said, actually clear enough for me to understand him for the first time that night. Dang, his accent was thick, especially when he said his own name. The way he rolled his "r's," it was kind of sexy. Which I was surprised and disgusted with myself for even letting my mind go in that direction. I'd also begun to admire him in that kilt. Clearly, he was not self-conscious and, in fact, was bold enough to come here tonight wearing it.

"Gordon?" Mary repeated as a question. He nodded.

"I'm Mary," she replied.

"Nice to meet you," they both said, almost simultaneously.

"Soooooooo," she began tentatively, which was not Mary's personality, "I met a new friend, and he and I are leaving here and going to breakfast. What are you guys gonna do?"

"What?" I asked, incredulous. "What do you mean by that? I rode with YOU, remember? Where are we going to eat breakfast at two-thirty in the morning?"

"Denny's!" She practically spat it out, eyes wide with brows raised. She pulled me in very close, and not in my ear, nose to nose, eye to eye, whispered through clenched teeth, "You don't need to go with us. Why don't you hang out with your new friend and get to know each other better?" It became abundantly clear that the trip to Denny's didn't include me. She needed me to have a "Plan B" for getting home, which I didn't. I just stood there, awkwardly silent, as she continued to hold the collar of my sweater in a little wadded-up ball, pulling my face down to her own. She was smiling broadly and never took her eyes off mine, waiting for my response.

Gordon piped up, "Ok, no problem. I'll hang out with you while they go to breakfast." My new Scottish friend was obviously way more astute than me. He smiled at me and said, "Let's go for a walk." I shot a glance at him, mortified. "I'm not going for a walk with you at three in the dang morning!" Then I turned my attention back to Mary.

"If you're going to Denney's you can ride with your new friend but you're leaving your car keys with me, Sister!"

"Okay!" she agreed quickly. Then she grabbed her purse away from me and hurriedly dug her hands around inside it. Finding the keys, she thrust them into my hand. She then closed my fingers around them, squeezed my hands, and, before departing, whispered, "Where are you going to be?" I had no idea how to answer her at this point. I was still quite dumbstruck by the whole thing. Gordon quickly answered again. "I'm staying over at the Hampton Inn. Room 117. Just come there when you're done with breakfast. I'll take good care of her."

As they spoke, my head was jerking back and forth from his face back to hers, reminiscent of watching a tennis match. "Wait, WHAT?"

"It's okay. I'll stay outside with you," he reassured me.

"'K, bye! See you in a while!" And with that, Mary dashed out The Waterhole's double doors and disappeared. I stood there staring as the hem of her red dress flapped out as she fled. I turned to Gordon. "Ok, now what?"

"Let's go." He took my right arm, and out we walked. "Are you hungry?" There happened to be a Huddle House right beside the Hampton Inn where he was staying, so we climbed into Mary's car and drove over there. We were both awkwardly silent, and I had absolutely zero appetite. I pulled the car into the parking lot that was shared by the Hampton Inn and the Huddle House, turned off the ignition, and just sat there, looking straight ahead.

"So...do you want to eat, or do you want to go in and listen to some music?"

"Go in? Go in WHERE?" Again, incredulous. Still staring straight ahead, looking out that windshield. I didn't want to make eye contact with him.

"We can go in my room. And listen to music. Nothing else, I promise."

By that time, I could no longer contain myself. I spun around and faced him. "I am NOT going inside your hotel room! What? Are you crazy?" I practically shrieked out the words as I glared at him, eyes wide. No doubt I resembled a caged animal at this point.

"What do you think's gonna happen?" he asked me, laughing.

"I have NO IDEA, and I'm NOT trying to find out! You're from a different country; I know absolutely NOTHING about you!" I returned my gaze to the front and noticed I was shaking my head in an unspoken but reinforced "no." I also heard myself repeating the word "no" as I continued the vehement shaking of the head. I was also thinking about how very wrong it was that I was even sitting here alone with him. Everything in my being was anxious.

"Ok, so we should just sit out here in her car until she comes back? That could be a while, Jackie." He was still chuckling and looking right at me. He wasn't the least bit awkward; it was all me. I couldn't help but notice that I liked the way he said my name. Dang it! I refused to get distracted! But that ACCENT, though ... and those green eyes. "I promise I won't do anything at all. Apart from maybe shoot your kneecaps off..." he trailed, still laughing.

"What the...?" *That's a strange thing to say*, I thought. I suddenly found myself laughing too. I realized I liked this guy's sense of humor. He seems harmless, really. And honestly, I thought, *what's he gonna do to me? Kill me? Mary and I both know his name, where he is staying, and where he is working. Why the heck not?* I took the keys out of the ignition, dropped them in my purse, and opened the car door. "Alright, but you better not kill me!"

We got out, walked to the ground level door to his hotel room, and he unlocked it. I followed him in. And I really was surprised that I wasn't scared. There was something about this guy I trusted. Once inside the door, before he closed it, he paused, looked at me, tilted my chin up to his, and leaned down to kiss me. I backed away.

"No, no, please. I can't." I looked down. *Oh my God, Oh my God.*

"It's okay. Let's just listen to some music. You like Chris DeBurgh?" Clearly, he was "trying" me. He didn't know how stubborn I was.

"Sure," I shrugged, having no idea who Chris De-whoever was. We sat down and listened to the music and talked about random nothing, really. Easily and comfortably. After an hour or so, Mary was knocking on the door. I stood up abruptly, almost guiltily, like I had just been caught.

"Coming!" I called through the closed door. Once again, he turned me toward him, looked into my eyes, and softly lifted my chin. "Still, no?"

"Still no. I'm sorry. I hope I didn't send you the wrong message. I've really enjoyed hanging out with you. In spite of my crazy friend deserting me tonight. You're a good guy. Goodnight, Gordon." *Of course, I sent him the wrong message! What am I even doing here?*

"Goodnight," he said before opening the door. "Will I see you again?"

"Probably not." I smiled, then gave him a hug before walking away. He stood there leaning on the doorframe, watching as I walked toward Mary, who was already standing by her car. "You got the keys?" she shouted through cupped hands.

"Yep!" I answered, as I turned around one more time. He had begun to walk toward me, which caught me by surprise. I stopped, returning his gaze.

"Can I ask you something? Just before you go, I have to know..." he trailed.

"What?"

"Are you married?" I was initially shocked at the question before immediately realizing it was a valid one. *Was it obvious?*

"Long story," I said and simply walked away.

"Goodnight, Jackie," he said softly.

"Goodnight," I answered without looking back. I remained determined to stick it out with Alan and try my best, which also meant I was doubly determined that the last thing I needed to do was get involved with another man. I reasoned that would be easy since this guy didn't even live in the same country as me. *But there was just something about him...*

12

Click Your Heels, Girl ... You're Not in Kansas Anymore

The Wizard of Oz is my all-time favorite movie. As a little girl, I'd sit cross-legged in front of that big ol' console television set and, after watching it so many times, could recite almost every single word right along with the characters. I was especially glued to the scene where Dorothy gets swept up into the storm and woke up in an enchanted land ... beautiful and colorful, yet unfamiliar. She had dreamt about the land far, far away where the dreams she dared to dream might come true. Dorothy had felt misunderstood by her family, and all she wanted was to escape and travel to a place somewhere over the rainbow. Where blue-birds fly ... where the sun shines.

I wanted to be Dorothy. But, unlike her, I'd never click my heels together and chant, "There's no place like home ... there's no place like home..." I was determined to get as far away as I could and never go back. I would create my own version of over the rainbow. And it would be just as enchanted and perfect as the Land of Oz.

I returned home to Alabama after that night at The Waterhole. And, as I had promised myself, I tried to work things out with Alan. He really was a good guy, and we had spent the last seven years trying to make it work. I had grown up to become extremely guarded and tried to pretend I was a very hard person on the inside, but I knew the truth. My efforts to harden my heart were so that I could keep it from breaking. I could no longer stay with Alan. It wasn't fair to him that I was selfishly holding onto yet another futile effort of mine to establish the happily ever after I had been determined to have. When I explained all this to him, he admitted that he had been seeing someone else anyway. He confessed that he knew as soon as I moved out to "think things through" that we would never reconcile. We both reluctantly admitted that we had jumped back into our relationship without weighing the consequences of such a sudden decision. We both wanted to recapture the high-school puppy love we had, to no avail. We filed a non-contested divorce; it felt like it was inevitable. It was my second failed marriage, and I wasn't even thirty years old. At the time, I justified it by convincing myself I was a strong and determined woman who would never settle for less than perfection.

Looking back, I now see myself for who I really was back then—a stubborn, insecure young woman who was terrified of failing ... even after I continued to do it. But I'd fix it. I wouldn't stay broken and insecure. I'd fix myself and anyone in my life that would let me. And I couldn't get that handsome Scottish guy out of my mind. We reconnected by phone and would spend hours and hours just talking, getting to know each other. This segued into random rendezvous where we'd meet at hotels between Birmingham and Jackson. We were falling in love. *Oh dear, Jesus ... help me not to make another mistake...*

After a whirlwind romance, my Scottish Braveheart and I knew that there was something different about our relationship. Something special. Maybe it was because we were both past the young love stage, heading toward thirty and thinking now is as good a time as any to get serious about settling down. He invited me to just pack up and move, leave all the past behind, and move over to the UK. Another chance to start over. So, I fell—no, I jumped—at the chance. My mantra was still "Little girls dream, but big girls make plans." I had always wanted to be far, far away from Alabama and any reminders of the life I had there, so even better that this time, I was going to start new in another country.

Peterborough, England, United Kingdom
Summer 1988

Packing up my apartment in Birmingham before boarding the plane was daunting. What do I take? What do I leave behind? Finally, I decided to say the heck with it all, leave the stuff as well as the memories behind, and just do it. Go. Why not? Everything I had tried in the States had failed, so this time would be different. What I didn't realize at the time was the old saying, *"Wherever you go, there you are,"* is truth. I had unresolved issues and no matter where I moved, or what man I was with, there I was. I couldn't run away from me.

Gordon and I lived in a small rental house in Peterborough, England, along with one of his best friends whom he worked with. The arrangement reminded me of the sitcom *Three's Company*, except Gordon and I had decided to start making forever plans. This would be a trial. I immediately set out to decorate and make the little house a home. The guys would go to work every day, and I loved the prospect of making dinner for them every night, complete with flowers on the table and placemats set out. They would arrive home and be genuinely pleased as they walked in the front door, delicious aromas wafting up their nostrils. I would stand by the door to greet them, kissing Gordon as I welcomed him home, then I'd step aside and wait for them to notice the pretty, little table, all set up with steaming bowls of homemade southern dishes I had carefully prepared.

As was typical in Britain, Gordon and his friend wanted to have a beer with our dinner every night. I didn't drink, and anything I knew about drinking was negative, but I wanted to change my mind about this subject. Also, being with Gordon helped me to see that not everyone who drinks alcohol would end up angry and picking a fight. It had been a decade since I left the angry alcoholic home of my childhood, and I wanted to broaden my perspective. Loosen up. Have an open mind. So, I always made sure to have cold beers ready and available for them.

My goodness, looking back, I might as well have donned a ruffled apron, wore high heels, and put a ribbon in my hair, all the while standing with clasped hands and the biggest smile I could muster up as I dutifully served them. I wanted to be the prim and proper southern girlfriend. It was the after-dinner routine that I had trouble wrapping my brain around, because the saying "Old habits die hard" is true. It was rather customary for all the guys to go out to the pub and have a few more drinks either after dinner (which they called "tea") or, worse, before even coming home to eat. I'm pretty sure Gordon chose the aforementioned over the latter because, after all, he was still trying to court me, and part of our decision for me to move over there was to see how well I could acclimate to the British way of life. He waited until after dinner so I could go too and see for myself that it was a perfectly acceptable way of life. It's not that I had never tried alcohol—I had—but the fear was always lurking in the back of my mind that it was not a good idea. I didn't like the way it made me feel, and I'm pretty sure that's because I had formed an un-healthy opinion of anything associated with alcohol. After all, I had never seen anything good come from it.

Still, I didn't hesitate; I was so desperate to get to know him, in his own element, that I happily obliged and headed out the door to the pub. Of course, in my mind, the pub was equal to a beer joint where I come from, and couples didn't just go casually hang out for a couple drinks and then go home. On the contrary, mostly the men went, got drunk, and ei-ther came home and passed out or got into a fight with their wives and ignored their children. That would become my biggest fear … how might this be any different?

Gordon's friends would always offer to buy me a drink and I'd al-ways say, "No thank you; I don't drink," trying not to sound too religious or to appear to be a puritan. And again, even then, I didn't recognize the unhealthy mindset. I now see it as part of my unrecognized effort to re-main in control and to stand by at the ready to help Gordon, or any of his friends, if they had one too many. The fixer. Not a prima donna, not a stick in the mud. Just be the one who keeps it all under control.

A few weeks after moving in together at the house in Peterborough, Gordon decided it was time for us to go to Scotland and meet his family. I was so nervous. *What if they didn't like me?* I knew that Gordon and his mother were very close—he was a self-admitted "mama's boy" and loved her more than anyone else on earth. While the thought of this made me a little uneasy, especially after my relationship with David's mother, I made up my mind to go to Scotland with high expectations. I believed this was the man I was going to marry, and by God, I was determined that the third time would be the charm. I needed his family to accept me.

Largs, Scotland, United Kingdom August 1988

The road trip from Peterborough up to the west coast of Scotland was amazing. I felt like a kid on a trip to Disneyland—everything was so mag-ical. The hillsides were the greenest I had ever seen. All the fields were dotted with fluffy white sheep grazing, and I had my face plastered against the car windows, trying to see them better. Gordon was driving so fast up and around those curvy roads, and all I wanted to do was sight-see.

"Aww … are those sheep?"

"Yep. And wee lambs." I loved his accent.

"Oh, my goodness ... pull over ... pull over, please!"

He did, and I couldn't wait to jump out of the car and run to the edge of the fields.

"I've never seen a sheep in my life! Aw, and the baby lambs..." I was walking quickly to erase the distance between the animals and myself, fingers touching parted lips, wide-eyed.

"Och aye—we love our lambs here in Scotland. Especially for dinner."

"What?!" I snapped my head around and glared at him. "No, no, no," shaking my head in denial but understanding this was part of the culture. Still not wanting to admit my naivete, we laughed, got back into the car, and continued the drive. We enjoyed every minute of it. Gordon was the acting tour guide, while I was the awestruck, little Alabama girl who'd never been anywhere in her life and had never even laid eyes on a real sheep. As we neared his hometown of Largs, I became more and more nervous, so he broke the tension by teaching me common Scottish phrases. And the "correct" pronunciation, which was mostly just slang. Of course, I was teaching him some good ol' southern slang as well. We really celebrated our different cultures and had fun with it.

As we drove through the glen and over the Haylie Brae, I had my first look at the beautiful seaside town of Largs. Or, as Gordon called it, "Here's mah wee toon." With panoramic views of the Firth of Clyde across to the Isles of Cumbrae, and all the dotted, smaller isles and peninsulas surrounding it, I gasped, awestruck. It was so dramatic and honestly the most beautiful place I'd ever seen. All my nerves melted away as Gordon drove me all around the town to see the sights before making the drive up the road to Alexander Avenue, his boyhood home and where his parents were waiting to meet me. We parked along the road in front. Uncharacteristically hesitant, I remained seated while he opened his door and immediately got out.

"C'mon, then." He ducked his head back into the car where I sat, still buckled up. I couldn't pinpoint the reason for my nerves, but my heart was pounding. I pasted on a smile and slowly got out of the car. Before we reached the end of the path to the front door, it swung open and there she stood. She had light blonde hair and bright green eyes, which seemed to dance as she smiled from ear to ear. Her raised and prominent cheekbones indicated that her smile was genuine and often. Unlike David's mom had, she acknowledged me first, and I instantly felt her warm sincerity.

"Huh-LOOOOOW, Jackie! Pleased to meet you!" She extended her hand to mine. I quickly reciprocated.

"Hello, Mrs. Van Dyke ... pleased to meet you too ... Gordon has told me so much about you!"

"Och! Call me Irene!" she replied, with a wave of her hand and a shake of her head. She rolled the "r" in Irene, just like Gordon had in his name when we first met. She leaned in and gave me a hug as she spoke. Then she turned to Gordon.

"Huhlow Mum." He leaned in, and they kissed each other simultaneously on the cheek and gave a quick embrace. We entered the foyer and took off our coats. Gordon's dad was standing just inside the parlor and was equally friendly. "Hi, Jackie, I'm John," he said, in his more English accent because that is where he was born and raised before moving to Scotland to marry Irene. He also leaned in for the traditional kiss, which I reciprocated, although this was totally not the way most American families introduce themselves. *Hey ... when in Rome?* I thought to myself. The atmosphere in their home was warm and friendly, unpretentious. Irene immediately offered me a cup of tea, which I accepted. This was my first time having a "real" British tea—traditionally hot and served with milk—and quite frankly, I wasn't sure about it. Being raised in Alabama, the only tea we drank was overly sweet and always iced. *Another "when in Rome" moment.* I sat sipping the tea as the conversation was flowing. The entire family had a talkative, joking nature and were very courteous. I felt immediately comfortable there.

"Would either of you like a drink?" his dad stood up and asked, as he walked into the tiny kitchen just off the parlor. He looked at each of us, gesturing with his hand. My immediate thought was *We just got a cup of tea ... so...?* But I was learning that the Scottish people typically offer a cup of tea and/or a cocktail. I waited for Gordon to answer.

"Och, alright. What are you having?"

"I'm having a wee hauf," his dad replied.

"Alright ... I'll take a wee hauf. You wanna wee hauf, Jackie?"

"What is it?" I didn't want to sound stupid but had never heard of such a thing.

"It's half whisky and half lemonade," Irene explained. *Whiskey and lemonade?!* I tried not to demonstratively gag.

"Lemonade is what Americans call Sprite®," Gordon explained. "Or Seven-Up. Sparkling soda."

"Uh, no thanks ... the tea is fine for now."

The rest of the evening was spent talking and laughing, Gordon and his parents regaling me with stories of life on Alexander Avenue and all the mischief Gordon and his pals used to get into. It was so easy hanging out with them; I never felt one bit uncomfortable there. They were great. Even when it was late and our tongues were tired, we said our good-nights as they disappeared into their bedroom. They assumed Gordon and I would just go to bed in his old bedroom upstairs, which we did. It wasn't awkward at all. We were adults, and they knew we were already living together down in Peterborough. I must admit, however, that when I saw that his bedroom contained two separate twin beds, I was a bit relieved. Easy night. I was glad to be in Scotland, meeting the family of the man I had fallen in love with.

The next day was the celebration of much acclaimed Cowal Highland Games, which were held annually in the Scottish town of Dunoon located on the Cowal peninsula in Argyll and Bute. While part of me was excited to experience it and heard it was a lot of fun, most of the stories were about how I could most likely expect that the fun involved a lot of drinking. I was still excited to go and was looking forward to meeting Gordon's childhood pals. Irene decided not to go, as she was not feeling well that morning, so she saw us out as we made our way down the road into the little town of Largs. Off we went, Gordon, his dad, and I, to catch the ferry. I remember standing down at the ferry, and literally everyone around me was in full holiday mode and attire. All the guys were wearing kilts, and there were plenty of bagpipers playing down along the seafront. I had to pinch myself as I looked around at all the scenery, heard all the pipe music playing, and watched all the people gathering and just laughing and enjoying themselves.

I genuinely did feel at that very moment that I was in a fairy tale. A story from a land far, far away and nothing this Alabama gal had ever expected to experience. I mostly hung out with Vikki, who was Gordon's cousin, "Wee Bobby's" girlfriend. I loved how she immediately took me under her wing and began to tell me everything to expect at the event, which was, of course, my first time attending a Scottish Highland Games gathering. We all boarded the ferry and set off to the next island. I couldn't help but notice that almost every single person was already drinking alcohol and it was only nine in the morning. Gordon was hanging out with all his pals, so I was thankful that Vikki stuck beside me … she knew I was but a virgin highland-gamer, innocent to the type of revelry I was about to be witness to. What she didn't know, however, was my history—my past life of witnessing drunken alcoholic rages, which had caused a deep secret fear of being around almost anything involving booze. I tried to make up my mind not to remember those times … today was new, fun, and exciting. Nothing like back then, I prayed.

And it *was* a lot of fun! It was an atmosphere of people participating in the highland games, watching the pipe bands, the parades, and all in camaraderie. I was shocked that no one was fighting. Everyone was laughing and enjoying themselves. I even had a couple glasses of wine with Vikki and some other gals we met at the games. Everything was all in good fun, and I thought to myself that I had finally gotten past all the negative ideas and opinions I had formed based upon my life growing up.

Around four p.m. is when everything began to wind down, and people were lining up to take the ferry back to Largs. I couldn't find Gordon anywhere! Vikki also didn't know where Bobby was, so she just shrugged and suggested we take the ferry back ourselves and they'd have to catch up with us later. I was flabbergasted … leave without Gordon? But what other choice did I have? Someone had told me that Gordon's dad had already gone back to Largs, and I could be certain he'd be in one of the pubs downtown waiting for us. We took the ferry back, and Vikki and I walked over to the Bowling Club, where she thought we might find him. Irene, Gordon's mom, was a champion bowler and the whole family spent a lot of time there. When we arrived, Vikki asked the bartender if John was there; he was not. I had yet to meet Gordon's sister, Elizabeth "Liz," who also lived in the town, so when Vikki suggested we walk over to her house, I was adamant that we should not. I was already a bit embarrassed that I had become separated from Gordon and in a bit of a panic trying to decide what to do. I was an almost twenty-eight-year-old woman, confident and able to take care of myself, but reminded that I was in a different country and not used to their customary fixes for a predicament such as this.

"How about I just phone you a taxi, and they'll give you a wee ride up the road?" She also had a lovely Scottish accent, with a friendly lilt, and I had felt comfortable after spending the entire day with her.

"Ugh ... okayyyyyy. I guess I don't have any choice, do I?" I was exasperated and didn't have another solution. The typical "fix it" me felt lost and didn't have an answer for this one. The taxi came around, and Vikki walked out with me and gave him the address. I slid into the backseat and retreated inside myself. *What am I going to say when I get there? Would Irene even be home? How could Gordon have left me alone?*

In literally two minutes, the cab driver stopped the car in front of the house, telling me, "Nay bothah," when I said I didn't have any British currency on me, and as I looked up, I saw Irene coming out of the front door. Someone had apparently called her from the bowling club and told her that I was headed up in a taxi. Alone. She walked down the path to meet me and held her arms out toward me. The sobs that had been trapped in my throat finally escaped, and I just stood there, in her arms, crying. I had no words.

"Come on, then," she said softly, as she walked me into the house. "Where's Gordon? And Johnny?" Her lovely Scottish lilt remained upbeat, even though she was clearly annoyed. I just vomited out a bunch of words, in between the sucking in of the cries ... completely disillusioned, sad, and a little tipsy from having two glasses of wine.

"I don't know, I ... um ... we ... Vikki and I ... couldn't find him or Bobby. We looked everywhere; last time we saw them was at the pole vaulting. They went off with their pals, we planned to meet up with them, but we didn't know where they were..." I rambled on, words just falling out. Unable to finish my sentences, I was mortified, embarrassed, and very mad at myself that I couldn't hold it together. I was also one hundred percent certain I had completely blown it with Gordon's family. *Jesus ... how did this happen?*

"Alright, let me get you a wee cup of tea and just you sit down, and I'll go find them." With that, she poured my tea and out the door she went. Walking. Strong lady. Way stronger than me. Or anyone else I'd ever met. After an hour, I went up the stairs and fell onto one of the twin beds in Gordon's old bedroom. I was exhausted and passed out.

It was about an hour later when I felt Gordon's breath in my ear as he whispered to me, waking me from a fitful sleep.

"Hey ... I'm sorry." I also couldn't help but smell the alcohol on his breath, which just infuriated me, so I pushed him away.

"Oh. My. God! Where WERE you?" I didn't even want him to answer me and at this point, I was still half asleep and wasn't awake enough to remember we were at his parents' house.

"Jesus, Gordon! How could you leave me alone??!" I hissed through clenched teeth before feeling more tears streaming down my face. At that moment, Irene appeared at the bedroom door, standing with arms folded.

"Gordon, why don't you go downstairs?" She was so calm, and he did as he was told. She walked over and sat on the edge of the bed. I was embarrassed I had let her hear me so angry, not to mention see me crying like that. Once again, there is nothing I could do to fix this. *Oh my God, I hate feeling so frickin' helpless!*

"There, there, now, Jackie. It's oh-kay." She enunciated each syllable. Again, her voice was so soothing and pleasant that I couldn't stay mad.

"I'm sorry, Irene. I don't mean to be so upset. I was scared, and I didn't know what to do when I couldn't find him." I sat up in the bed and wiped my face before looking up into her eyes.

"Don't you worry yourself over this. I'll talk to him. Just you lie back down. You must be knackered!"

I allowed myself to lie back and close my eyes—a little from being overtired, but mostly because I was so embarrassed and at a loss for words or a solution. She patted my folded hands, and I heard the bedroom door close softly behind her. I heard their voices and knew they were downstairs probably discussing the day's events, but I eventually drifted off to sleep. *What am I going to do?*

The morning came early—a little too early. I rolled over and looked three feet across from me to the other twin bed in Gordon's old bedroom. Gordon's face was smashed into the pillow, open mouth slack and drooling while snoring like a bull. And yet, he still had the best face I had ever seen. I wanted to stay mad at him, but I couldn't. I was really in love with this guy. And his mum and dad. Everything about being with him, and there in Scotland with his friends and family, felt right. After being treated to my first traditional Scottish breakfast—square lorn sausage, a couple of links, a fried egg, streaky bacon, baked beans, black pudding, tattie scones, fried tomatoes, and mushrooms, and of course, toast—I felt fat and happy. After a few Scottish teas to wash it all down, we just relaxed and hung out. Their home was full of so much joking around, sarcastic humor, laughter, and just doing nothing really that I almost didn't know how to act. It was so utterly different from anything I had ever known. Even after all the drinking from the day before, I was perplexed, yet pleased, that nobody was mad at anyone else, and there was no arguing and pointing fingers at each other. No one was giving anyone the silent treatment. No furniture was broken. And nobody had a black eye or any other bruises on them.

I realize this is a very sad thing to even comment upon, but, unfortunately, it was how I thought. I had nothing else to compare it to, except what had happened inside the four walls of my house growing up. Gordon's family was unlike any family I had ever been around. And I liked it. I had completely forgotten about the nonsense from the day before and enjoyed just hanging out with them. Gordon's sister, Liz, and her family had come over that day, and I had been pleased to meet them all. Liz and her husband Johnnie had two beautiful, little girls who I was immediately smitten with. I realized I had not only fallen in love with Gordon but with his family as well. And I felt accepted. They didn't have expectations but seemed to accept me warmly. I believed this would be my family for the rest of my life.

13

Goodnight, Irene

Fall into Winter 1988, United Kingdom

That first weekend spent in Scotland with Gordon's family had educated me in so many ways. Aside from the obvious, it was unlike any other lifestyle I had ever been around. Being from small-town Alabama, where there were the haves and the have-nots, Gordon's hometown had those same people. They just talked funny, but they had said the same about me. And like American Southern folk, they were kind. So full of humor—laughing was easy with them. And they loved family. I felt very welcome there, as everyone was so warm. I knew I would be accepted if Gordon and I decided to marry. But I was still struggling with that, being torn between what I felt my heart wanted and what my overactive, controlling mind was telling me. I knew I had made so many poor choices in the past, and this time I was hell-bent and determined not to mess this up.

I loved my new life with Gordon. It was different. Exciting. A whole new life in a whole new world, with whole new people. I wanted it. And I loved him. But getting married to him scared me. He drinks; I don't. I tried to and wanted to see casual, social drinking as acceptable … normal. To Gordon, and all his family and friends, having a couple drinks is *okay!* Why couldn't I just get over my fractured past and accept it? But there's this little thing called a stronghold mindset that I just couldn't shake off. Every experience I had ever had with alcohol involved something bad happening. I literally had *never* seen anything good come from drinking. It was an oxymoron in my little, closed mind that people go out to enjoy a couple drinks with friends. Because ninety percent of the time, a couple of drinks became a few; a few became several; and several turned into too many. "Oh, I must've had too much to drink last night. I don't remember everything I said, and I have a headache." I had heard that so many times in my life growing up. There must be something to it, right? But I was willing to change my mind. Grow up and forget my childish mindset. Live a little. Loosen up. I would try.

The next few months would make it easier, but not in a good way. I knew I'd do almost anything to keep Gordon. I loved him, and I needed him. And I refused to fail this time.

Shortly after my first weekend in Scotland and meeting Gordon's family, his mother Irene was diagnosed with colon cancer. She had been having some symptoms for a few months, but she was a very private person and had not wanted to talk about it, especially with Gordon and his new girlfriend. She confided in her daughter, Gordon's sister, Liz, as they were best friends. Confidants. And because Liz was already happily married with children, she was certainly more stable than Gordon, who had left the UK, moved over to work in the United States, and surprised them all by inviting his American girlfriend back to live with him. Irene did not want to upset him or interfere with his dreams.

But Liz had phoned Gordon just after dinner one evening with the news after we were back at the house in Peterborough. They exchanged their normal cheery brother/sister greetings, then I saw Gordon's countenance become grim. They spoke for a few minutes, and I heard only bits and pieces. "How is Dad? What do you think we should do? Do I need to come up there now?" I had no idea what the conversation was about, but I could tell it wasn't good. When Gordon put the receiver back into the cradle of the phone, he kept his head down. I just sat there looking at him, waiting.

"What is it?" I finally asked, softly.

"Mum's not well. She has cancer." Tears had already started to fall down his cheeks. He covered his face with his hands, and I immediately went to him, holding his head on my chest and stroking the back of his head while he cried like a baby. I had never seen my happy-go-lucky Scotsman like this. And, I didn't know it then, but he would never be the same after that. We sat and talked for hours that night, finishing two bottles of wine between us. I guess I needed it too. I couldn't bear to see him in so much pain, and he couldn't bear the thought of losing his mother. I realized that night that alcohol was not just for laughs and socializing but also to help numb pain. We finally fell asleep, having been successful in drowning our sorrows and putting our fears to rest, even if just for that one night.

The next several weeks flew by. We had immediately made the decision to get engaged—no reason to postpone what we both believed was meant to be. And we felt the urgency to move forward. Celebrating the engagement was bittersweet, but I remember both of us smiling as he popped the question one night after we had gone to bed—he literally pulled a ring case out from under his pillow, where he had hidden it earlier that evening after work.

"So, will you marry me?"

"Yes!"

That was all there was to it. We were lying in bed, ready to go to sleep. Let's face it, neither of us were kids ... we'd both been "around the block" a few times. We didn't need a lot of pomp and circumstance, just a wedding as soon as we could arrange it.

We went up to Scotland a few times in the weeks since the diagnosis. Irene had been in the hospital, and we knew she wasn't feeling well at all. But neither Gordon nor I really knew all the details of the extent of her illness. Liz did, John did, but Irene was fierce about keeping as much as possible from Gordon. He was her baby, and she wanted to protect him. She was such a strong lady, always putting on her bravest face when we would visit.

When we finally set the date for our wedding, December 16th, we had little time to put all the plans in place. Irene seemed to be feeling a tiny bit better—she was out of the hospital—so she suggested I come up to Scotland and spend some time with her and Liz so we could make wedding plans together. Undaunted, I immediately agreed. I was extremely inexperienced with travel of any kind, much less in a different country, so when Gordon dropped me off at the train station in Peterborough, destination Largs, I was nervous but confident. After the rather long train commute, I stepped off the train in Largs, and there stood Irene and John, smiling and waiting for me. John took my suitcase, and we climbed into their little car: destination Alexander Avenue.

I knew this trip was primarily about making the wedding plans, but I also knew it was my opportunity to get to know Irene, and vice versa. We both loved Gordon very much, and there was no secret about how much he adored his mum; she was his person. I hoped and prayed that she and I might form a bond as we made plans for the wedding, hoping also it might take her mind off her diagnosis even for just a little while. At that time, neither Gordon nor I knew the gravity of the situation. If I'd known, I probably wouldn't have been so relaxed around her … the fixer in me would've spent the entire visit trying to work out what I could do to alleviate the situation.

So, Irene, Liz, and I, along with Gordon's dad, John as our driver, ran from photographers, to florists, to their local church, and some of the hotel venues in town to plan the wedding reception. It was a flurry of activity and together, we were decisive and satisfied with our efforts. Gordon called in once or twice, mostly to check in on us more than to give input into the wedding plans. I know he was worried about his mum, as well as a little concerned about whether she would be able to connect with his soon-to-be American bride or not. Because, in his mind, we couldn't be more different. But the fact that we both loved him was the glue that would create the bond between us.

We had one special night together that I will never forget. I didn't realize it then, but now I know it was all part of God's greater plan. Irene and I were going to make a connection that would last for my lifetime, and I wouldn't trade a million dollars for this experience.

That night, after dinner, John had gone to bed, and Irene and I were sitting in the living room talking about the day. She lit a cigarette and asked me if I'd like one too. I didn't really smoke but had picked up the habit of occasionally having a cigarette with Gordon if we went out for drinks. So, I thought, *Why not?* She lit one of her Benson & Hedges, extended the open pack to me, and after I slid one out, she leaned over and lit it for me.

She sat back in the gold-patterned, velour sofa, legs crossed Indian-style, and blew a circle of smoke up and away from our faces. I sat only two feet away from her, on the other end of the sofa, and choked back a cough as I tried to take a puff without gagging. She was smiling at me, head tilted in her familiar way, with one arm across her lap and the other bent upward holding her cigarette. I was still facing forward, both feet on the floor, looking straight ahead and trying my best not to look like a novice.

"Sooooo…" She stretched out that word in her sweet Scottish lilt. "You're not really a smoker, are you?" She laughed, and so did I.

"Not really. How could you tell?"

"Well … good for you! You shouldn't smoke just because I am." Again, the sweet laugh, eyes still looking at mine.

"No, I know that. I like to smoke," I lied. "But only when I'm drinking." Truth.

"Well, what would you like to drink, Jackie? Wine?" She uncrossed her legs and started to walk into the kitchen.

"Sure, that's fine. I'll have whatever you're having."

"Oooh, look! I bet you'll like this!" She smiled, holding up a brown bottle with a gold label on the front. "Tia Maria! It's like a dessert; I usually keep it for special occasions!"

She brought in the bottle of Tia Maria and two little, fancy cordial glasses, sitting them on the coffee table. Before the night ended, the entire bottle would be emptied, as well as that pack of Benson & Hedges. We talked about anything and everything. Laughing about stories of Gordon as a "wee boy" and all his mischief. I told her a little bit about myself and my family, and how I wish I had happy stories to tell. It was late into the night when the conversation turned serious.

"Jackie … I want you to know something. I didn't know if I'd ever see Gordon actually get married. He got engaged a few times, but it never lasted."

"Why do you think that is?" I genuinely wanted to know. Because unlike me, who jumped at getting married to anyone I even remotely thought might love me and be a good husband, I didn't understand why Gordon kept getting engaged but never going through with it.

"Well…" she said, before taking another long drag of her cigarette and blowing a smoke circle up above her head before dropping her eyes back down to mine. "I don't think he ever loved anyone as much as he loved himself … or me. Until you." Her eyes never left mine.

I felt tears well up in my eyes, so I looked away, stubbed out my cigarette, and took a long drink, finishing off the last of my Tia Maria.

"Oh, don't get me wrong," she continued, making an effort to lighten the conversation back up. "He had plenty of girlfriends … he thought he was quite the stud." I couldn't help bursting out laughing at her using that word to describe him.

"But he honestly never really loved any of them. He wanted to advance his career and travel, and just didn't want to settle down with one person."

"Well, I sure hope he goes through with it this time!" I replied, also still laughing and wanting to veer from the seriousness of what she was saying.

"He will. But, Jackie, please promise me something, will you?"

"Yes. Anything."

She hesitated, stubbed out her cigarette at that point, and finished off what was left in her glass.

"Don't give up on him. He might hurt you, but he won't mean to. Stick it out. He has a good heart."

Trying to process what she meant by that, I simply said, "I won't." I am not exactly sure why I said that, because God knows I had walked away from David and let him die without me. And poor Alan I just walked away from because I knew I had rushed into marrying him in the first place, determined not to have to move back in with my mama and daddy. How could I make such a promise to her?

We finished the bottle of Tia Maria and said good night, both of us left with nothing more to say. We were tired, and this had been a heavy conversation. Maybe it had just been the alcohol we'd consumed. We'd never bring it up again.

The next night, in contrast, was my last night in Largs before heading back down to England. It was also the day before Irene was to receive the trophy and given the title of "Lady Champion" at the bowling club. It was to be a fancy dinner and a fun celebration. That last night, our conversation was different. Light. Fun.

"Jackie, how do you put your eyeliner on so straight? And your eyeshadow, it's so sparkly! And what color blush do you use? And that bright pink lipstick?"

"Irene, I'm from Alabama. We KNOW how to put on some makeup! I'll teach you!"

The next couple of hours were spent in her kitchen: she perched on a stool, holding a hand mirror, and me standing inches in front of her face as I applied each component of her makeup, instructing her and showing her each step. A couple of times when I'd tell her to hold still, keep her eyelids closed and stretch her lips, she'd open one eye, look at me, and then we'd both burst into laughter, unable to continue until we regained our composure. She made me write her a list with everything she needed to buy the next day so she could do it herself. I ended up leaving her my makeup.

"You GOT this," I promised. "Good luck tomorrow night!"
I took the afternoon train back to Peterborough.

November 1988

The next few weeks flew by. Gordon and I continued our life in Peterborough, with him working and me continuing to play house, cooking dinner every night, and practicing for what I prayed would be my final attempt at a wedding and a marriage that would last forever. I traveled back home to Alabama in November and made arrangements to borrow my best friend Gerri's wedding dress, and to make all the air travel arrangements for my mama and Gerri to come over to Scotland in December. Meanwhile, Irene's health was not improving; she had returned to the hospital for surgery, but anytime Gordon called her, she put on her best act and kept saying she was "fine" and excited about the wedding. He knew from talking to Liz that his mum was getting worse but, as they tend to do in Scotland, didn't want to take away from the plans we were making for the wedding. Irene was the most unselfish person I had ever met. And Lizzie tried her best not to upset Gordon, while she bore the pain of their mum's declining health. Gordon's dad just never really spoken of it; I think he was probably in denial.

On December 12th, my twenty-eighth birthday, Mama, accompanied by my friends Gerri and Carla, flew into London. We went sightseeing and spent a couple of fun days together before making the road trip back up to Scotland for the wedding. Car packed down, we arrived in Largs on Wednesday, December 14th. We all went up to Alexander Avenue, along with Liz, Johnnie, and the girls, so we could open some wedding gifts and share toasts for the upcoming nuptials. All the plans were in place. My mama, of course, met Gordon's mum and for the first time, it all felt right. Admittedly, it hadn't with either David's mother or Alan's. Mama was just a different bird, and not everyone "got" her. Of course, she had to make some sarcastic (yet funny, in her mind) comment about how maybe "this-go-around," I would be happy. Despite all the different cultures and personalities represented that night, we all sat around and shared plenty of laughs, looking forward to the rehearsal dinner the following night and the wedding celebration scheduled for the 16th. Gordon and his mum had a special relationship, and even she quipped that night, "Gordon, as long as you and I are happy, that's all that matters, right?" I was glad they were so close.

After a couple of hours, Mama and my friends went down the hill to stay in a bed-and-breakfast they had rented and settled in for the night. Gordon's Uncle Stan and Aunt Pam had come from London, so they had also booked a room in the same place. Liz, Johnnie, and the girls went back to their house just a few blocks away. It was just the four of us who remained: Gordon, John, Irene, and me. We had one last celebratory drink before turning in for the night. Irene appeared to be in some pain, but when Gordon asked her about it, she denied it, waved it off with her typical, "Och, I'm fine," and we all said goodnight and went to bed. Gordon and I, of course, in the bedroom with the twin beds, right next to his mum and dad's room. We fell fast asleep.

December 15, 1988

The next morning was the day before the wedding. I was startled awake when Gordon sat on the edge of my bed and fell into me, crying.

"What's wrong?" I asked, still semi-conscious.

"My mum ... she's dying..." He could barely speak. His full weight was on me, so I struggled to sit up in the bed while still holding onto him.

"What do you mean? What's happened?"

He could barely speak at all. Through the tears, he choked out the words, "She's *dying,* Jackie ... I know she is!!"

"No, Honey, she's not ... she was fine last night..." I had wanted to believe that, but honestly had been unable to tell. With all the people there, it had been hard to determine. She was always so cheery.

"She's dying..." were the only words he could say. I had never seen him so upset. I immediately scrambled out of the bed and went straight into their bedroom, only pausing briefly to tap on the door as I pushed it open. John was sitting in a chair at the end of the bed; he didn't look up. My eyes fell onto Irene, still lying in her bed. I sat down beside her.

"Are you alright?"

"I'm okay, Jackie." She could barely speak. The words came out in a raspy whisper.

"No, you're not ... what can I do? What can I get you? What do you need?" I felt both desperation and dread at the same time. Gordon had also come into the room. I looked at John, but he wouldn't look at us.

Gordon and his dad were inches apart but neither looked at the other nor spoke.

"You need to go to the hospital!" My voice was pleading.

"No!" She was very firm, and her eyes flew wide open. "No..." she said, more softly. I could see she was weak. I wasn't sure what had happened during the night. "Just you go ... go with your mum and friends. I'll be okay."

Gordon had turned around and taken my arm lightly. He had a new-found sense of strength, it seemed, and I was so thankful he felt better. I wanted to think he had been wrong earlier ... that she really would get better. I prayed so hard that morning!

"She'll be okay ... let's go pick up your mum and Gerri." His voice was firm.

I reluctantly got up and allowed him to guide me out, but not before turning to his dad and giving him a knowing glance that said, *you take care of her.* Gordon and I got dressed and went down to get Mama and my friends, then we went into the town for breakfast. We had planned to spend most of the day sightseeing before heading to our wedding rehearsal at six p.m., but after breakfast, Gordon asked me to show them around and go into some shops, and that he was going back home to check on his mum.

Approximately three hours later, we were outside of a little boutique in Largs when I saw Gordon's car careen around the corner and pull to an abrupt stop at the curb. He rolled down his window and said, "Get in." His face and eyes were red and swollen. My best friend Gerri must've sensed what was happening, because she immediately said, "Don't worry about us; we'll get a taxi." I jumped in beside Gordon and before I could ask, he said, "We're taking Mum to the hospital." I didn't ask him anything, and as soon as we pulled in front of the house, I ran upstairs to her room where John had gotten Irene up out of the bed. She was dressed and sitting on the edge of the bed but didn't look up when I barged in. She looked extremely weak. I sat beside her and put my arm around her.

"Gordon said you are going to the hospital. Is that right?"

She didn't reply. John answered for her. "She's going."

By then, Gordon had walked into the room. "Mum, Lizzie's on her way." Irene still hadn't responded and never looked up. I awkwardly started packing a bag and just started rattling off random stuff. "Okay, I'll get your pajamas. What about your book? Want to take your book? Where's her toothbrush? She'll need her toothbrush..."

Just then, Liz and her husband Johnnie arrived and came up to help Gordon and his dad gather her belongings. We heard the ambulance sirens just before the paramedics ran straight up the stairs with the stretcher. Mama, Gerri, and Carla had hailed a taxi downtown, and all three of them were standing in the living room as I raced down the stairs.

"Y'all go on. We'll be right here when you get back. And we'll be praying." Gerri reached out to hug me. She was such an encouraging friend.

"We'll do whatever you need, Baby ... whatever ... you just name it." Mama said, speaking like the mother she had always been to me ... willing to do anything. She wanted to protect me, but, as always, she never could. I had to steel myself. I had been strong in the past, and this time was not going to be any different.

"I'm good, Mama. Don't worry. I'll see y'all later." With that, Gordon and I headed out the door and jumped into his car. I'm still not sure how we made the drive to the hospital in Greenock. We were both in shock; he was silent, and I was praying under my breath, "Please, God, please ... heal her!"

It was about twenty minutes later when the nurses told us that we could come into her hospital room. John had been with Irene the entire time and when Liz, Johnnie, Gordon, and I entered the room, she was lying still, eyes open. I am still not sure if I imagined this or not, but when Gordon walked in, I swear I saw her eyes follow him—from the second he walked in the door. He went over and took her hand, speaking very softly to her. To this day, I have no idea what he said. I stood aside as Liz and Johnnie took their turns speaking to her privately. She was aware that we were with her; I could tell by her eyes. Finally, it was my turn. I felt undeserving—I had only met her a few months prior, and I couldn't help but feel I had no right to be in there with her at such an intimate moment. As I walked slowly to the side of her bed, I took her left hand, leaned in, and whispered, "Tomorrow night is the night we've planned for ... I know you're going to be there ... I know you are..." I was saying this to myself as well.

The night, only a couple months prior, when she and I had sat up all night drinking Tia Maria and smoking cigarettes, might sound like an unhealthy memory to have, considering my past, but it was just the opposite. I was so very thankful for that night. That's the night I fell in love with Irene Van Dyke, my mother-in-law. And I like to think she felt the same way. We connected in such an amazing way and spoke about some things so special, only she and I will ever know.

"You get better so you can put on that pretty dress you bought, and I'll even do your makeup," I whispered, smiling. She squeezed my hand. "And, if you aren't out of here by tomorrow, why then, we'll just do it the next day ... or the next. But you *will* be there!" I promised.

This time, as she was squeezing my hand, I felt her gently pull me closer in. She couldn't speak but her eyes locked with mine and she mouthed, "Yes." I kissed her cheek and turned to Gordon before we walked out of the room, leaving John, Lizzie, and Johnnie with Irene. The nurse stopped us and said, "You can stay. You should stay."

"I can't do it, Jackie. I can't stay here and watch her like this," Gordon said to me through tears.

"Honey, yes, you can ... I'll be right beside you—your dad and your sister too..."

He was shaking his head no. "I can't."

I opened the door to her room and called Liz outside. "Gordon can't stay." She went over to him, and they embraced for what felt like an eternity. As he pulled away, Johnnie came out and offered to take us both back to Largs. The three of us walked back into the room, to her side, and leaned down to give her a kiss. Her eyes were on Gordon the entire time until we walked out and closed the door.

It was cold and raining as we drove away from the hospital in Greenock. To this day, it was one of my hardest goodbyes ever. Within an hour, she was gone.

We reluctantly proceeded with the wedding the next evening, paring the guest list down to include only immediate family; we all knew it was what Irene wanted. And it would be a very short ceremony. Gordon's dad, John, walked me down the aisle, and as he placed my hand into Gordon's, we all paused and held on for several seconds, tears falling onto our hands as we kept our heads down, not being able to look into each other's eyes. As Gordon and I said "I do" that night, we promised to never leave each other's side ... that we'd stay together forever. And this time, I meant it.

14

The House at Pooh Corner

We left Scotland a few weeks after the wedding, and, of course, after attending Irene's funeral. Gordon and Liz had spent most of that time with their dad, all of them just trying to make sense of it all and to reconcile their feelings, which was an impossible task. Gordon realized it was time to get back to work and to decide what kind of life he and I would build together. Neither of us wanted to just go back to life as usual in England. And what was "usual" anyway? The previous six months had been a complete whirlwind and life-changing for both of us. Neither of us had a clue about what to do next. What would be our next move? Would we remain in the UK and Gordon continue in his current job, or would we roll the dice and head back to the States to start our new life there? I was conflicted—not truly wanting to move back "home," but making up my mind that this marriage, this life with Gordon, would finally become my "real" forever home. Life with this man would last; it had to. He needed me, and I needed him. It wouldn't be like my previous marriages, which had been nothing but my futile attempts to escape a life like my mama had. This time, we'd make a family of our own: happy, perfect, full of love. I would not let myself fail again. I had to keep things under control.

In the weeks following the wedding, Gordon's employer's next assignment was to send him to a temporary job in Zeltweg, Austria. Together, we reckoned that would be a good distraction, maybe even a honeymoon of sorts, because obviously we had not done anything remotely resembling celebratory, nor did we have alone time. How could we? Neither of us had cared to, but we knew that now we needed to get our focus back on each other. We managed to enjoy the next couple of months spent in Austria, but when his company offered the next temporary assignment, which was to be in Russia, we both immediately knew this was our sign to take the plunge and move back to America. The plan was that Gordon would go through the months-long legal process of immigration, while I would work full time as the breadwinner and was happy to do so. Saying goodbye to Liz and John, who, by now, I was also calling "Dad," was difficult. They both knew that this time, Gordon was returning to the States with his new bride to live—permanently.

Atlanta, Georgia, February 1989

We landed in Atlanta, rented a car, and drove back to Alabama—first stop was Mama and Daddy's house until we were able to establish where we wanted to live, work, and begin raising a family of our own. This was NOT an easy task for me. My daddy and I had never reconciled or even had a conversation about the past and how our relationship had been permanently scarred. Perhaps not completely broken, though; time would tell. He had not approved of my moving away to the UK and certainly didn't approve of my marrying Gordon.

"He's a damn foreigner, Jackie! Hell Girl, you done tried two American boys and didn't neither one of them work for you, so you just up and decide to leave where you's born and raised to take off to a whole damn 'nuther country!"

Of course, he had a point, even though I didn't share his opinion, I could see where he was coming from. He had also said, "I gave you away once, Girl, and the other two times, you's on yer own! I ain't never gonna approve of this." I thought about trying to talk sensibly to him and attempt to explain myself, but then I thought better of it. Mainly because I didn't really understand it either. I just knew, if it took me the rest of my life, I would get it right. I refused to settle. After the initial hoopla and arguing, of course, the good side of my daddy rose to the surface ... the one that was always there, underneath all his childhood hurt and pain that had turned him into a seemingly cold, hard man. Inside, he had a heart. I guess I might've always known it, but until now, I just refused to think about it. Or him. Or all the crap I'd witnessed growing up.

"Ok, Daddy ... I get it. I've messed up. But this time will be different."

"Yeah ... ha ha ... suuuure it will!" he chuckled. "I've heard that shit before!" He kept laughing, like he was happy to be right. "But you know one thing's fer sure ... I love my young 'uns ... all of y'uns." He reached up to wipe an accidental tear away from his cheek as he spoke, revealing his signature three fingers on his left hand. Several years prior, he had accidentally shot two of his fingers off and had been given the nickname "Three-fingered John" by all his buddies at the beer joints. And it had stuck. So anytime he would get emotional, he always wiped away the rare tear with that three-fingered hand. Weirdly, there was something very sweet about it. A rare vulnerability.

"I know you do, Daddy." Did I? Did I really believe my daddy loved us, or was it just the right thing to say because here stood Gordon and I needing a temporary place to stay until we could figure things out? I think, deep down, I knew.

"Alright then, go on back there and use that bedroom for now. But what y'all gonna do about a car? How y'all getting' to where y'all wanna live? And do ye even know where that's gonna be?"

"Mr. Brewer, can we borrow your car tomorrow so we can go buy ourselves something to get us around until we get jobs?" Gordon asked, very politely I might add. Not only did Daddy agree, but he even co-signed a loan with us on the 1979 Toyota van we decided upon, trusting we'd pay the loan off as soon as we got jobs. And we did. I felt like my relationship with Daddy was finally starting to even out. No more arguments, no more hatred. I sincerely want to believe there never was any real hate—just an enormous amount of dislike—our personalities were too similar, and as I had grown up, I had dared to stand up to him. Seemed the older we both got, the more amicable we became. Mama sure was relieved. Finally.

Within a few weeks, I had secured a great job with an ophthalmologist in Atlanta. Gordon and I had decided we didn't want to live in Alabama—we wanted to be close to my family, but not too close. And all my memories of Alabama at that point in my life had not been happy ones. I was all about the fresh, new start; it was time for my fairy tale to begin. Again.

"Third time's a charm!" Mama had giggled. No matter what I did, she supported me and loved me through it—even the hard stuff, much of which, as an adult, I had brought on myself.

After several weeks of living in Georgia, Gordon had completed the immigration process and was offered an excellent job at Siemens in Alpharetta, so we chose an area of metro Atlanta that was a reasonable commute for both of us.

We bought our first house together, a pale-yellow two-story house with honest-to-God gingerbread trim on the white posts all along the big front porch. Inside there was a big kitchen with more cabinets than I had ever seen in an entire house, much less just one room. All three bedrooms were upstairs, and a large bathroom with a soaking tub AND a separate shower. I remembered Jean and I used to think people that had a separate shower must be rich. Heck, we never even had one at our little concrete block rental house in Steele. This house felt so fancy to me. I chose corn-flower blue wallpaper with little, mauve-colored roses for the kitchen. The living room had a big stone fireplace, so I decided upon beige grass cloth wallpaper for that room. I bought white custom curtains with big ruffles all the way down the front and tied them all back with huge mauve bows. We bought a new living room set, a sofa with a matching loveseat, that was also country blue with tiny flowers dotted all over. And Gordon had always wanted a recliner, so of course, we bought him one. The room was finished with shiny oak end tables and a large round oak coffee table with claw feet that sat in front of the sofa.

I decided to decorate my walls with old quilts and woven baskets, very much in style back then. There were French doors that opened off the living room to a screened-in porch. I had never seen a prettier house anywhere. It felt like the house in the Loggins and Messina song "House at Pooh Corner." That song was always so magical to me, as it felt like a song that would be sung in a house where everybody loved each other. I had always dreamed of that house, and this felt like it might be it.

Within a couple of months, we found out that I was pregnant, and we were elated. It had not even been a full year since we had moved in together in Peterborough, planned our wedding, lost his mother, and made the decision to move back to America. The roller coaster ride of emotions in that period of time was hard to think about. We decided to turn our focus onto this miracle—this new life—growing inside me, as well as the one happening outside around both of us. Nothing could take away the joy we felt.

A few short weeks into the pregnancy, I began to feel mild cramps. My doctor had told me that this was relatively normal and not to worry unless I had further symptoms. I took his advice and did my best to push past the fear that was trying to creep into my thoughts. Until one morning, I could tell something was not right. I was trembling, and my heart was racing as I climbed out of bed and went into the bathroom.

"Gordon." My voice was weak and barely audible. I closed my eyes. "Gordon! GORDON!"

He had been sleeping but was startled awake as soon as he heard me scream his name out.

"What is it?"

"Something's wrong," I squeaked out, a raspy whisper. I was feeling dizzy and too weak to speak.

"What's wrong?" I could hear the bed squeak and the muffled sounds of the bedspread being tossed to the side. Within seconds, he had made the ten-foot journey from the bed to the bathroom. He looked from my face, which went from wide-eyed to eyes fluttering shut, down to my panties. He saw the blood. We both became frozen, rooted to the spots we were each in and unable to form words. The dizziness overcame me, and I felt myself wobbling, about to fall onto the floor. He reached out and grabbed me. I don't even remember him cleaning me and pulling up my pajama pants.

"C'mon … come … get back in the bed." He began to gently lift underneath my arms. I managed to stand, and he guided me back to bed. "I'm calling the doctor."

Within an hour, we arrived at the office of my obstetrician and were escorted back for an ultrasound. Because it was still early in the pregnancy, the ultrasound tech used a special type of device whereby she could place the tip of the ultrasound wand directly against my uterus. That's when we saw them … the two fetuses, each in their own individual sacs, nestled side by side.

"Here are your babies, Jackie."

Neither Gordon nor I could take our eyes off the image she was showing us. We couldn't really tell exactly what we were looking at, but we definitely saw two tiny circles amidst the waves displayed on the machine's black-and-white screen. And each circle had a very faint pulsating pattern within it.

"Babies?" Gordon was leaning in, squinting at the image, forehead wrinkled. I couldn't speak but could only stare at what all mothers can relate to … seeing the beating heart of their first child. And in this case, children. There were no words.

"Yes." Her answer was flat. She pressed a button and called for the doctor, who appeared at the door and into the room in seconds. He peered at the image on the screen, took the wand from the ultrasonographer's hand, and moved it around. Gordon and I just continued to stare at the image, unsure of exactly what we were seeing.

"You see this?" He used a pointer on the screen to illustrate what we were seeing. "There are two gestational sacs, which means there are two babies." Gordon and I, never taking our eyes off the screen, held hands even tighter.

"Twins?" Gordon asked, then swallowed hard.

"Technically, yes…" The doctor trailed off before completing his answer. "But, as you can see, one of the sacs is smaller than the other," he said, as he was moving the arrow pointer around on the monitor.

Finally, I managed to form words. "What does that mean?"

"It means…" he sighed and hesitated before completing the sentence. "One of the babies is not doing well." He gestured to show us exactly what he was talking about, but at this point, I couldn't understand a word he said. Just a jumble of words through the ringing in my ears and the inner pounding of my heart. I heard something about the heartbeat being very weak as the little one was "detaching," just before I passed out.

The nurse wheeled me out to the car as Gordon had pulled up to the front entrance, those doors that we had, only an hour before, walked through with strength and hope that everything would be okay. The doctor had given us instructions on strict bedrest for me, stressing to Gordon that I was ONLY to get up when I had to go use the bathroom. He explained that the more I reclined and remained still, the better the chances of the "little one" staying attached. I don't remember ever feeling such helplessness and fear. Looking back—as I have with so many of these memories—I can remember feeling determined to fix this. I felt that my baby's life depended solely upon what I did or did not do. I couldn't let anything happen to it; again, I believed it was up to me. I couldn't fail my child!

After what felt like the longest ten days of my life, we returned for the follow-up visit. I had followed doctor's orders to the T, hoping and praying the entire time … yet, I had noticed a few more tiny drops of blood on my underwear when I went to the bathroom. He had told us that, ideally, there should be no more. There was, so they wheeled me back into that same ultrasound room. This time, however, the doctor came right in to do the test himself. He inserted the probe and began to move the tip around and around inside me. You could've heard a pin drop as we all waited in that cold, dark room for the image to appear on that screen. When it did, I couldn't tell exactly what it showed but I saw the doctor faintly frown—for just a second—before painting on an obligatory smile as he turned to face Gordon and me. He indicated with a tip from his head toward the screen. We could see and hear the pulsing from that tiny sac we had seen ten days previously. There was just one. Maybe I just didn't know what I was looking at.

"Hear that? It's a heartbeat. A strong one." Gordon and I didn't know how to respond. Did he have more to say?

"This baby is going to be just fine. You should have nothing to worry about. He's a fighter." He paused, taking his eyes off the screen and turning his gaze directly at us. "I'm sorry, but the other little one just didn't make it through ... we knew that he was struggling when you were here last, but we thought there might still be a chance..." his voice trailed, and he averted his gaze away from mine and looked only at Gordon.

Did I do something wrong? Could I have done something different? Did I get up and walk too much? I didn't wait for answers. I felt like I could hear my words inside a cavern, echoing inside my head, or that room; I couldn't distinguish which one. The doctor went on to explain how this is not uncommon—that early in some pregnancies, there are sometimes two fetuses, and often the weaker of the two detaches from the lining of the uterus because it doesn't get as much nourishment. He even told us that many parents are never even aware that they had two gestational sacs in the first trimester, because a little bleeding is not uncommon; the weaker of the two just flushes itself out. I couldn't bear to hear any more of this medical jargon. I didn't like how the conversation turned to calling my other baby a "gestational sac" that wasn't strong enough for the duration of the ride, vanishing twin syndrome, blah blah blah.

Bottom line, the doctor assured me I had done nothing wrong. "It's just something that happens," they'd said. The only thought I had was that I was unable to fix this. I was convinced it was my fault.

May 1990 Northside Hospital, Atlanta, Georgia

Thursday, May 3, 1990, was the happiest day of my life. I looked into his sweet face for the first time, and my life was forever changed. It was a type of love I had never experienced before, and I still have no words to accurately describe it. The delivery had been unconventional, and not what I imagined when I dreamed of having my first baby. I don't know exactly what I had pictured, but I'm sure it involved lollipops and rainbows, smiles and wide-eyed wonder. A state of euphoria. Like everything else I had dreamed about when I was a little girl, painting the picture of what my perfect life would look like. Instead, aside from the initial scare we got when he was the sole survivor of what had been fraternal twins, the issue happened during the last month of pregnancy when he had been transverse lie, which meant my baby was sideways versus head down, as is typical for a normal delivery. The doctor had attempted to turn him up until the last minute, but it was to no avail. He remained sideways and was not going to turn around. Stubborn even before he was born. Only approximately 2% of babies remain transverse up until the day of delivery. And when they will not turn, they must be taken by C-section.

Afterward, when they handed him to me, with each leg pressed straight beside the corresponding ear, he opened only one eye and let out the most beautiful cry I'd ever heard—and the loudest. I swear he was winking at me, as I imagined him saying, "Get ready, Mama—this is only the beginning of how different I will be from everyone else in your life. Ever." He was right.

But here's the best thing he taught me. I didn't have to do a single thing for him to love me. I didn't have to look right, dress right, say the right things, be from a certain education or income level, have the nicest house in the neighborhood: none of those things. He loved me unconditionally, and he trusted me. He never questioned if I was there for him; he just had to cry, and there I was. I'd never leave him. If he was sick, I'd take care of him. If he cried, I'd hold him and kiss away his tears. There would be nothing I would say or do to make him doubt that truth. I had never felt that kind of love before—the kind that didn't require something from me. But there it was. He felt like an angel sent from heaven; I still think he really was. We named him Hayden.

Within the next few weeks, we would have lots of visitors, as everyone wanted to meet this child. Mama had made the drive from Alabama the day we brought him home. Because I had a C-section, my recovery would take a few days longer than a normal delivery, so she came to help me settle into being a new mother. To my utter shock (no exaggeration), three days later, my daddy drove the hour-and-a-half drive from their little trailer in Gadsden to our house in north Atlanta. He was thrilled to meet his new grandson and treated me with tenderness that I didn't recognize. It was the first time I could remember him speaking softly, gently hugging me, and then reaching to hold Hayden. He sat down in the recliner and rocked him, cooing and smiling at him the whole time. I was in disbelief; it was a side of him I had never seen. I wasn't around him much when Jean had her babies—I imagine he did the same with them—but the image of him sitting there, holding my new baby, changed something in me.

Gordon's dad came from Scotland before Hayden was even a month old. It was less than a year and a half since Irene had died, Gordon and I had married, and moved back to the States, and he missed us. We had not seen him since and were so glad when he arrived at the Atlanta airport. He walked into our house that afternoon and saw me sitting there holding Hayden. He leaned down and gave me a kiss, then immediately reached out to hold him. He didn't say much, just sat and looked at the baby who would be the first to carry on the Van Dyke name. He looked up at me, eyes brimming with tears, and said, "I wish Irene was here to see this." So did I, Dad, so did I.

Hayden Alexander Van Dyke would forever change me. And he was the first person in my life whom I ever considered might be able to, even though he'd never try. Feeling that kind of love from him and for him, for the first time in my life, there was no compulsion to try to change anything. Neither of us needed "fixing," for he was absolutely perfect. And I didn't have to worry if I'd be enough for him; I just was. And being his mother was the greatest gift and honor that I had ever experienced.

15

Brother Love and
the Circle of Life

I was finally happy, settling into the life I had always dreamed of. I had a perfect husband, a beautiful little boy, and a career that I was proud of. I had grown past some of my old, outdated ideas of what I thought I had to control to make it all happen. It seemed it was happening all by itself. When Gordon got a great job offer in the mountains of western North Carolina, we said, "Why not?" and packed up and moved from Atlanta. This would be an amazing new chapter for my little family of three.

Asheville, North Carolina 1993

We built a lovely new house, and I found another great ophthalmology job shortly after the move. Three-year-old Hayden and I loved to drive around together and play games and sing songs. I worked full time, and the days were long, so I would wake him up and drag him, usually half asleep, to the daycare, feeling guilty the entire drive. I loved my job, but I despised having to wake my toddler and get him out of his cozy bed, get dressed quickly, and strapped into the backseat of the car usually before sunrise. Every single time, the first game was always how the early bird catches the worm. I'd have him pretend he was the early bird, and I'd point at nothing, just randomly out the window, into the great pretend, and excitedly say, "There it is!! There's the worm! Hurry, catch it!"

This seemed to make me feel better about myself for not only driving him to the daycare at the butt crack of dawn, but we were also always the very first human beings to arrive in the parking lot before sunrise. My heart would sink when I swung the car into the daycare's driveway and, invariably, we'd have to sit and wait for the first worker to arrive. And to make matters worse, I'd have him unstrapped and halfway up the sidewalk, causing the three of us— Hayden, me, and the daycare teacher—to walk in together. I'd give him a quick kiss and a hug and tell him I love him before passing his bag onto the teacher, then spinning around and striding toward my still running car.

Just before getting inside, I'd throw him one last wave and shout cheerily, "You did it, Hayden!! You caught the worm this morning! Way to go!" Then, as I backed the car out, I'd glance back and see his little self, standing there in the doorway, waving goodbye. *Dammit! I'm such a bad mother!!* I'd drive the rest of the way to work mentally kicking myself, but, oh my goodness, I didn't want to be late ... I was never late.

I was the practice manager at a large ophthalmology practice, and I had early morning meetings with the physicians before all the rest of the staff and the hundreds of patients arrived. They needed me, which was what I needed, too. I was hired to make that practice run smoothly. To fix it. And I desperately needed to accomplish that. But, of course, that is who I was. The fixer. The controller. It was required of me, at least it was in my mind. It was how I had learned to cope growing up, always looking for an opportunity to be needed. I was even proud of it. Before Hayden was born, it was the only thing that I felt made me worthy.

Gordon also had a busy full-time job. He worked long hours and had moved up in his career, accepting an Engineering Manager position at his company. We both had goals of attaining the "American Dream": a nice house, great jobs, a kid, and a dog. In our thirties, we were well on our way to "arriving" before we reached age forty.

One day, the strangest thing happened. I had picked Hayden up from daycare in the evening, and we were headed home for dinner, listening to music and singing songs aloud together. One of our favorites was Neil Diamond's *Greatest Hits*, so we knew all the words and would belt out each song, staying right in sync with Neil. That day, Hayden abruptly asked me to turn down the music because he had something to tell me. "It's important, Mommy!" I complied and asked, "What is it, Son?" Quite honestly, I continued driving mindlessly, still humming "Cracklin' Rosie" in my subconscious and tapping my fingers on the steering wheel as I halfway listened.

"I'm going to get a baby brother."

"Wait, *WHAT?*" He had my attention now. Gordon and I had no plans to have another child and had decided one was enough.

"I'm going to have a baby brother, when I turn five," he spoke very matter-of-factly. Thankfully, we had just stopped at a red light, so with my foot on the brake, I took my eyes off the road in front of me and made eye contact with him through the rearview mirror.

"Who told you such a thing?" I giggled and asked incredulously.

"God." Again, answered without hesitation and with certainty.

"Oh … okay, Son." I just shook my head and laughed it off. *Where did he come up with these things?*

That night after we gave Hayden his bath and tucked him into bed, it was our practice to say bedtime prayers, and we always encouraged Hayden to pray aloud too. It was usually something like, "Thank you God for my mommy and my daddy, and my school and my friends, etc.," but this night he added, "And I especially thank you for my baby brother." I had not even told Gordon the story yet. When we spoke later that night, we both agreed that it was a "cute" thing to say, but it wasn't happening. Not in the plan, but Hayden continued to mention it often.

Several months passed, and we were still living our best life, never dreaming anything could burst our little family bubble until I got a call from Mama one afternoon. She and I had set Sunday as our normal day for our weekly chats, so I was surprised when she randomly called on a Wednesday.

"Jackie? Hey … I just wanted to let you know that I just got home from taking your daddy to the doctor. He has some spots on his lungs. It's not good."

"What do you mean 'spots on his lungs'?

"It's cancer. Your daddy's got lung cancer."

"Wait, what? Are you sure?" I couldn't even imagine John Henry Brewer ever having anything physically wrong with him. Aside from the accidental hand shooting, he had always been healthy and strong. And mean as a snake. I couldn't picture him weak or vulnerable.

"The doctor told him it was bad. I haven't told your sister yet. Do you want to talk to him?" My mind was reeling. *Talk to him? What would I say?* I had no idea, but before I knew it, Mama had handed him the phone.

"Hey, Girl." His voice was as gruff as usual. I hesitated before responding.

"Hey, Daddy. How are you feeling?"

"How the hell ya think I feel? Like shit, Jackie." We both sat silent for several seconds, which felt like an eternity.

"Well, I'm coming down; I'll leave in the morning."

"There ain't no sense in all that, Jackie. That's a long-ass drive, and you ain't got no business driving all the way down here. Ain't nothin' you can do, anyway."

"I'll see you tomorrow, Daddy," I choked out the words and hung up the phone.

The next day, I made the seven-hour drive to Alabama. When I arrived, my sister Jean and her husband Steve and their kids were there. None of us really said anything. Daddy was sitting on the couch, as usual, and Jean and Mama met me at the door, where we hugged in silence. When I pulled away, I looked at Daddy. His face appeared soft, but he didn't look directly at me. I walked over and bent down to hug him. He reached up as I leaned down, and we exchanged an embrace that I had never experienced with him. No words necessary. We both softly wept, even though Daddy shook his head and turned away. And I desperately wanted him to see that I had grown up to be strong. I needed him to know that I was no longer that scared, little girl, that I was in control. It's all I had ever wanted, really, for him to see I had made it, that I hadn't failed this time.

I stayed at their house for a week or two, took Daddy to his oncology visits, and, for the first time in our lives, we seemed to share a mutual love and respect. No one yelled, no one got angry. Daddy and I treated each other like adults—we talked about things that I had never dreamed we would. It was about time; I'd waited a lifetime for this, and so had he. I guess he knew his life was about to come to an end.

Jean also spent a lot of time over there with us, and she and I prayed over Daddy together. We told him about our relationships with God and how wonderful our lives had been as we discovered our faith. We weren't sure if he'd believed any of it, but Jean and I stood strong together and trusted God with our daddy. I finally had to return to North Carolina to be with my toddler, but before I left, I had my last conversation with him.

"I'll be praying for you, Daddy. And I want you to know I love you. You probably don't know this, but I always have."

was getting a baby brother. When we tried to get him to forget what he had supposedly "heard from God" and help us think of names for his little sister, he refused.

"I'm getting a baby BROTHER!" He was insistent. *Bless his little heart.*

We eventually chose her name, Irene Claire, her first name to honor Gordon's mother. Of course, I did what any normal pregnant gal would do. I immediately went out and bought some pink frilly dresses, which made Hayden frown. One day, he asked, "Mom, are you *sure* it's a girl? Can we check again?" We did, and guess what? Hayden had been right ... we re-measured and discovered it was a baby boy after all. I knew right then and there that this baby really was a special gift from God to our family. Dr. Steve measured him and checked all his little organs as they developed. He was perfect. We looked forward to the day we would hold him in our arms, and Hayden would finally have that little brother he had been talking about for two years.

December 19, 1995, Memorial Mission Hospital, Asheville, North Carolina

The time had come, and I was ready to deliver our second baby boy. Dr. Steve decided to admit me to the hospital, and I had an uneasy feeling. Something wasn't right. It started when I was packing my bag to take to the hospital, and Kristi had reminded me to pack the matching-colored Mother/Baby outfits for the trip home from the hospital. She had bought me a blue oversized tunic and matching pants that had the exact same pattern as the little blue onesie that I would bring the baby home in. Our baby boy. Hayden had been right. God promised him a baby brother when he was five. He was five and a half. And we had all celebrated and been so excited because the new baby was going to be our Christmas baby. A gift to our family. He would be the best gift ever. We had already chosen his name; it would be Cale Gordon Van Dyke.

So, that morning as I packed the bag, I hesitated when I was folding our matching outfits to place inside it. I felt a single tear roll out of my eye, down my nose, and drip onto the onesie. I froze. Gordon noticed immediately.

"What's wrong?" He placed his arm around me, but I couldn't answer him. He turned me around by the shoulders to face him. "Are you

crying?" he asked softly, his eyes peering directly into mine, full of concern. "Why?"

"I don't know." And I didn't. I continued to pack the bag.

"Okay, I'm ready when you are. Let me know, and I'll warm up the
car. And the car seat is in place." He shot me a big smile as he turned to
walk out to the car. We had already arranged for Hayden to stay with our
friends, Katherine and Keith, while we would be at the hospital.

"Gordon. Wait."

He turned around and looked at me, his mouth saying no words but
his eyes said plenty. They were pleading.

"He's not coming home from the hospital with us." My mind tried to
refuse to believe what my mouth was saying.

"Oh, stop that, Jackie. Of course, he's coming home with us. Don't
say that!" Gordon was shaking his head and continuing to walk toward
the door, keys in hand.

"I don't think he is…" My heart was filled with fear, and I couldn't
shake it. We drove to the hospital, not speaking. Silently praying. After
we checked in to Labor and Delivery and got settled into a room, we finally spoke.

"Don't think negative thoughts, Jackie. Where's your faith?" Gordon
needed me to be strong. But I didn't feel strength. I had a sickening feeling in my heart.

Dr. Steve induced labor and left me overnight to allow the Pitocin to
do its work. Even though the baby was in good position—head
down—and my body was in labor, he felt that many hours would pass
before delivery. He had instructed me to move around as much as I felt
like and encouraged me to walk often, as this would help put pressure on
my womb. Gordon stayed in the room with me but was soon fast asleep. I
could not get comfortable, so I got out of bed, dragging my IV pole
around with me, and began to walk the halls of the maternity ward.

I distinctly remember walking past the double doors labeled "NICU
Parents Only." This was, of course, the Neonatal Intensive Care Unit, and
every time I walked past those swinging doors, I would see random, tearful parents entering and exiting. All appeared to be exhausted. We'd
make brief eye contact, and I would mostly force an awkward smile and
duck my head down as I continued the slow walk up and down the halls,
IV pole rolling beside me. I remember thinking and then praying, "God, I

can't imagine how difficult that must be. Give them strength." And I really couldn't imagine. My head was swimming with unclear thoughts all night, as I agonized with sharp labor pains. I was ready to have this baby and hold him in my arms.

December 20, 1995

Around six a.m., I saw Dr. Steve walking down the corridor toward Labor and Delivery. I had been in hard, very painful labor all night. Thank God; let's do this.

Dr. Steve told me that he expected the baby would come easily, but he had been wrong. I was not progressing at all, and I was feeling more and more anxious. I didn't know exactly why. I just began to feel fear. After awkwardly clambering back into the bed and waking Gordon up, we waited to hear the news as Dr. Steve checked me. He frowned before gently re-covering my legs with the hospital blanket. "You're not there yet, Jackie. I'm going to increase the Pitocin to help move things along." *Oh, Dear Lord.* I couldn't imagine continuing with labor pains any longer. But, of course, I agreed to whatever we had to do. We would wait.

Dr. Steve was in and out of my room all day long to check on me. He approached my bedside, grinning from ear to ear, as always. His handsome face was forever reassuring, but I knew him way beyond the physician/patient relationship. I knew his heart, and I knew it was heavy. I was not progressing, and my baby was in distress. As he stood over me, before he said a word, I felt myself choke up, and tears began to roll down my face. Gordon was on my other side, his face leaned down, cheek to cheek with mine, while squeezing my hand. Kristi had arrived, and she stood beside Steve, her left arm crooked through his right, with her right hand resting on my leg. Her beautiful face trying to smile but her eyes looking deep into mine, bottom lip tight but revealing her effort to conceal the quiver. She bit down as Steve spoke.

"We're going to get you ready for surgery now, Jackie. We can't keep waiting, and it's best for you and the baby. I know you wanted to have him naturally, but it's not going to happen that way today. God has a different plan. Don't worry, we'll take care of you." Kristi and Gordon nodded in agreement, assuming this would reassure me. It didn't. My heart was breaking, and I did not understand this. Why?

"Let's pray," Steve said. And we did. As we always had, throughout my pregnancy. But this was different. I wasn't sure why, but I was scared. So scared. "Have faith … it's ok," they all kept saying. I just closed my eyes and cried, praying silently. The next thing I remember is counting from 99 … 98 … 97 … darkness.

Then, the darkness became a blur of confusion. I was awake but not fully coherent. I was only slightly aware of a flurry of activity in the operating room, along with a cacophony of sounds … hurried conversations … machines beeping, and an oxygen mask being forced over my nose and mouth. I had come out from the initial anesthesia, not fully but enough that I believed I could feel the scalpel cutting into my flesh. Maybe I didn't actually feel anything, but I was in such a delirium that I imagined I did. I began to panic, my eyes searching for Gordon amidst all the chaos. "Take this mask off! Take it off!" I was gasping for breath. Gordon leaned his face down to mine and said, "You're okay, Jackie … you're almost there … hang on!"

"I feel it!! I feel the knife! You're cutting me! Stooooop!!!" Was I out of my mind temporarily? Yet, I persisted with the notion that I could feel it. I heard Dr. Steve's voice, remaining professional and calm, as he instructed the anesthesiologist to administer another small dose of propofol. He had come too far to stop now and just wanted me to be able to tolerate the remainder of the cesarean section procedure. It worked. I was out like a light and remember waking up very groggy, only to find Gordon sitting right beside me, holding my left hand in both of his and squeezing tightly while whispering, "Thank you, Lord" in my ear. I could also hear but not see Kristi. "He's here, Jackie!! Cale is here!" She sounded gleeful.

I found out later that she had gowned up and had been in the surgical suite with us. She was an obstetrical nurse by trade, so she was allowed. As I slowly came out of anesthesia, I saw Dr. Steve and Kristi, as well as a bunch of other masked and gloved people whom I didn't know. I found out later that it was the surgical team, joined by the team of neonatal professionals who had been called in to stand by. The medical team had all expected there to be "issues" with my baby. Nobody told me that, and it was a good thing. I was already crazily doped-up at that moment. One of the nurses brought my tightly swaddled baby to me and leaned down, holding his face next to mine. I kissed his head and shakily reached up to touch his face. I didn't even notice that he hadn't cried. Then they whisked him away, and I fell asleep.

After a while, I woke up and could see two blurry faces within a foot of my own. As their features gradually came into focus, I could see that it was Gordon and Kristi, peering hard at me as I fluttered my eyes open.

"Where's my baby? Where's Cale?" I was groggy, but my words were clear. "Where is he?"

Gordon leaned in. "He's okay ... they had to take him to get all cleaned up and do some tests."

"Tests? What kind of tests? Where did they take him? I want to hold him!" Kristi and Gordon exchanged a look. Kristi answered first.

"He's down in NICU. They're just making sure he's perfect!" Her ability to remain so positive was amazing. She smiled the entire time she spoke. "You can see him soon!"

"What is she talking about?" I had turned my attention to Gordon now. He wasn't smiling and looked like he didn't know how to answer. "Is he okay? Gordon, tell me!"

"Ok, let's go see him. I'll take you there." I was confused. Why weren't they bringing him to me?

At this point, Dr. Steve came in and checked me, satisfied that I was recovering nicely. He removed his mask and smiled. "You're doing great. Now, do you want to go see your baby?" He was obviously my doctor—his job was to take care of me. He had delivered my baby and made sure I was doing well, but Cale was no longer in his hands. The neonatologists had taken over. Before giving the post-operative recovery room nurses the go-ahead to wheel me down to the NICU, he leaned in and prayed over me. Just as he and Kristi had done from the time I found out I was pregnant until now. He truly had a heart that trusted God with every single patient.

"Amen," he finished, touched my hand, and said, "God's got this." He hugged Gordon before disappearing through the swinging recovery room door. I began the journey, still on the surgical stretcher, down the halls toward the NICU. Once in the NICU, the nurses sidled my stretcher up beside Cale's incubator. I couldn't reach him. He was connected to so many machines, not breathing nor did he have a beating heart without the aid of those machines. They were so loud. So mechanical. So surreal. He was not premature. He was a fully developed baby, and I didn't understand why he was in here.

"I need to hold him!" I cried. "Why can't I hold my baby?" My eyes searched from Gordon's face to all the surrounding NICU nurses. No one answered. "LET ME HOLD MY BABY! I'M HIS MOTHER … GIVE HIM TO ME, PLEASE!!"

"Tomorrow, okay, Mama? Let us take care of him tonight," one sweet nurse leaned down and whispered in my ear.

"WHAT DO YOU MEAN? *I CAN TAKE CARE OF MY BABY!*" I stretched my hands toward the incubator, reaching but unable to touch him. Gordon gently took my hands, folded them into his, and kissed them. I began to sob uncontrollably. The NICU team and Gordon quietly gave me a few minutes to get it all out.

"I want to pray over him, please … Gordon … let's pray over him, please?" My pleading eyes returned to Gordon's. Even though we couldn't touch him, we laid hands on his incubator and prayed. I was too weak to have faith. I felt helpless that I couldn't take care of my baby. I couldn't fix him. I couldn't even hold him.

The next morning, the neonatologist came in and explained to both Gordon and I, as well as Dr. Steve, that Cale had been born with the diagnosis of IDM, "Infant of a Diabetic Mother." The doctor explained that the amount of sugar in my system was extreme and so out of control that it had crossed into the placenta and had caused serious complications with Cale, and, as a result, none of his organs were functioning properly. He had to be placed on full life support. Within days of his birth, he was diagnosed with a heart defect that required emergency surgery. I fell into a deep despair. Not being able to hold and care for my newborn was completely unnatural. I didn't want to leave his side.

Dr. Steve kept me admitted for as long as he could so that I could spend all my time recovering, while remaining with my newborn. Christmas came and went in a blur for us. Cale would remain in the NICU for almost seven weeks. From the beginning, the doctors and nurses had told me that he was the "sickest baby in the NICU," even though he was the only full-term baby there. Surrounded by so many tiny preemies in incubators, all with concerned parents by their sides, there lay my 8 lb. 8 oz., full-term baby, hooked up to full oxygen and other life-saving machines. They had administered a paralytic agent to keep him still because he was intubated, and they didn't want him to "fight against it" by trying to breathe on his own.

One of the neonatologists told us that we shouldn't "get our hopes up in case he doesn't make it," and that they were doing the best they could. His pulse ox was low, and his heart wasn't pumping properly. The

NICU nurses told us that they just wanted us to be aware and prepared for anything. Gordon and I were determined to keep the faith and trust God with Cale. We knew he had been born for a purpose.

Over the next several weeks, our pastors, Kirk and Suzette Bowman, from The Rock Church were by our sides daily. And the congregation also rallied to make sure Hayden was taken care of—he was in kindergarten, so we didn't want his life to be too disrupted. They came by daily to bring food, clean our house, do our laundry, and keep our house stocked with groceries. This church taught me what true servanthood was about. I had never imagined a group of people being so generous and willing to do whatever it took for us during these weeks of uncertainty. But the best thing they did was to stand with us in prayer, trusting God to take care of Cale. One gentleman in particular—his name was Ray—prophesied over baby Cale and told us that he knew for a fact that God had great plans for Cale, that he would serve God and bring many people to know of His faithfulness. That he would "live and not die, and declare the works of the Lord," which was a scripture reference from Psalm 118:17. I wanted desperately to believe it and didn't think I could bear to lose baby Cale. I pleaded with God. *Please let him live, God. Please!*

Gordon, of course, returned to work during this time. I spent most days and nights by Cale's side in the NICU, only coming home to take a shower and sleep a few hours. I wasn't allowed to even hold my baby until he was three weeks old. We, and some of our friends at church, had all written down scriptures on index cards and taped them all around his little NICU bed. Gordon, Hayden, and I also made a cassette tape of all of us praying and singing to Cale. The nurses promised us that they would keep it playing on the little cassette player right beside Cale's little ears, even when he was fully connected to breathing machines and life support. We were allowed to bring Hayden to visit Cale, and the three of us were amazed at his progress. He had a few setbacks, but we saw that he was getting better, and we had confidence he would be coming home.

On a cold day in February, we went to the hospital, gowned and masked up as usual. As we walked through those NICU doors, we saw Tessa—our favorite NICU nurse— standing there, grinning from ear to ear and holding Cale. He had been disconnected from all the machines that had been keeping him alive all those weeks.

"Look, Cale ... here's your mommy and daddy ... and your big brother!" she said into my healthy baby's ear, never taking her eyes off us.

"Oh, my goodness ... thank you, God!!" The three of us cried and hugged each other as I reached to take him from her arms.

"Y'all ready to take him home? Or we can keep him a couple more weeks?" Tessa teased.

Best day ever. I hadn't been able to fix him, but I knew the One who could. Looking back, this was probably one of my earliest memories of truly understanding the fact that things will happen in life that I can't control or fix. I can only trust God.

16

The Slow Fade

Life after bringing Cale home was wonderful. I knew that having Hayden had changed my life for the better, but when we brought Cale home, our family felt complete. I had been able to quit my job for a while and stay home, while Gordon continued to advance at his job. I honestly thought that life could never get any better than this.

Of course, life changes when you have two kids. In many ways, it gets better. Fuller, more rewarding. Our two boys were wonderful. The apples of our eyes. Smart and perfect. But the relationship between Gordon and I began to change. After all, I was not just his wife now. I was a mother, the mother of his two sons. And no one had taught me that just because I had children, I couldn't hit the pause button on being a wife. I had gained a lot of weight during my pregnancy with Cale and losing weight after age thirty-five, well, it's just not as easy.

I took a hiatus from work for several months after Cale was born. After the harrowing experience we had endured immediately after his birth, I was extremely overprotective of him. I suppose I subconsciously thought he was too fragile to ever let out of my sight. The doctors and nurses in the NICU had warned us that there was no way to be sure what, if any, long-term effects he might have. He had often been low on or without oxygen and underwent heart catheterization while in the NICU, so they had basically advised me to "be careful" and to "watch him." Oh, I watched him alright. Truthfully, I went completely overboard because it had frightened me so much when it felt as though we might lose him, and, as much as I hate to admit it, I lived in fear. I would wake up in the middle of the night terrified that he'd stopped breathing. I felt it was all up to me to make sure that he was okay; fixing him was my responsibility.

Cale was a perfectly healthy, bright child with a ready smile and a sweet spirit. Hayden certainly played the big brother role to the hilt, constantly reading to Cale and teaching him about anything and everything. He was also very overprotective of him while simultaneously being the typical, aggravating big brother, which he did very well. Suffice it to say, ninety-nine percent of my attention went to my boys.

Gordon had begun working a lot more and was very successful. He was climbing the proverbial corporate ladder, and his position at his job was extremely important to him. He felt needed. Important. And he was. I always told him, "You're the smartest man I've ever met!" It was true. He was a perfect combination of smart, witty, funny, and an amazing provider. He told me that when I decided to go back to work, it could only be part-time (if that's what I wanted), and he said we would use any money I would earn as a vacation/adventure fund.

During the first year of Cale's life, we faithfully continued in church being very active in ministry. The Pastors had asked us to become part of the Leadership Team so we led Connect Groups and began teaching in children's church. Hayden was beginning elementary school, and I was happily becoming a homemaker. This was something I had never imagined myself doing, as I always saw myself as a hard worker with such grit and determination to succeed professionally. Turning that same fierceness to mothering and managing our home felt odd at first, then became the delight of my life. It had felt like my fairy tale come true.

But things slowly began to change. I had stopped making being a wife a priority. And Gordon had stopped being a husband. All our attention was on our kids and making enough money to support the lifestyle we had always wanted for our family. Things began to fall apart, and neither of us could stop the unraveling. It appeared as though our marriage would not be able to survive the disconnect that was happening between us.

Summer 1997

When Hayden was seven and Cale was eighteen months old, Gordon and I broke up—maybe broke down is a better description. Split. I know this sounds blunt, but here are no good words to describe one of the most painful and difficult periods in all our lives. All four of us were affected, but only two of us played a part in the decision; Hayden and Cale were simply victims of their parents' inability to work through these difficulties. Which, at the time, felt too big to fix. All my life, my goal had been to make a better life than the one I had been born into. I would make sure of it, wanting to fix anything that even looked like it might break. And I believed I could. How wrong I was.

We were still living in Asheville, North Carolina, and we'd designed and built what had always been our dream house. It was a white southern farmhouse with a wraparound porch and, of course, my signature gingerbread trim on each post. I laugh to myself as I think back upon and now write the descriptions of the houses we lived in. I attribute my ornamental obsessions to when my sister Jean and I used to draw pictures and look through house catalogs. I guess it had been part of our fantasy of the fairy tale we dreamed of. Like, somehow the outside of the house would make what was happening inside prettier too. It was adorned with deep burgundy shutters on each window and white rocking chairs on the porch beside the double front glass doors. There were hanging ferns and potted flowers dotted all around, from the front to the back. It was on a beautiful grassy knoll in a cul-de-sac of a family neighborhood. Children would play in the streets while moms and dads barbequed on their back decks, families hanging out and waving to their neighbors. Reminded me of the old song "Pleasant Valley Sunday" by the Monkees. Status-symbol land. It looked like perfection, my dream come true, at last.

We were also still actively involved in our church, The Rock of Asheville, and had begun to see our friends there as family. We had a great church, great friends, Gordon had a great job, and what a great little family we had made. Lots of "greats." However, we had blinders on and didn't notice the gradual, slow fade.

It was a sultry summer day, right around lunchtime, when there was an unexpected knock on the door. I had been taking care of my baby, as well as trying to clean the house, do laundry, and decide what I would cook for dinner. I had not bothered to get properly dressed—wearing only sweatpants and a T-shirt—and I didn't have on makeup. My hair was in a messy, frizzy ponytail. I grabbed Cale up onto my hip and plodded to the door. I looked out the side glass before I opened it. She was pretty. Beautiful, actually. Smiling broadly, perfectly straight white teeth, dressed to the nines, and holding a basket of goodies. Her long, auburn hair was cascading down past her shoulders. Wondering who this lady was, I reluctantly opened the door. *Is this someone from our church whom I have not yet met?*

"Hi?" I noticed I said it with a question mark ... because it was more of a question than a greeting ... Hello stranger, and who are you coming to my front door unannounced?

"Hi, Jackie? I'm Cathy, Gordon's new secretary ... I wanted to drop by, see your new house, and meet the new baby! Oh, and I brought you something!" She thrust the basket toward me, already looking past me into the foyer of the house.

"Oh, hello, Cathy..." I stammered a bit, caught completely off guard. Why would this girl stop by in the middle of the day? And did Gordon know she was coming? Why hadn't he called and "warned' me? All I could do was step aside and invite her into the house. Remembering how sloppy I must look, and realizing Cale needed a diaper change, I was quite embarrassed, bordering on mortified. "Um ... C'mon in..." I gestured with my free hand.

"Wow! This is beautiful!" Her eyes were darting around, checking out the house. I still hadn't taken the basket, and, noticing this, she turned back around. "Oh, wow ... I'm sorry, I have heard so much about this beautiful new house you guys had built, I forgot that your hands were full! Would you like me to take it into the kitchen and put it on the counter?" She had already begun to stride out of the foyer, past the dining room, and into my kitchen, making sure to notice every detail.

"Sure..." It wasn't like me to be at a loss for words, but I honestly didn't know what else to say.

After placing the basket on the counter and then admiringly rubbing her hand across the island, she whispered, "Nice granite!" and then turned and faced me, still standing there, a hot mess holding my baby on my cocked hip. Reaching out for him, she cooed, "Well, hello there, Cale! I've heard so much about you ... come see me..."

"No ... let me change his diaper first ... and put a shirt on him." I was still in a bit of shock and felt so ill-prepared. I really wanted to feel thankful that it was a nice gesture, but the whole thing felt contrived. Fake. Not to mention, she and I had not even been properly introduced. I felt myself pull away from her as she thrust outstretched hands, with wiggling fingers in the direction of my baby, wanting to hold him.

"Oh ... and I'm Jackie ... but I guess you knew that." What the heck? How awkward could this get?

"Oh, my goodness ... yes, of course! And I recognized you from the photo on Gordon's desk ... I'm sorry! I obviously knew who you were, and I guess I feel like I already know you. Gordon talks about you all the time!" *Hmm ... I just bet he does ... and no doubt that photo on his desk was my pre-pregnancy weight and when my hair was long and pretty ... probably had makeup on too...* I tried to hide the sarcasm as I answered her.

"Oh, okay! Well, nice to meet you, Cathy. I've also heard a lot about you." *I heard you were "attractive," but my husband never mentioned you were so young ... and perky ... and ... over the top...* I tried to push the cynical thoughts out of my head as I excused myself to go into Cale's room and change him. I shot a glance at myself in the mirror hanging on his bedroom wall, paused, and tucked a stray wild hair behind my ear before heading back into the kitchen. *This is as good as it is gonna get.*

Cathy only stayed about twenty minutes after that. Of course, she wanted me to give her a tour of the new house, gushing over my decorating skills as we entered each room. She apologized again for popping over unannounced, reached out to tweak Cale's cheek, and flittered down the steps off my wraparound porch, underneath my gingerbread trim, and past the flowers along the front path, smiling and waving the entire time. I had the sudden, sinking feeling my perfect, little, happy home had just been violated. I couldn't shake the notion that she had only come by to check it out, as well as check *me* out. I felt like this woman wanted my life. And she was going to do her best to get it.

Looking back, the next few months seemed to pass so quickly. Gordon began to work more and more, going in earlier and staying later, often missing dinner. I stayed busy running Hayden back and forth from school, spending my days playing with Cale, and making extra certain to keep my house spotless, all the laundry done and put away, and always making sure to have a delicious hot meal on the table every evening by six. Even on the days Gordon worked late, I was faithful to make him a plate, wrap it in foil, and keep it warm until he came home. Sometimes he would eat, but often he'd make an excuse by saying he had picked up something to take into work ... not wanting to interfere with our schedule. Most days, he came home in time to help bathe the boys and read them a story at bedtime, but after that would often fall into bed, claiming exhaustion and rarely seeming interested in spending time with me. I had been working on losing all the baby weight, as well as making sure to wear makeup and have my hair fixed most days. I sensed he was losing interest in me, and I wanted to do anything I could to gain it back. When Gordon stopped going to church with us on Wednesdays and Sundays, I still went and took the boys. Then we stopped leading our Connect Group. Gordon's schedule was just too busy. I was furious, and I didn't try to hide it.

"What is happening?! Since when did work become more important than church? What is *wrong* with you?!" I whined and cried.

"It's not more important, but *someone* has to work and support the lifestyle you want!" I felt that he resented me for that. Since we'd decided to have another child, he had promised me I wouldn't have to go back to my 50- to 60-hour-per-week job. Now, I felt as though I was being punished. "And you need to get off my back about church!" He would demand and just leave me pouting and crying.

Looking back now, I see how jealous and controlling I was being. Ever since I met Cathy, I began to notice things changing with Gordon and me. We began to fight over the most trivial matters. I'd scream and cry; he'd sulk. I accused; he defended. I believed I knew there was something going on, but he would deny it and tell me I was just jealous. When he told me that he wasn't sure if he was in love with me anymore, it felt as if my world had crashed. I begged and pleaded with him to go to counseling, but he refused. He was done. Some of it was my insecurities and my tendency to inflate things in my mind. I was so afraid of something going wrong, something that could disrupt the perfect life I had finally managed to attain. That I felt I had *earned.* I wish I had thought more about how I could be a more loving wife instead of the "good wife" I had always thought would be enough. The one who was better than Mama had been. It makes me so sad to admit this now. Mama had done her best. At least Gordon wasn't beating me up, I rationalized. But he was also not paying any attention to me. We became parents only, not husband and wife. *What could I do to fix this? How can I make things better? I just need him to love me ... like he used to.*

August 31, 1997

It was the same day that people all over the world received the news that "The People's Princess," Princess Diana, had died. I had been up all night watching the news and didn't get a wink of sleep. Cale slept in his bed all night, no clue that his family was falling apart ... on the same day the world watched Princess Diana die; the day my seven-year-old son was asked to be "Daddy's helper" while he moved out. The day I watched two of the three people I loved most in the world slowly and methodically move boxes and random pieces of furniture into a moving truck. Gordon was leaving me. I held my eighteen-month-old son tightly in my arms as we stood in that gingerbread clad doorway and waved goodbye, as the truck backed out of the driveway and down the street. I blinked back the tears, kissed Cale on the cheek, and turned around. I wouldn't let him see his mommy's heart breaking. Hayden had seen it but tried his best to remain neutral. So sad that my seven-year-old son had to do that.

Gordon had leased a brand-new apartment, and it appeared as though he wanted to begin a brand-new life. Without me. He and I had promised to make this as easy as we possibly could for our sons, whom we both loved and never wanted to hurt. But how could it not hurt them? That night, after I put Cale to bed, I sat up and watched the unfolding coverage. I remember the newscasters saying, "This will go down as one of the saddest days in history."

Yes, it would. My heart was shattered.

Within a month of Gordon moving out, we decided to sell our house, and within a week, it had sold. I didn't want to stay in Asheville, so Gordon and I agreed that the boys and I would move to Alabama so I could be close to Jean and Mama. The irony of moving back to the very place I had always determined to escape was not lost on me. I had to hold things together, never wanting the boys to see the pain I felt. I was no longer that broken, little girl from Steele. The girl who had tried to force the fairy tale she'd always dreamed about. Who had never really learned how to just love and have faith in God. I thought I had, but I now see how clueless I had been. I was still as broken as I had always been, just an adult version now. The woman who was determined to succeed. All my efforts to "fix it"—life and people—had failed. Again. Would I ever learn?

After Daddy had passed in 1994, Mama had moved into a little trailer next door to Jean and her family in Attalla. Gordon bought a nice home for the boys and I that was only a few miles from Mama and Jean. He stayed in North Carolina and continued to do well in his job, making sure to make the six-hour drive at least every other weekend to spend with the boys. Weird as it was, we were both determined to remain friends and do right by the kids, and each other.

On the planned days when Gordon would be enroute to visit, I'd get the boys ready, playing games where I'd say, "Guess who's on his way?!" And they'd both squeal, "DADDY!!" Then we'd laugh and plan what fun stuff we'd do when he arrived. Amazing what two people will do for their kids, even as the chasm between them gets wider and wider. Hayden was old enough to understand and while he was often very sad, something in him rose up and he became my little helper. He was not just my son, but oddly, my little best friend. He was wise beyond his years and had a deep, spiritual understanding. He and I bonded in a way that no mother and son should ever have to. Fortunately, Cale was too little to even understand what was happening, which both Gordon and I were very thankful for.

After two years of back and forth, "do we get back together or do we make this separation permanent?", we decided to file for divorce. It was an extremely difficult decision for both of us. And telling Hayden almost destroyed me. The questions I asked myself were, "Do I curl up and die, or do I pull up my bootstraps and get stronger?" I decided there would be no in-between. I made up my mind to dig in, study the Bible, memorize, and learn scriptures, and begin to understand the Word of God, making it real in my life. I had to learn to activate my faith and really lean in and trust God. I had tried to control everything for so many years, and I finally realized I sucked at it. I can't control my own emotions, much less anyone else's.

But when I decided to get stronger in my spirit and my walk with God, my "flesh"—the human being—was still the same, old fixer/controller Jackie Brewer, the girl who still had scars from all the years of growing up in an abusive, dysfunctional home, watching my mama get beat up and downtrodden by my daddy—and part of me just got angrier and angrier. I began to hate myself and felt unworthy of all the things I had dreamt of and prayed for my entire life. I had failed again, but I loved my boys. And I still loved Gordon. So, I pressed on. What was slowly simmering inside me, what had begun as a child, would take years to come to the surface. I wouldn't even know what hit me: unresolved anger, the pain of deep insecurity, and holding on to years of unforgiveness can destroy a person.

And it almost did.

17

The Best of Times;
The Worst of Times

Gordon remained in North Carolina the next two and a half years, the boys and I in Alabama. We continued with the same routine—Gordon would try to come down to visit every couple of weeks, only to turn around and head back that Sunday afternoon. The goodbyes were often tearful, heart-wrenching for all of us. The boys and I would always walk down to the driveway to see him off, inevitably with Hayden holding on to his daddy's legs and me having to quite literally pull little Cale out of his daddy's arms, legs wrapped tightly around his waist. Gordon and I would always lean in and kiss each other goodbye, pausing to look into each other's tear-filled eyes. We knew we couldn't carry on this way and were only two weeks away from the final divorce decree.

One Sunday, after a particularly harrowing goodbye experience, I put Cale down for his nap and walked back into the living room to find Hayden standing at the top of the stairs, looking at me, his eyes pleading. I walked over to him, and we both began to softly cry. We sat down on the stairs, leaning into each other, hugging.

"Mommy, will you and Daddy ever get back together?" he spoke without looking up. I hesitated, knowing what I wanted to say but being painfully aware the impact my words could have on my little boy.

"I don't know for sure, Baby, but I think we will."

"Why don't you know for sure?' This time, he slightly pulled away and leaned back to look at me. How do I answer him? I believed we could … we might. Gordon and I had spoken about it many times, both of us wanting to make it work, but so unsure if perhaps too much damage had been done. The last thing either of us wanted was to hurt our boys, or each other, anymore. I couldn't answer Hayden definitively.

"Why don't we pray about it?" I felt like that was such a lame answer and was so obvious that I couldn't tell my little boy what he really wanted to know. I didn't have the answer, but I knew who did. So, we prayed. Which we did a lot, but this time it was different. There was something about it ... both of us so vulnerable, sitting side by side on those narrow stairs, holding onto each other crying. We were sincerely seeking a real answer from the God we had all trusted in for the last several years. We both prayed aloud, each taking a turn as we just simply asked God to help us get our family back together. We said our "amen" and just continued to sit quietly, holding each other and wiping our tears.

I'm not sure exactly what came over me, but suddenly, something rose up in me, and I looked at Hayden and said, "I know your daddy and I are going to get back together." *How am I suddenly so confident? Was I crazy making a promise like this to my kid?*

"How do you know, Mommy? Did God tell you? Like He told me that time that I was going to get a baby brother?" *This kid didn't forget anything! Geesh.*

"Yeah ... I think He did." *What am I saying?*

"Do you promise?" His eyes pleading, as a single tear slid down to his chin. I hesitated. Like for a full minute. I had to be careful. I guess on the inside, I quickly "checked in" with God, and that's when a faith rose up in me that I had forgotten was possible. I hadn't felt too sure of anything since we had prayed for Cale to "live and not die and declare the works of the Lord." I had known Cale would survive and somehow, I now knew that so would Gordon and I, so I blurted out my answer.

"Yes, Son. I promise!" *Oh my goodness ... what have I just done?*

We hugged and cried happy tears before Hayden went down the stairs to play in the den, and I went immediately up the stairs to my bedroom, closed the door, and got in God's face.

"Ok, God ... I've done it now ... I just made my kid a promise; now I really have to trust You. I believe You told me what to say, so I am just gonna wait for You to do what only You can do ... cuz, I got nothing left, God. This is all on You." I had no clue, really. And I just kept kicking myself for making a promise to my kid.

Six months later...

Just when you think you have gone as low as you ever thought you would, God opens your eyes to see things from a lens—one you thought you'd never pick—referring back to my eye exam analogy. Gordon and I were seeing through a glass darkly, a faint reflection of the riddles and mysteries, but our understanding was incomplete. We never doubted that we still loved each other (1 Cor. 13;12-13). This time, Gordon and I went to the "physician" together and got an "I" examination. We had both struggled with so many issues in the past few years: insecurity, pridefulness, anger, and bitterness, just to name a few. But what we discovered was that our love for each other and our boys, coupled with our faith in God, was way bigger and more important than our emotions and our circumstances. Sounds simple when the preacher says it, doesn't it? I can't tell you how many sermons I've sat through and heard the words, "Let go and let God! God is in control! Cast your cares on Him!" All true, by the way, and I am in no way making fun of those preachers or those sermons. But let's just get real ... those are EASY words to say, aren't they? Like it's just that simple? It's NOT. If only ... but then again, God never said it would be, did He?

After almost three years total that we lived separately, divorce papers just two weeks from becoming a final decree, Gordon called me one morning and said, "What are we thinking?" I agreed. After many more long, heartfelt conversations and much prayer, we both called our attorneys and told them to cancel the court appearance and rip up the papers. We had decided to get back together. It really was not as simple as it sounds, but we both just knew. Neither of us could imagine life without the other. Hayden was elated. Little Cale still never really understood what was happening, which made my mother's heart happy. No need. But I didn't know I would struggle with abandonment issues for the next several years, and that I feared I would never be able to trust Gordon again. But I had to try.

We sold the house in Alabama, and the boys and I moved back up to Asheville with Gordon. Being back there just never felt right to us, though. Asheville reminded us of all the trials and struggles we had gone through from the time Cale was born and stayed in the NICU to the day our family became separated. Of course, our church, The Rock of Asheville, stood by us the entire time we were apart. They had been praying for us throughout the process, and they celebrated with us when we reconciled. We went to Pastor Kirk for counseling. We both remember the day we went in and told him that we had decided to start over as a family. Gordon would find a new job, and we'd see where that would take us. He agreed and prayed over us, standing with us and believing God to take us to new levels in our relationship with each other. Leaving Asheville was bittersweet, but the right thing to do.

Within a few short weeks, Gordon had an amazing new job offer with General Electric and his new boss said, "Pick a city ... just make sure to be close to a major airport." What an opportunity! We could choose anywhere we wanted to live! Because Gordon's entire family was "across the pond" in Scotland, and mine was still in good ol' Alabama, we chose a little town in west Georgia that was "close enough" to Mama n'em and was also an easy trip to an international airport. We knew absolutely nothing about it, but for some reason, it felt right. Gordon and I had always been quite spontaneous, and this time was no different. We held up a map and pointed right to the place: Villa Rica, Georgia. There would be MANY memories made there as well as more life-changing experiences. And we were excited for the ride!

Villa Rica, Georgia, June 2000

"I found a great little neighborhood, Gordon! It is a community that will be designed around a golf course. It's what they're calling a 'Master Planned Community,' so there will be grocery stores built, new little shops, and they will even have tennis courts. There are many house plans to choose from!" I remember being so excited to share my new find with him. We had been looking online, and nothing had appealed to us until now.

"How far from the airport?" Gordon had asked. This was a very important consideration because his new job with GE guaranteed up to seventy percent travel for him. An exciting opportunity for him, but, if I'm honest, I wasn't thrilled. We had been separated for almost three years prior, and even though we had reunited with the determination to be stronger than ever, I was afraid. Still insecure that what had happened before might just happen again. I couldn't shake my fear.

"Only about thirty-five minutes. And I'll be about an hour and a half away from Mama and Jean." Crazy as it sounds, I was comforted by knowing that I could get to them easily, if need be. They had been so very supportive of the kids and I over the last few years. But, at the same time, a hundred percent thrilled to see that Gordon and I had reconciled. Our prayers had been answered.

"Sounds good to me. What's the house like?" Gordon was great in that he really yielded to me in that regard. If I loved a house, so would he.

"Well, there's several different plans to choose from!" I was practically salivating as I thumbed through the options.

"Whatever you like. If it's within budget." And with that, he moved on to looking up all the details of the golf course he would, most certainly, be joining as soon as we moved.

This would be the third house we'd build from the ground up, from the foundation all the way up to the roof. And all the houses we'd built had been based on the fantasy I had ever since I was a little girl, imagining my grown-up life. I always wanted what I never had: a beautiful home filled with love, laughter, and great memories. Third time would be a charm, just like my marriages. I had this weird belief in that old saying—like there might be something true about it. People try things, and when they don't work out, they are reminded of the old saying, "If at first you don't succeed, try, try again!" And I had certainly done that.

I had a lot of faults, but giving up was not one of them. Ever the fixer. Always the one in control. And always concerned with how things might look from the outside. What will people think of us? I would concern myself with every little detail until I got it just right. Another new house, no gingerbread trim this time, but all the other pretty stuff I wanted, *needed*, to achieve the look of a blissful, perfect, little family living in their perfect house. I would NOT fail again. But, deep down, I was very afraid that I just might.

After the house was built and we had completely moved in, life just got better and better. We found a great church, kids enrolled in schools: Hayden was in the fifth grade by now, and Cale was just at the age to start preschool. Gordon's job was going great, so I decided to go back to work part-time. Three days a week, just for some extra "gravy money" for family vacations or extra stuff we didn't need but wanted. My thoughts were always on holding all this together. I simply refused to lose this again.

Hayden was that "extra" kid. The overachiever. He was winning awards upon more awards at school, sports, anything he put his hand to.

He was so smart and so accomplished in everything. Cale was the sweetest kid. He was also very smart in school, but his focus seemed to always be on caring for others. He was extremely sensitive to feelings and had a unique gift to get along with everyone, always knowing what to say or do to keep everyone in his group happy. Both our sons were very special, young men. We had no doubt they would grow into well-established strong men, despite the fractured past we had put them through. Gordon and I were determined to do our parts. We loved our family, we loved our home, we loved our church, and we loved God. What could go wrong?

Each year, we went on special vacations. It was back in the early days of "all-inclusive resorts," and we always picked this type of vacation package because, as the name implies, EVERYTHING was included. Having two growing boys who wanted to eat all day long, these types of vacations were the best option. It was also when Gordon and I started drinking more. The resorts always included all the food we could eat *and* all the alcohol we could drink. We felt so much stronger by this point in our marriage, so we decided to indulge. Why not? I had also been working on my "fear" of drinking. I wanted desperately to get rid of my old mindsets and learn to relax a little. And because I secretly worried Gordon might leave me again, I wanted to loosen up and stop being so controlling about everything. I found it easier to just go along with it. And I discovered I liked it!

We'd always come home from those awesome vacations with great stories and so many fun and memorable times had by all. I still look back at all our photos and smile when I think about the experiences we had and how we grew even closer as a family of four. We NEVER ran short on laughter, and our love for each other was what I had always dreamed of.

I'm not exactly sure when things began to change—again. I don't like this part of it, but it's necessary in my understanding the growth and the revelations God gave me in these latter years. And it solidifies my "why" of even telling my story at all. I think I see how slowly, and how tricky, life's circumstances can be if we're not always on our spiritual guard. I've realized that the better life is going, and the easier things seem to be, is when we take our eyes off the subtle things that can creep in. The Bible calls these things "little foxes." Another reference to that "slow fade" that I had become familiar with a few years prior. The trouble was I never gave it any more thought after that one experience. I was determined that would never happen again. Ever.

Our so-called perfect family life continued for the next several years while we lived in our house in Villa Rica. For the first time in our marriage, we had lived in one location for more than a couple of years; we were established in our church; the boys had made great friends and were excellent students at their schools, both playing soccer and tennis. Gordon was excelling at his job, continuing to receive promotions and more responsibility. I had a wonderful part-time job with an ophthalmology practice full of people I loved and believed would be lifelong friends. Everything I'd ever dreamed of.

In May of 2008, Hayden graduated from high school with top honors and had been accepted into the prestigious United States Naval Academy in Annapolis, Maryland. We had always known he'd excel and be able to get into any school he wanted, and we were extremely proud of him. What we didn't expect was the gaping hole his moving out of our home would leave in our family. As his mother, this was my firstborn child, the "strong one" who had fought through and made it when his "vanishing twin" sibling had not. This, too, was something I thought I had recovered from but have come to find out I had NOT.

Hayden was also the wonderful big brother and mentor to Cale, who felt a tremendous loss at the notion of his brother no longer being there at night to sit up late and tell stories with. And of course, Gordon ... our fearless leader, the strong father who had locked arms with me together to bring our family back, stronger than ever before. He certainly had not expected the pain that was to come.

This was not like our eighteen-year-old son was graduating high school and moving on to college like all young men and women are expected to do, a normal part of life. This was not like a "normal" college. Not even close. We didn't get to go view his dorm, buy IKEA furniture, and help him decorate it. We didn't take him to get settled in and know that we would be able to see him anytime ... a graduating senior who was off to college, not fully moving out. Who could come home anytime, as much as he wanted to, like other normal kids who go off to college. NO. This was the United States Naval Academy. He was not only going to one of the top universities in the country, but he was also signing up to be a full-time military officer. He would belong to the United States Department of Defense for the next several years.

He didn't get a choice to get homesick and just drive on home anytime he wanted to see his family. And vice versa. We couldn't just pop in for visits anytime we felt like it. Cale couldn't just call his big brother anytime he needed advice on school or girls. It felt a bit like another breakup, a serious divide in our family, something we all wanted but none of us were prepared for. Suffice it to say, after we said goodbye to him, as we left him on the banks of the Severn, there was this weird combination of pride and mourning that took place. All four of us felt it. Life had changed. Albeit, a normal expected change, but a large void was left. Gordon, Cale, and I cried together, hugging each other tighter every day after Hayden moved out, but it was all part of God's great, divine plan.

The next few years would test our family strength again; and we didn't know if this would be yet another test we'd pass.

December 2008

Hayden had been away only five months, and we were still adjusting to being a family of three while missing him terribly. It was a cold day just before our first Christmas without Hayden, and things were about to change again.

"Wait, what?" I walked into the living room when I heard Gordon speaking into his phone that morning. His face ashen and his countenance fell. My heart leapt. *Has something happened to Hayden?*

"I don't understand. Yes. Yes. Okay. Thank you for calling." He ended his phone call before dropping his chin to his chest. He didn't look at me.

"What happened? What's wrong?" My heart pounded.

"I just lost my job."

"*WHAT?* Why?"

General Electric had sold a portion of their business, Plastics, which was the division Gordon worked for, to a Saudi Arabian company called Sabic, and they were reforming this sector of the business. Gordon was one of the many chief executives that had been let go. "Made redundant," as they called it. He was devastated.

"What are we going to do?" I asked, partly just thinking out loud, but also feeling a little bit panicked. He had never been unemployed during all our years together, and his job had always been extremely important to him.

"I have no idea" was his only answer. We both just sat in silence. After an hour, Gordon said he was going to the store to buy a bottle of wine. We would share it and discuss what we might do in the face of this devastating news. We weren't getting any younger; our oldest son had just moved out of our home, and our youngest was only in the eighth grade. We had to come up with a plan.

We drank the bottle of wine, and we prayed. Neither of us were sure if we could hear God better after a few glasses of wine, but at least we felt better and were able to relax a bit.

The next day, we broke the news to Cale, who honestly wasn't one bit concerned—he had always been well taken care of so the thought never occurred to him that this would change anything. None of us were really worried about it, as Gordon had always easily been able to find a company who considered themselves lucky to employ someone of his knowledge and expertise. And we lived in metro Atlanta—the largest city in Georgia—so surely there must be plenty of local opportunities. Or so we thought.

After a few weeks, he got a call from a recruiter. He had found the perfect job for Gordon: six-figures, great benefits, executive level position. Exactly what he was looking for. None of us had expected anything less.

"Where is it?" I had nonchalantly asked, as we poured ourselves a second glass of wine that evening before dinner. This time of drinking was becoming our norm.

"Tucson, Arizona." Blank stares, no words necessary.

"Do we have to move? Or can you work remotely?" I broke the silence.

"They want to fly us out there next week. We'll talk about it then."

"What do you mean 'fly *us*' out there? Why do I have to go?" I only had to pause and think about it for five seconds before stating the obvious, "They've already interviewed you and offered you the job." It wasn't even a question; I knew.

"Yes. They want us to see the area and look for houses."

"Oh. My. God." I shook my head and closed my eyes. "What about Cale? Are we just going to take him out of school? Uproot him from all his friends?"

"What other choice do I have, Jackie? I need this job!" I had never seen my husband this anxious.

We finished another bottle of wine before going to bed, promising to continue to pray about it. The next day, we met with our pastors, Tony and Sheryll. They loved us, and we knew they would give us good advice. "Trust God. He'll tell you," Pastor Tony said, with his signature expression of faith. The one we knew and trusted. "Always go back to the last thing God told you and ask yourself if you've been obedient." We tried that, but neither of us were sure we knew. After several bottles of wine late one night, we made a decision.

Tucson, Arizona, February 2009

After Gordon accepted the job, we found a nice house that we were able to rent while Gordon started his new job. We got Cale enrolled in his new school, and I began to, yet again, set up and settle us into another house. Dear Lord, when was all this going to end? We had believed that Villa Rica would be our forever home, where both of our sons would grow up, move out, go to college, and get married. Everything had been so good there. Why was this happening? Was this another test? Because if it was, I was not only growing weary of being tested, but I was also getting hard-headed and hard-hearted toward God. Why was He testing us, again?

Unfortunately, Gordon was not enjoying his new job, and he began to suffer mild panic attacks. Anxiety. Then, as if things couldn't get any weirder, I began going through the beginning stages of menopause, which I still refer to as "meno-HELL" to this day. At first, I thought the hot flashes were because we were living in the Arizona desert, where 100-plus-degree weather was the norm, but when I also started having panic attacks, it was clear to both of us that things were just "not right" here. Cale had enrolled in his new school, and all his new friends were completely different from all the good ol' boys from Georgia: the ones he went to church with, hung out in our country club neighborhood with, and whose parents we knew well and trusted. No, these boys were different. Not that there was anything wrong with them—in fact, they all seemed like nice kids, but the whole family dynamic had changed.

In a time frame of seven months, our oldest son had moved out of our family home, 800 miles away from us; my husband had lost what he thought would be his "forever job" and had to start over in a job almost 2000 miles away and was experiencing panic attacks; I had walked away from the absolute best job and friends I had ever had, coupled with starting to go through menopause, hot flashes, anxiety, and depression; and our sweet, little Cale had been snatched away from his buddies and one of the best schools in the state of Georgia; we all had to leave our beloved family church; and now we were even farther away from Hayden and everything we ever knew that symbolized a settled family life. When I first spoke to my doctor about this, her reply was, "You do realize you are describing a combination of the top stressors in life, right?" Great. Just great.

"Would you like for me to prescribe hormone replacement therapy for you, or just give you medication to help you through this?" I just looked at her, unable to answer because I didn't have one.

"The hormones are hit and miss," she continued. "It usually takes a while to figure out exactly which hormones you need that can help you. And the pills can also cause unpleasant side effects."

"I don't want anything. I am strong enough to get through this."

Gordon told his doctor the same things when he had suggested Xanax and Lexapro. Neither of us wanted to rely on medication. So, every evening after work, we'd eat dinner, talk about Gordon's day at work, Cale's day at school, and my useless, damn day at home by myself. All of us were over 2000 miles away from Hayden, our home, our church, and our friends. Wine was a good idea. A really, really good idea. And we drank it every night. I remember one night in particular, as we sat outside by the pool, looking up into the bluest sky I had ever seen. We were surrounded by the purple desert mountains and the gorgeous flowering cacti, citrus, and palm trees all around, sitting in our reclining pool chairs and sipping our fourth or fifth glass of wine. We had both been dealing with all this anxiety, depression, and racing thoughts of wondering where we might end up and how we'd gotten here, in Arizona of all places. Ever the one to quote scripture I had memorized, I asked Gordon this one simple question.

"The Bible says that we 'have the mind of Christ' ... We know that Jesus, Himself, never struggled with panic attacks, anxiety, and depression!! Then why are we? We need to take a stand!" It was a desperate plea. I waited for Gordon's reply. And in his typical, very strong Scottish brogue, he said, "Jackie ... Jesus only lived to be thirty-three ... we were fine when we were thirty-three. Remember?"

I laughed out loud and thought to myself, *Even Jesus is laughing at this.*

For the life of me, the one who looks for something good in absolutely every single experience of life, I could NOT figure out what good came from our time in Tucson. I have mostly hellish memories from those days. None of us were happy, and we couldn't imagine why we had to move there. Why did Gordon lose his job? Why did we have to be uprooted? Why was it so horrible there? And I swear I heard the voice of the Lord whisper, "Cale..." At first, I didn't understand. Then it dawned on me. It was in Tucson where he found his own personal experience with God. He had been in church his entire life, so he knew all about God, Jesus, and the Bible. But he was young and had mostly been riding on our spiritual coattails. It was only when he was surrounded by friends, most of whom were not believers, thrown into a church where there was absolutely no youth group and no planned activities for a young teenage boy that he began to search inside himself.

One of the best things about the small church we went to in Tucson was—because they didn't offer anything for the youth—the worship leader asked Cale if he might be interested in playing drums on the adult worship team. Cale had always loved drumming and dreamed of getting his own professional set. This was an opportunity he didn't want to pass up. So, we bought him a new set of good drums and paid for professional lessons, and he was given a place on the worship team at Catalina Church. It was during that time that he was able to grow spiritually in many ways. He was using his musical gifts at church, and soon he began to witness to his friends. Other kids were drawn to him, as he came into his own ministry. Now, we know that the move to Tucson was not in vain. God never does anything without a purpose.

As for Gordon and me, well, that's a different story. Tucson was a struggle for us. He hated his job, and I was bored. Our spiritual lives waned, and we both became more and more dependent upon alcohol to get us through the tough times. It was a daily activity. We both felt out of control in Arizona, and the only way either of us knew to fix it was to drink; we called it a "coping skill." Neither of us dared to believe our drinking might be becoming a problem. We pressed on and after a year and a half, Gordon's company agreed to allow him to work remotely, which meant we could move back to Georgia. We all felt this was the right thing and that we'd all look back on Tucson with a wink and a nod. A blip in the radar. No big deal.

But things had changed. Gordon and I had changed. Even when we moved back to Villa Rica in late 2010, we were different. Life was different. Church was different. Mostly, it was we who were different. We had allowed the disappointment, coupled with the onslaught of emotional challenges we went through, as well as the physical changes that were happening in us (Gordon hurt his back, and I became a menopausal basket case) to change how we viewed life. We used to enjoy an occasional glass of wine with a meal, or at a special occasion, or even just to unwind at the end of a long workday. But now, we didn't just "enjoy" a little wine. We seemed to need it. To rely upon it. And what happened in me was unexpected, yet not unusual, knowing what I know now. Everything I had ever thought about alcohol, deep down, were the negative feelings I had associated with it as a child. I resented it. All I had ever seen of alcohol was connected to anger, fighting, or crying. It had never been something I could ever see as a good thing. So, any time Gordon wanted to go to a happy hour, or attend a party where alcohol was being served, I did it, resentfully. I would suppress my anger and try to remain in control.

We both began to drink more. And more. And it would be only after both of us had too much and passed out that the horrible thoughts began to haunt me. Was this becoming a problem? Would we eventually have more problems? Would I ever become like my mother and just accept it to keep the peace? Or worse, would I become like my daddy and explode with anger?

I must never let that happen. God help us.

Part Three

Realizing that my life, and everyone else's that I loved, was out of my control—finally. No more fear of what I couldn't fix. Starting with myself—my own shattered pieces. My feet were finally ready to leave the ledge I had been perched on my entire life. I'll give in to your gravity, God. Knowing that I'll free fall into Your grace.

—paraphrased from "I'm Letting Go,"
a song by Francesca Batistelli

18

Douglas County
Inmate #6935801

Back to the beginning of this journey, on that rainy night in Georgia, as I remember sitting in the backseat of that police car, I knew that was my turning point. My "rock bottom," whatever that term really means. The experts have told me that everyone has one of those. A personal rock bottom. I look back and shake my head, as I think how tired God must've been having to deal with me. It was like He almost had to knock me upside the head about absolutely *everything*.

I knew I had put myself in the backseat of that car. I couldn't blame anyone else. Oh, I had tried to. Gordon and I had individually and collectively made some really dumb choices through the years. If it wasn't for the grace of God, we both might've ended up dead. It's funny how I've heard so many jokes about that subject all my life. People don't understand the nonchalance of many of the phrases we use. I've probably heard it a hundred times in conversations about people's foolish escapades.

"I tell ya what, it's a miracle I didn't end up either dead or in jail!"

And everyone laughs. It's funny until it's true.

I remember as I sat in the back of the police car on that cold night, I had grown numb and stared ahead in disbelief. With some people, disbelief may be stunned silence. Pondering. For me, disbelief is a LOT of talking. To myself, or anyone who might listen. Questions. Rambling. I still didn't fully understand what was happening. And I was still drunk. The man driving the car had refused to speak to me.

I felt myself slide to the center of the backseat, as he swung the car into the circular driveway. Arms still cuffed behind my back and unable to brace myself, I lurched forward as he abruptly stepped on the brakes and shifted into park. That's when he grabbed that crackling radio and practically barked out one single word to whomever was listening on the other end.

"INTAKE."

Everything happened so quickly that I barely realized he had exited the driver's seat before jerking open my backseat door, reaching across my trembling upper body, and unbuckling my seatbelt. For just that moment, I felt a tiny bit of relief. *Is it freedom?* The mere thought felt ironic. In the days ahead, I would come to understand freedom on varying levels. I would also gain a deeper insight into the meaning of the word bondage and how my perspective—how I viewed myself—colored the meaning of those words. I would discover that I could be both captor and liberator; and that I played both those roles equally for most of my life.

I looked up at the officer's face, my eyes questioning. His hard eyes were staring back at mine. Squinting slightly, he smirked and said, "This is your stop, Lady. Get out." I felt him cup his rough hand under my left elbow and lift my arm. He seemed to think I would know what to do at this point. I didn't. He tugged my arm. "I said, GET OUT." His voice was gruff and commanding. Did he think I was deliberately not cooperating? I attempted to slide my hips toward the open door and swing my legs around and out. It's amazing what one discovers they cannot easily do without the use of their arms or hands. When I tried to stand, my body was weak; I couldn't hold myself up. As I slumped forward, I felt his arm quickly hook underneath my armpit and lift me by the shoulder. It hurt. I was trembling. For a second, I imagined that the tone of his voice softened a bit.

"You got it? Can you stand up?"

"Yes, I think so."

"Alright then. C'mon." The gruffness was back. I just stood there, my feet paralyzed and my legs wobbling. I did, however, manage to lift my downcast eyes for just a second to see the building in front of me. The facade was large and grey, with just a few tiny windows perfectly lined in little rows, and I could see a tall fence surrounding it just beyond the area where we had parked. I could barely make out any details due to the bright lights shining directly onto my face. I'm pretty sure that was by design—it wasn't as important for the officials who managed that building to be seen as it was for them to clearly see all who would enter its doors. Almost blinded by the lights, I instinctively attempted to lift my hand and shield my eyes before realizing they were still cuffed behind my back. I let my head drop back down. Once again, I felt new tears falling from my eyes in huge droplets down my face and spill onto my sweatshirt.

"I said, let's GO!" The man was clearly getting impatient with me. His arm returned to underneath my bent left elbow as he tugged, urging me to walk. I shuffled forward, reluctantly.

I heard a loud click and what sounded like a type of alarm—more like a loud buzzer—as the large iron door began to slide open slowly into a vast room. Immediately, I saw a sea of faces turn and look in my direction. They were all staring directly at me. What WAS this place that all attention fell on the door that I had just walked through? I instinctively turned my head, attempting to look away. The man led me down a center aisle, between rows and rows of seats, the staring eyes getting closer with each forward step I took. No matter which direction I turned my head, I could not escape those eyes. Assessing me. Looking me up and down. Everyone fell quiet. Or was that just my imagination? Maybe the ringing inside my head was drowning out the sound. I couldn't tell; it felt like I was floating in a sort of dream-like state. I decided to try my best to look straight ahead and not make eye contact with anyone.

As we approached a chest-high counter surrounded by glass, I decided the easiest thing to do was to fix my eyes on the person sitting on the stool behind the glass. I remember thinking she looked bored. Or was she just tired and fed up with her job? I couldn't really tell. Her head was down, pen in hand, ready to take notes ... like something that she had already done dozens of times that night. As we approached the counter, without looking up, she slid open the glass. Then she raised her head and looked at me first, ignoring the man who had walked me in and who was still holding onto me, arm hooked underneath my shoulder. I just stood there at this weird angle, one shoulder hiked up, as he maintained his grip on me, and the rest of my body slumping against him, mascara-streaked red face. I was a mess.

She put her pen down and stared directly at my face. Something in her expression looked gentle. Her countenance softened. Her dark brown curls framed her face, and she tilted her head slightly, as she made eye contact with me. I tried to look away, but where could I look? It seemed everywhere I tried to turn my eyes, I could not escape all the other eyes staring directly into mine. Deciding not to drop my head down, nor look up, I chose to continue to stare directly ahead, my eyes focusing on nothing. She spoke, and I heard compassion in her voice as she directed her question to the man holding my elbow.

"Charge?"

"Simple battery."

Hearing those words made my tense shoulders drop and I felt my eyes close, tightly this time; it was futile then to try and stop the tears. Unable to wipe them, I just gave in to them and did my best to blink them away. My bottom lip was raw from biting it. The voice in my head was telling me to try to stay strong, but I couldn't. She hesitated before responding and briefly nodded to the man before returning her eyes to mine.

"Ok, thank you, Officer. Identification, please?" I realized she was now talking to me. Confused, my thoughts began to race. At that exact moment, it occurred to me that I hadn't brought anything with me. No purse, nothing. I couldn't hide my sudden sense of panic.

"Where's your ID?" Now it was him, with that same condescending tone.

Pausing briefly, still in shock, I shook my head and opened my eyes, glancing into hers before turning my face to him. I was incredulous.

"What did you say?"

"I said, DID YOU BRING YOUR I-DENT-IF-I-CA-TION?" He enunciated each syllable slowly, independently, as if I didn't understand the question. He thought I was stupid. My first thought was, *You supercilious asshole!* It was a miracle I didn't say it out loud. Instead, I answered, "My ID? No, I didn't bring anything ... I couldn't. You didn't give me the opportunity to even speak. Or get my purse. You just put my arms behind my back, cuffed my wrists, and sat me in the backseat of your car!" I rambled on incessantly, not making any sense. This is what I always did when I was nervous. I continued my rant. "Remember? You didn't even give me a chance to speak! I saw you talking to my husband ... what did he say? What were y'all talking about? And did you seriously just say the word 'battery'?" It was mostly incoherent babbling, and he never looked at me once as I continued to fire off a mixture of statements as well as questions, never really giving him a chance nor expecting him to respond.

I noticed that he looked at the female officer, shaking his head piteously just before demonstrating the age-old gesture of tipping an imaginary drink to his lips, snapping his head back, and then making small circles with his finger around the side of his head beside his ear, all with brows raised and smirking while looking at her. No words were necessary; it was clear what this gesture implied.

"What? Are you trying to say that I'm crazy?" I heard my voice rise an octave higher and with a shrill tone and wide eyes.

"You're drunk!!" he said with a pshaw. He lifted his head, with face turned toward me, and was staring at me over the rims of his glasses, his eyes mere slits. Then, with an overexaggerated eye roll, he began shaking his head and returned to filling out the required form. My mouth hung open.

"Name?" He drawled the word out, smirking.

I directed my burning stare to the floor, avoiding eye contact with this person who was obviously taking great pleasure in his effort to reduce me to nothing. And, of course, I was already filled with self-loathing, still in shock over it all.

"I said, what's your NAME?" He was practically shouting now.

"Hey ... it's okay ..." the lady behind the counter spoke with the same softness I had noticed before. I mumbled my name aloud. It felt and sounded like I was in a tunnel; I had a distorted sense of time and place. This couldn't be real. Could it? He briefly continued to write and eventually thrust the form under the glass to the female deputy. With that, he turned his back and began to walk out. He looked like he was triumphantly marching as he kept that faint, smug smile on his face and accompanied it with a sharp, upward chin thrust. He arrogantly winked at all the other congregants in the room, as if to say, *Yup ... got another one off the streets.* There was a cacophony of squawks and scuffling, loud boos, and even a few sounds of what I thought might be pitiful cheers for me. Will these people like me? Because it was clear that none of them liked him. The man who brought me in this place was quite obviously the enemy. I quickly allowed myself to entertain the thought that I would not want to get on their bad side.

After completing the required paperwork, the female deputy had allayed most of my irrational fears. However, the confusion and dread of what was to come remained. She advised me that the processing would take a couple of hours and pointed me toward the seating area. I chose one of the few empty chairs that I would be occupying until the paperwork was complete. I tentatively walked over to an open seat surrounded mostly by other females. They were varying in age and all walks of life.

As I looked at them, I wondered what their stories might be. Would I get a chance to find out?

This vast room, which I had learned was called the intake area, was only the first stop in this experience. There was a wide variety of folks in there: both male and female, young and old, black, white, brown, red, and yellow—all colors, all backgrounds, and all locked up. This place didn't appear to discriminate. There were those who looked angry and defiant, and those who appeared to be frightened and humiliated. I was simply overwhelmed, still mentally numb and unable to focus.

Everyone was still in their regular clothes, whatever they had been wearing before they knew they would end up in this place tonight. As I was assessing everyone's outfits, I couldn't help but think, *How would one dress for this occasion? I mean, if they knew. Would they go for comfort, style? Or perhaps they'd choose the more "bad-ass-don't-mess-with-me" attire?* It was only when I realized the situational irony of it all that I could laugh, recognizing that it was possible to be both extremely proud and mortified at the exact same time. I looked down and noticed my own attire. I was wearing my "Proud United States Naval Academy Mom" sweatshirt. It silently screamed, "Ask me about my navy officer!" Aghast, I shook my head and heard a slight, sardonic laugh escape my lips. Funny, I could still find a modicum of self-amusement at this point. But that quickly changed when the female deputy came over and advised me that I could make my phone call right now.

"Phone call?" I asked, as though I was surprised. I wasn't, but I was certainly unprepared. "But I don't have my purse or my cell phone." My mind was racing.

"Do you not have anyone's number memorized?" She waited for my reply.

"I can't remember!" I shook my head wildly, as I willed myself to think, *Who do I call? Definitely not my husband, as he is no doubt still reeling from the night's events. He's either furious with me or passed out by now. I know … I'll call my son … I just need to hear his voice. But what can he do? He'll be devastated. And embarrassed. He'll be angry too. Ugh. I am disgusted at myself, so of course everyone else will be too. God, oh, God … how did this happen? How low have I fallen?* And I couldn't recall anyone's cell phone number from memory. I snapped back into reality as the deputy spoke, urging me to make my phone call.

"Do I just get one call?" I had seen my share of *Investigation Discovery Channel* episodes about this very thing. Not to mention, of all things—and you can NOT make this up—*Law and Order* was playing on repeat on the single, small TV that was mounted in the corner of that massive room. I began to sober up and realize exactly where I was and how on God's green earth this had happened to me.

"No," she answered. "But you DO only get three minutes ... so make your call, or calls, count." She patted my arm, and I noticed a faint, piteous smile on her face, as she led me to the single phone, right in the middle of that room. I could feel everyone's eyes watching me. The only people that I knew had a landline, that I had memorized from the many years they had it, were my sister Jean and her husband. I cringed. But it was my only option.

Of course, I was required to go through the facility operator, and all calls had to be made collect. I spoke the number out loud into the phone, slowly and carefully. Then I forced my slumping shoulders back and attempted to stand up straight. I hoped this might make me appear to be strong, even though inwardly I was freaking out. It was late on a Friday night, and I knew Jean and Steve would be in bed. I recognized my brother-in-law's sleepy voice as he picked up.

"Hello?" His tone was quizzical. My heart sank.

"You have a collect call from an inmate at the Douglas County jail named..." I had pre-recorded my name prior to the call, as was the custom inside the jail. The operator then played the recording of my own voice.

"Jackie Van Dyke."

"Will you accept the charges?"

"Yes."

I took a steeling breath, inhaling through the nose and exhaling slowly.

"Steve?"

"Jackie ... what's wrong? What happened?"

I began to cry and blurt out words in run-on sentences that were incomprehensible. I don't even know what I said. I couldn't think because I could hear my sister's voice in the background, asking her husband what was happening. My heart was breaking.

"Hey ... hey ... hey ... slow down." He paused between each word, as his voice remained calm. Strong. "What happened? Are you in jail?"

"YES! I'm sorry, Steve! I'm so sorry! Yours is the only phone number I could remember!" I rushed through my words, knowing I only had three minutes. And I knew I still had to call my son. I had no time to give details right now.

"I don't have my cell phone with me, so I need Cale's number! Can you please give it to me? Just look in your phone contact list and call it out to me please. I have a pen and paper. Please hurry!" I obviously didn't have much regard for what he was imagining this scenario to be, not to mention he would have to explain this to my sister. But none of that mattered at the moment. The clock was ticking. He quickly gave me the number, and I muttered a thank-you before pressing the hang up-handle on the wall phone. I was instantly reconnected to the jail operator. I blurted out Cale's number and asked her to please place the call. She did. My heart leapt out of my chest when I heard his voice. The repeat of the phrase, "Collect call from an inmate, blah blah blah."

When I heard my recorded voice state my name this time, I had a sickening feeling in the pit of my stomach. This was my son. My baby. This was way too much for a twenty-year-old young man to have to deal with. Unlike Steve's voice, Cale's voice wasn't uncertain, but rather tentative. Fearful. Clearly, he already knew.

"Yes, I accept ... Mom?"

"Son..." I was sobbing uncontrollably. I had no words.

"Dad told me. Are you okay?"

"Yes ... I mean, I'm okay, but I'm not OKAY. I'm so sorry, Son. I'm so, so very sorry..." I was hyperventilating and gasping out each word.

"Mom ... Mom ... it'll be okay. We're going to get you out of there. I promise we WILL get you out. Dad and I are working on it right now. Be strong!"

I had shrunk into the wall as he spoke to me. I don't think I had ever—in my entire life—felt such pain and shame inside my heart. It felt unbearable.

I just kept repeating, "Okay," muffled by the nonstop sobs.

"I'm going to pray for you now, Mom. You don't have to say anything. Just listen to me. 'God, I want to thank you that You are right there with my mom. That You hold her in Your arms and keep her safe and comfort her heart. Take care of her and let her know that You love her. That we love her. And God, use her to show others Your love and forgiveness. That You will make her stronger through this. That Your light will shine in the darkness…"

Then I heard the "click" of the phone call being disconnected. I could no longer stand up. I felt myself slide down to my knees, still grasping the phone receiver. Eyes closed and mouth open, the short cries escaping for anyone to hear, I collapsed into a heap, holding on to that phone. That's when I felt a hand on my shoulder. A strong hand. I looked up. She couldn't have been more than thirty years old: beautiful, perfectly straight and neat, long corn rows; large, gentle brown eyes that were looking directly into mine. She moved her hand from my shoulder and extended it to me. She took the phone receiver out of my hand and placed it back into its place, then reaching down to lift me up. I stood, shakily, and mumbled a "thank you" before she led me back to a seat surrounded by several other women. Their ages appeared to range from twenty to maybe mid-forties; I appeared to be the oldest in the group. Everyone was looking at me, but nobody asked me a single question. After I settled into my seat, one of the other girls spoke to me.

"Just try to sleep. You're going to be here for a while."

Sleep? What? How? While I was still slightly dazed and confused, I was much more cognizant than I had been two hours ago when that horrible man had brought me here. The effects of the alcohol had almost completely worn off, and the absolute shock of it all was settling in. I couldn't believe I was here, and I had no idea what was next. Exhausted, the last thing I remember was my head feeling very heavy and my neck too weak to hold it up any longer. I allowed my eyes to close and tried to shut my mind down, even for a short while.

Sleep would not come again for three days.

19

Stripping Down Shame

Humiliation. Self-loathing. I was degraded, mortified, worthless, and defeated. All these things are not only what I felt, but what I believed about myself. The words were screaming from inside my head. As I tried to wrap my brain around this situation, I couldn't come up with a solid excuse for it, and I spiraled into more shame than I had ever felt in my entire life. I continued to sit and wait, slowly becoming completely sober and painfully thinking about how I ended up here and what would happen next. I was, thankfully, spiritually mature enough to realize that I had made the dumb choices that landed me here.

But I also knew that I was here for a reason, and that somehow, in some way, God would use this situation. Too bad I hadn't been spiritually mature enough to not have landed myself here in the first place. Back to good ol' Romans 8:28. *Gee, thanks, God.* I also knew that the Bible referred to Jesus as both the Lion AND the Lamb. And I remembered hearing a preacher say one time, "He'll either lead us gently into His will like a lamb, or if He has to, he'll grab us and drag us like a lion!!" It was evident that He knew it would take Him dragging my butt like a lion to get my attention. *Why had I always been so stubborn?* Several hours passed. I was cognizant enough to realize I was in the intake area of Douglas County jail and that I knew I had to change my mind about a lot of things. And I had a lot of time to think.

I discovered that not all people who go to jail are bad people. They are broken people. They hurt. I thought a lot about my daddy. I always wanted to believe that in his heart-of- hearts, he was not a mean person. He had learned most of his behavior patterns growing up. He had seen that the only way to resolve conflict was to shout and fight. Starting with the brothers he grew up with, his own parents, then moving on to his wives, and then his kids. I remember realizing that I always knew deep down that he loved me, but he was never shown how to love anyone, much less himself. He had never seen it modeled. The only thing he learned was anger, and he used it to control everyone in his life. He was a broken child who had grown into a broken man. He was hurting. I have found that broken and hurt people often break and hurt others. They don't always intend to; it's just what can happen.

Another truth I learned was this: not everyone who breaks and hurts others will ever face real consequences for it. I knew that I wasn't the only person who had ever had too much to drink and did something stupid, yet here I was. My worst nightmare had come true. I felt I had become like my daddy. Shame and insecurity will make our minds go wild with fear of what will happen to us, how we'll never again be respected. I became convinced that church people might be the first who will judge. And whisper. The "Sister Sallys" of the world, the ones who judge and gossip, all in the name of "sharing" with other strong Christians who, they convince themselves, will pray for the wounded. I mean, it's not really gossip if you're telling a Christian brother or sister so they will pray … is it?

These people would never consider themselves in the same league as those who I spent four days in jail with. The folks I came to realize are good people with good hearts … they just made mistakes. Like we all have. Just different consequences. Some people think I'm crazy for saying this, but it's one hundred percent true: going to jail that night might be just one of the best things that ever happened to me. My eyes were opened to many things I had never understood until now.

After a while, the thoughts in my head were eventually halted and replaced with the reality of what was happening. I felt my slumped body jerk when I heard my name shouted above the fray.

"Van Dyke?" I heard the deputy's voice behind me.

"Me?" I turned around and pointed to myself, as if I really wasn't sure it was me she was talking to. It had been a few hours, and I had eventually dropped off into a fitful doze, more of a semi-conscious state. It still felt like a nightmare.

"Yes, Ma'am. Let's get your mug shot." *Oh, dear God. This is getting real.* As I snapped to attention, I looked across the holding area, and those same young ladies were still there too. Most of them had fallen asleep and had assembled themselves into a little stack—uneven, like newborn puppies. I especially noticed the one who had helped me up from the floor after my phone conversation with Cale. She looked peaceful. I stood up, straightening my clothes for some reason, then smoothing my jeans legs and tugging to make sure my "Proud Navy Mom" shirt wasn't riding up, while scanning the area the lady was calling me to. I tentatively walked toward her.

"Ok. What do I do?"

"You've got to get out of those clothes first," she said, as she handed me the orange jumpsuit. "Go on, take a shower." She indicated with her head toward the area just behind her. I looked past her and saw an open area with about five shower stalls in it, only separated by a large half wall with a sign that said, "FEMALE INMATES ONLY."

"You want me to go in there?"

"Yes. And just put your clothes in this bag. I'll be right here as soon as you come out of the shower."

Unsure of exactly how one undresses after being booked into the county jail, I tentatively took the jumpsuit and the bag and walked over to an empty stall, glancing over my shoulder to make sure no one could see me. I had never been a shy person, but this was a whole 'nuther level. I was shaking uncontrollably.

"Just get in?" I asked and noticed my voice was so small, weak. Like a child. And the feelings were not unlike the way I used to feel when I was that scared, little girl all those years ago. I had flashbacks of when Jean and I were little, and we weren't sure what we should say or do to keep Daddy from being mad. The deputy must've seen similar reactions in the past because her face softened. Since I had first walked in those doors, escorted by that police officer, I could tell this young lady had a big heart. She leaned in toward me and whispered, "Yes. But before you start the shower, I have to check you."

"Check me?" I didn't understand. Here came the tears, again. Eyes wide, I just stood there, crying and shaking, gripping the rough, orange fabric.

"Search you." She looked down and sounded almost apologetic about it. She looked back up and noticed I was still standing there, holding the empty bag in one hand and the orange jumpsuit in the other. I couldn't make my feet move. I was paralyzed.

"It's okay." She nodded toward the shower stall.

I could feel my bare legs wobbling and my heartbeat pounding like a drum as I pulled back the curtain and entered the tiny, dingy-tiled stall.

She came in right behind me and quickly tugged the curtain closed. I just squeezed my eyes tightly shut, as I felt her hand gently turn my chin so that I was facing her. She whispered, "Open your eyes and look at me. I'm not going to do this, but they must think I am. Okay?"

"Okay," I squeaked out, feeling my body become rigid. Nothing happened. My eyes flew open after a few seconds, and she jerked the shower curtain back, rattling on its metal hooks.

"Alright, Van Dyke. You're good ... now, get showered and changed!"

It sounded like she was intentionally making her voice sound a bit gruff and authoritative just because everyone else might be listening. I remember standing in that shower, feeling the hot water cascading down my body, washing away all the filth I felt. I turned and faced the shower-head and stood on my tiptoes. I wanted it to hit me directly in my face, and I prayed that it would wash away the many tears I had cried, and maybe even a little of the guilt I felt.

I was assigned to Cell Block F. After processing was completed, the jailers led us down the hall toward what would be our living quarters all weekend. They had separated us into groups—the group I had been assigned to were the ones where it was either a first-time offense or at least a misdemeanor. The jailers led us in a single file line, cuffed and with chains, albeit very loose ones, around our ankles. We were instructed not to speak until we got into the holding area, where they would give us further instructions. I was completely sober by this time, and reality had begun to sink in. I looked around at the fifteen other offenders walking along with me, assessing how afraid I needed to be, not knowing what to expect next.

We made it to the small ante room, where there were no windows and only a few narrow metal benches. They removed our handcuffs and loosened our ankle chains. We had to sit practically on top of each other, those benches were so small. One of the jailers came in with a bag and quickly handed each of us a plastic wrapped sandwich and a box of juice. The jailers disappeared, and everyone seemed to relax a bit. That's when all the questions began filling the room: "What are you in for? Is this your first time?" etc. I sat silently, taking it all in. I dared not speak a word. Truth be told, I was afraid to. Here I was, surrounded by "criminals" ... and I had mistakenly said that aloud one time, which I don't recommend. My lips stayed zipped.

There was a group of five or six women who had been staring at me since we were all booked in around the same time. And, because it was a Friday night, we discovered that we could not get bonded or bailed out until after we saw the judge, and that would not happen before Monday. We knew we would all be together for at least the next three days. Finally, one of them, a skinny, young thing who looked to be around the same age as my twenty-year-old son, decided to speak to me.

"How about you, Mama? What'd you do to end up in the pokey?" she asked sarcastically, as she laughed and leaned in toward me, tucking a strand of long, blonde hair behind one ear. I answered the same way I had when the deputy had called my name earlier, like I suddenly didn't understand the English language.

"Who, me?" They all looked at each other and laughed out loud. Then the gentle gal with the soft brown eyes and beautifully cornrowed hair elbowed the skinny blonde, as if to chastise her. She came over and sat on the bench beside me, leaning her head over against mine, smiling.

"You gonna eat all that sandwich?" At first, I was confused. And still scared. Just then, they all erupted into laughter—the genuine kind—not mocking. "Coz, if you ain't, I'll take it!" I felt myself relax—even if only slightly—for the first time in almost twelve hours. I handed her my sandwich and gave them all a small smile, as I exhaled deeply. What had been an attempt at intimidation ended up with a few of the others coming along side me ... an odd sisterhood was forming.

Within another hour or so, the jailer came back to the door of the ante room and I heard, for the first of many times that weekend, the sound of the extremely loud buzzer that indicated the large iron doors were about to slide open ... slowly ... followed by another ear-piercingly loud siren, which informed what could be half of Douglas County, that the jail door was OPEN. *Dear Lord, they really don't want us to try to escape, do they? Scared the Bee-Jeebus outta anyone who might even think about moving, much less, running.*

"Alright, stand up and get back in line!" We all did as we were told, the best we could while shuffling around in chains. You could hear the crackling of brown bags and the wadding up of plastic sandwich wraps, followed by the thumps of juice boxes being thrown into the trash cans.

"Now what?" I whispered to the gal who had been sitting beside me. She had become my unintentional best friend that night.

"Get up and get in the line. I'm right behind you. And whatever you do, DON'T CRY. Do not let anyone see fear." She was whispering through clenched teeth, glancing at me sideways. I felt the tears begin to fall down my cheeks, as if on cue.

"Where are we going now?"

"To our individual cells. Do. Not. Cry," she repeated and paused in between each word. This was not merely a suggestion. She said it as if my survival for the next few days depended on it.

When we got to the actual cell block, once again, there was that horrible, scary siren sound when the large, barred door opened. I must have jumped three feet off the floor; it was so startling! Some others were already seated inside at what reminded me of school cafeteria tables, complete with little, metal attached seats. All heads up and another sea of faces stared toward the open door. And many of those faces looked angry: defensive, bowed up, and ready to defend their positions within the cell block. Most just looked sad and tired.

We were instructed to enter and remain standing until the jail assistants called our names. They called us, one by one. As I watched my cohort's names called, each would walk over to where the assistants were standing, that would be at the entrance of the tiny, individual rooms with the hard, metal cots. Some already had one occupant; others were empty. I was praying I would get put in the same room as my new friend and I realized I didn't even know her name.

"Van Dyke!"

"Here!" I realized how ridiculous I must've looked, as I raised my hand. I quickly looked behind me at my friend. "What do I do?" came out in a frantic whisper.

"Go!" She nudged my back. I walked toward where the assistant jailer stood at an open door, holding a large roll of what appeared to be a thin mattress and blanket. I shuffled in and stood there, face to face, with a very large, very serious-looking woman who, with arms crossed, simply said, "I got the bottom bunk. You goin' up top." Alrighty then. I dropped my head back down and bit my lip as, yet again, the tears began to fall, softly at first. By the time I had climbed up on that rock-hard top bunk, grasping at my roll of covers, it was uncontrollable. My body was quaking, and the cries escaped in wails, echoing throughout the cell. And there didn't seem to be a single thing I could do to stop it.

Dear God … please help me.

After a couple of hours of everyone settling in, we all realized that since we were going to be spending the next few days together, we might as well get to know each other's stories. To my surprise and unexpected delight, before long, I began to relax a bit and even ended up making friends. Ok, so maybe that is an exaggeration, but at least we weren't enemies. There were no pretenses. Pretty soon, none of us were worried about what anyone else thought of them. Nobody cared about age, political views, race, or even what crimes their cellmates had committed. And we weren't bothered by who did their hair the best or whose outfits suited their shape, or worse, our style preferences. We were all happy to flaunt our ill-fitting orange jumpsuits and bond together in such an odd way that I honestly never knew was even possible. No one judged anyone else, because we all knew we were about to be judged by the one who could make the decision to set us free or keep us in those chains we'd all got ourselves into. Most of us stayed up all night, sharing stories; some horrific and others were actually quite amusing. But a sisterhood formed. A weird, unexpected sisterhood within a mixture of ages, ethnicities, backgrounds, educations. None of it mattered. We were in this together, rooting for each other.

I had somehow morphed into the "mama" of the group. Because I had initially been the one who just couldn't stop shaking and crying, they had all seemed to migrate toward me to protect me. They were in awe of how "somebody like me" ended up in jail on a Friday night. So was I. But after the first night, I had decided to toughen up and just get through it. I decided to use it as an opportunity. I pulled up my big-girl panties and jumped into the midst of my new friends, doing what I knew to do. Love on them. Talk openly with them. Listen to them. Tell them some truths. Hard truths. Others were as easy as breathing. But the best thing was that they wanted to listen to me. I told them my story, and, as a result, they trusted me.

I became more than the "older lady" who accidently got caught doing something wrong. I was just like them; the only difference was that I was supposed to be the older and wiser one who should've known better. But we were all in that cell block together because we were being punished for the mistakes we'd made. Many were just dumb choices. Maybe there were a few that were just straight-up rebellious and had no remorse. But mostly, they were good people who were broken and without hope. Perhaps I could offer hope.

The same lady deputy who had processed my intake on Friday night came to my cell on Saturday afternoon and told me she had a message for me. I had no idea what to expect. She just looked at me and handed me a book. I didn't understand. Didn't know I was allowed to have a book.

"Thank you." I looked at her quizzically as I took the book.

"Your son brought it. He dropped it off and asked if we could make sure you got it. He also sent a message...." Her voice trailed off. I didn't understand so I just stood there, waiting for her to explain. When she didn't respond, I opened the cover of the book to look inside. There were two sets of scrawled writing.

> You will always be my always. Love, Dad, Gordon, Husband
>
> P.S. I'm sorry for this.

Then:

> We love you so much. Dad is being strong for you. Call when you can; we want to encourage you. Just know we have done everything we can for now. Praying for peace in your heart. Love, Cale

I closed the book, then held it tightly to my chest, hoping the words would sink into my heart. Eyes closed, I took a deep breath, then exhaled slowly.

"Before your son came by with the book, he had called first and asked if he could speak to you. I told him that you could not receive phone calls from the outside, but that you were allowed to make phone calls at certain times of the day. So, he asked me if I could tell you something..." Her eyes were darting around to make sure no one was listening, her voice trailing off as she seemed to be having difficulty telling me. I admit at first, I was scared ... *Is there bad news? Had something happened at home? Was Gordon okay?* My thoughts were all over the place. I had just read the sweet notes they had both written inside the book, but why was she telling me that my son had also called, asking to speak to me? I immediately panicked as the thought occurred to me...*Hayden?* He had been on deployment during all this mess and he would have no idea what was going on. *Had someone been able to reach Hayden and tell him?* I froze at the thought. I knew he would be both worried and probably furious with me for being so stupid.

She took a crumpled piece of paper out of her pocket and quickly opened it up. She leaned in and whispered, tears welling up in her eyes, "I'm not supposed to do this ... relay phone messages ... so please keep this to yourself." She then glanced down and looked at the note she had obviously quickly written down as he was talking to her. It was also from Cale. She read; "He said, 'Please tell my mom how much I love her. And I believe in her. Tell her that God is holding her in His hands. And He will use this.'" She paused and swallowed hard. "So, I told him I would tell you those exact words."

I had no reply. I felt the tears again, but this time I wasn't afraid. I knew that there was a reason I was here. I didn't understand it, but I didn't need to. She immediately returned the wad of paper to her pocket and promptly turned and walked away. I was so thankful she took a chance and broke the rules just that one time.

The next few days were filled with conversations I had never dreamed I'd be having, in a setting I never dreamed I'd be in, surrounded by people who were nothing like the people I had always imagined I'd be having a girls' weekend with. We laughed, and we cried. We bonded in a very peculiar, special way.

You know all these church songs about "Chain Breaker," "No More Shackles," "Break Every Chain," "My Chains are Gone," and all the rest of those chain songs? These songs take on a whole new meaning outside our fancy sanctuaries, when you are physically locked up, in actual, real-life chains. And the old favorite, "Just As I Am"? We talk about how we come, without one plea? Another thing that feels way different is when you actually have to come, WITH a plea, before a human judge, and plead for mercy. On Sunday night, before we all had to go stand before the judge on Monday, we were all scrambling to secure a bail bondsman. I had no idea where to start. I called Gordon and asked him to call around and hire someone. The other ladies were telling me that some of the bondsmen were better than others. And they all told me to make CER-TAIN I had a good one. I didn't even know what that meant. So, I took an opportunity to share the first thing that popped into my mind. I asked them a question.

"What if there was just ONE really good bondsman who agreed to take all of us on tomorrow when we see the judge?" They looked at me like I was crazy.

"We have to pay them, and they all charge different prices depending on what we're in for. There's no way one person could take us all on as clients … that would be too much!" This was from my cellmate, and all of the other inmates nodded in agreement, still looking at me quizzically.

"Let me tell you a story…" I went on to tell them to imagine, in their wildest dreams, that one person walked right up to that judge, stood in front of all of us, and said, "I'll take the judgement for them. All of them. No matter the crime. Let them go, Judge." They wanted me to explain. I did.

I told them how that I had been introduced to the ultimate bail bondsman, the one who my Bible tells me walked straight up to that judge, over two thousand years ago, and stood there for me. He said, "Whatever she's done wrong, or ever will do wrong, I'll stand for her. Let her go. I'll pay the price. I'll take her punishment." I told them all about "that Guy" I had met at summer camp the summer when I was twelve; the one who not only took all our punishment, but He's also the one who paid the highest price to the Judge. One that no human bail bondsman would or could ever do. He paid with His own life. For ours. Many of us wept and prayed together. When we all went to sleep that night, I believe that many of them slept more peacefully than the night before.

I knew that weekend I had a lot of changing to do. I'd start with the obvious: I'll stop whining. And wine-ing. Neither were doing me any good at all.

20

Stop Wine-ing and Other Noble Jesus-Approved Addictions

Spending four days in the pokey, the slammer, the big house ... whatever you want to call it, will one hundred percent change a person ... I don't care who you are. It will either make you meaner and more bitter, or, conversely, contrite and have a desire to become a better person. Maybe even be willing to help others from making the same mistakes ... that is, if you're willing to fess up and openly talk about them. When I decided to do just that, I was nervous. (Ok so if I'm honest, God told me to do it, and I wasn't happy with Him about it.) I mean, what would my church friends think about me? Will it embarrass my kids? I didn't know how it would be perceived, but I knew I had to do it. I had to put myself out there, exposed and vulnerable, and tell my stories. But before I could write a single sentence, I had to be clear—in my mind and in my heart. I knew I had some things to change. I want to make sure to clarify that the following "definitions" are my own, based upon my own personal experiences, and in no way do I claim that any of these terms apply to anyone. I just have a few things to get off my chest and fess up to.

Let's start with the word addiction. Often referred to as "coping skills," since that seems to be the Christianese word that sounds better. Most people in my life have never even wanted to talk about it. It's uncomfortable and awkward and, if we're honest, most people have certain categories they put all these things into anyway. And absolutely everybody has an opinion, and some will argue to the death to prove they're right. I used to be one of those people. Now, I see how subjective opinions might be. I just know that I am forever changed. I also realize I have made that claim more than a few times in my life.

And what's wrong with that anyway? Why shouldn't there be more than one, two, three or more things that happen throughout our lives that change us? I like to think I have learned lessons and gained wisdom throughout my life, and I hope to continue to do so. I don't want to stay the same, dogmatic and determined to prove to the whole world that I know it all. I don't want to be that person who reaches a certain age or graduates to a new level and begins to announce to anyone who will listen, "You can't teach an old dog new tricks!" Or "I am who I am, and I'm too old to change!" I want to be willing to look back on my life and admit that there have been, and will continue to be, things that happen to me, in me, and even *because* of me that I am willing to learn from and make changes accordingly. I never want to plant my feet in a wide stance, fold my arms defiantly across my chest, thrust my chin up, and dare anyone to challenge me. On the contrary, I *want* to be challenged. Especially if I can grow stronger as a result.

I want my heart to be tender and malleable, accepting that I can always improve. I used to be so stubborn about establishing my authority on a subject that I would refuse to listen to the whisper of my spirit. Is this another form of control? Always the fixer, but unwilling to submit myself to being fixed? And I didn't want to exchange one "coping skill" or obsession for another. Which reminds me of a funny story.

Recently, as I was unloading my grocery bags, I noticed something that made me laugh. The ironic kind of laugh. You know, the stuff that makes you stop and shake your head as your mind wanders back to something you don't really want to remember? As I pulled out the milk and the bread—(it was a snow day here in Georgia, and you better, by God, grab your milk and bread quick before someone at the local Walmart runs you down trying to beat you to it)—I noticed at the bottom of the bag there lay a single Hershey's chocolate bar. Just the plain old bar that's been around forever. No almonds, no special dark chocolate blend, nothing fancy. It's my favorite. I have always said that if I could just die with a single piece of Hershey's chocolate slowly melting on my tongue, I'd already be halfway to heaven … but, I digress.

In another bag, there was a pack of turtle brownies, a box of white chocolate cookies, and a half gallon of salted caramel ice cream. It was all the stuff that gave me comfort, helped me cope, just plain ol' made me feel good. I was so excited. Until I had the realization that this experience was not unlike how I felt when I unpacked my grocery bags several years before that. Back then, it had been a couple of bottles of wine. Or three. Especially if the weather forecast was calling for snow and ice. It was whatever I didn't want to be without. Had I simply substituted one addiction for another? Or perhaps when it was wine, I was allowed to call it an addiction, but if it's candy bars and ice cream, I'll just call it a coping skill.

I would try to justify the difference by having a conversation in my head. *Well, at least this one doesn't make me act crazy and say things I regret! Nobody's gonna find me laying in a gutter somewhere crying and cussin' somebody out because I ate too much sugar! And I definitely won't go to jail for eating an entire bag of chocolate!*

Good rationale, right? I would say this to myself, and anyone who would listen. That is, if I was bold enough to talk about such things with my Christian friends. It's always interesting to discuss what's wrong, or a sin, versus what's acceptable and "not really a sin." Like gossip, backbiting, "a little white lie"...again, I digress. But you get it.

How exactly do we come to identify what real addictions are? I'm firmly convinced that there is an unspoken list of "Jesus-approved addictions," the ones we justify. The ones we don't feel the need to wag our judgmental fingers at each other about. But is sugar a "substance"? Like in the category in which we can use in the phrase "substance abuse"? Isn't caffeine a substance? Or was I simply wanting to rationalize that these things don't affect me negatively? Nobody gets hurt when I partake of these things. But I had to recognize that's not my point. For me, it became the things I think about, the things that I crave, long for; those things I make sure, if it's going to be a snowy day, I am not going to be without. This goes way beyond milk and bread, y'all.

Addiction is such a hot topic, yet such a sensitive one, especially among people who prefer to use the phrase "coping skills." Most church folk focus on what I call the big four: smokin', drankin', cussin', and druggin'—as we say down south, or at least where I come from. But no one ever wants to talk about the 400-pound preacher who's spitting hellfire and brimstone from the pulpit and talking about all the "alky-holics," yet he's the first one to belly up to the buffet at the Golden Corral. I'm sorry if that offends anyone; that is not my intention. I'm just attempting to illustrate how double-minded people can be. What we are quick to judge and declare someone "has a problem" with ... you fill in the blanks. And it's typically something that the person doing the judging DOESN'T struggle with. I'm guilty of doing it too, but now I just notice it in myself more.

I wonder if most people really see overeating as an addiction. Or sugar? We usually say something like, "Eating is my coping skill," or "Well, I just have a sweet tooth!" I personally began to rationalize whatever I was seeking to defend. But I also began to see that it's not just about having cravings for food, sugar, or alcohol. I understand that just because someone eats food, that doesn't make them a food addict. Or if someone enjoys a good dessert that they are sugar addicts. Or even if someone drinks daily wine that they are an alcoholic. I know that you can do any of these things and not "have a problem."

I guess it just makes me sad when I see and hear—quite often—others passing judgment on anyone who struggles with something that they don't. It seems easy to decide when we don't have a problem, only others do, but there are non-substance addictions too. These are called behavioral addictions. There really are so many definitions of the word "addiction," so take your pick. Depending upon how you Google it, you will see a combination of terms, phrases, and descriptors. It might be having a craving, tendency, or proclivity for a substance, thing, or activity. I've also heard people describe it as more of a neuropsychological condition that causes cravings or desires to perpetuate and undermine one's self-control. In other words, anything we think about too much, have a difficulty controlling our desire for—maybe more often when we feel sad or depressed—but something we feel comforts us when we do it/partake of it.

In theory, there is nothing wrong with that. We all have things we enjoy, things that relax us, help us unwind, etc. It's just how we're wired as humans. In my opinion, it only gets messed up when we tend to point our fingers (either literally or figuratively) at others, mostly because we can't personally relate to whatever someone else's chosen thing is. I admit that I've said to myself, "I can't even imagine being addicted to *that*" ... again, you can fill in the blanks.

Shopping is another such addiction. Some folks will straight up knock you over at those Black Friday sales, especially after they spent all Thanksgiving Day looking ahead, clipping coupons, or whatever else compulsive, obsessed shoppers do. Ok, I must confess, I did this—but only one time back in 1998—and it was only because Cale really wanted that Tickle Me Elmo that everyone was raving about. And I almost died that day in Toys 'R' Us. Never again. Seriously, there are people who struggle with compulsive shopping. And doesn't the term "struggle with" sound so much better than being "addicted to"? There are people who think about shopping all the time, and anytime they feel lonely or sad, they head straight to the mall and spend hours and many dollars, only to bring home thirty items that will remain in their closet for years, many with price tags still on them.

For others, the all-consuming coping skill might be coffee (guilty!), or soft drinks— anything with caffeine. Gaming. People spend hours—often all night—sitting in front of a computer playing games with people they've never met, obsessed with winning. Working ... there's a highly defended addiction. No one can judge anyone else for being a hard worker, can they? I'm talking about those who live, eat, think, sleep, and dream about their jobs. Climbing the corporate ladder, achieving the American Dream, often at the expense of their relationships. What about exercising? I really don't "get" that one, but apparently, it's a thing. Chronic exercisers will forfeit social events and enjoying relaxing family time so that they can be at the gym or on a long run that can keep them occupied for hours at a time. Then they come home only to think about the next time they'll exercise. Money, popularity, internet, who they "follow" on social media, Facebook, Instagram, and TikTok. I know I'm stepping on more than a few toes with this one.

We all want to shake our heads and deny these things that many of us, not all, are obsessed with. We reason these are not addictions because they are not substances. They don't affect our minds, bodies, or spirits. They don't change the way we behave. But don't they? I now notice more than ever just how many people gathered in one place, whether it be at the dinner table, at home in our living rooms, at work, school, church ... almost anywhere ... you will see the dim light of an iPhone or some other device illuminating faces all over any room at any given time. No one having conversations with each other. And, God help us, now we even get weekly reports of exactly how much time we are on said devices. That'll get our attention, won't it? But most of us either don't want to know or we rationalize why we do it.

Guess what? So do alcoholics and drug addicts. What starts out as having the occasional glass of wine at social events can often sneak up on us in such a subtle manner that we don't even recognize it's happening. I know, for me, I don't remember exactly when that happened. I just know that what I used to do occasionally, with a nice meal or at the end of a long day, began to happen more often. What started out as a justified thirst became too much for me, and I didn't like the person I was becoming. It was not helping me with anything; in fact, it was hurting me and my relationships. I decided one day I was done. And I was. I have never looked back and have never had to fight the desire or urge to drink again. Not even once.

Some clinicians, or otherwise experts in the field, have told me that I never was a "true" alcoholic in the first place, whatever that means. I didn't care then, and I don't care now. I don't understand why we have to slap a diagnosis or an official clinical title on everything. I recognize now that I first noticed my problem with alcohol when I began to justify needing it. To relax. To sleep. To be happy. That's when I knew I was giving it a place in my life that was too important. A place it didn't belong. I became weak. I spiraled. Descended into a pit of despair. I was not who I wanted to be. I know it was the power of God in my life that changed everything. My mind, my stubborn will, and the fact that I thought that eventually, I would fix it. I couldn't; only God could. Just like everything/everyone else I had tried to fix.

I'm not an expert in any of this. But now that I am looking back at my story in its entirety, I recognize how I unwittingly evolved into a person who was so afraid of life and anything bad that might happen. I also had to take a hard look at all the people whose coping skills, addictions, unhealthy habits (another new generational term for it) affected mine. I needed to recognize that I was molded through the years by all the people in my life. It started with my parents and the attitudes and opinions about life and people that they ingrained in my mind during my formative years. Was my daddy really an alcoholic (clinically), or was he just, like many people I know, using alcohol as a security blanket to cover and protect himself from all the fears and insecurities that he felt? Did he turn out "mean," or were anger and violence his outward signs of fear and defense? Was my mother really a coward and/or a weakling, or was she retreating as her form of defense from all the pain and insecurity she felt?

Upon reflection, what was really happening in my family growing up? And how did my sister and I become such totally different personality types, yet now we are both confident and secure in who we are? All these are rhetorical questions, of course, but certainly ones that caused me to take a look at myself and examine why I felt and reacted the way I have in my life. I wanted to stop being so judgmental of everyone else and deal with my own stuff. I wanted to be better, happier. I can say with assurance that since I stopped wine-ing, I've been able to stop whining. Well, maybe not a hundred percent; I might occasionally still whine a bit, but I'm getting there. I see things now that I had never wanted to recognize. The things I had inadvertently filled my life with. Things that ended up taking up many of the waking hours of my days.

So, I said all that to say this... think about if there might there be some things in your life that you spend more time thinking about than you do of your loved ones? Or, if you are a person of faith, more time than you spend with God? I just challenge you to consider it. I wish I had not waited so long to do it. I didn't want to admit that there were things that had become my standard "go to" when I wanted to unwind, have some peace, respite, or comfort, which are all the things that God tells me He has already provided for me.

That is something only we as individuals can answer. For me, I began to see the hypocrisy in some of the things people sometimes do in the name of Christianity. We might be quick to judge those who have what we deem as "bad addictions" and overlook, even justify, some of what might be our own tendencies and proclivities. And "fixing" often pops up in churches. We talk about "being a fixer", or even a "control freak" as if it's something to be proud of. Like perhaps it's one of our spiritual gifts ... as if God chose us specifically so we can fix others. All the other poor, little saints who just can't seem to get it right. It makes me sad.

I know one thing's for sure ... my going to jail certainly gave me a little more objectivity. Changed my mind about "bad people go to jail and good people go to church." That's just not always true.

I look back now and see how many years I had spent either feeling sorry for myself or making up my mind that it would be solely up to me to fix my life, and that included all the people in it. And for the last sixty years, my attempts at many things I thought would work have not. I had my mind made up that good girls do this, and bad girls do that ... you fill in the blanks for both. I had inserted behaviors, things, and relationships that always felt right at the time, trying to fill a gaping hole that was within me. The little girl who never felt loved, needed, wanted, or appreciated. I used whining, and wine-ing, for all the wrong reasons. I decided to stop.

I recognize now that it was up to me to decide to love myself. Quirks and all. God had accepted me, and He loved me even when all the things were "wrong" with me then, and the things that still are "wrong" now. I dislike that phrase immensely. "What's wrong?" As a society, we ask each other that question all the time. And "Are you okay?" Most of the time we answer each consecutively with, "Nothing," followed by, "I'm fine." But it's often a lie. It took me quite some time to admit it to myself. I never wanted to admit that things were wrong, and I was not fine.

In pursuit of changing myself, I was urged by a friend to go to my first Al-Anon meeting. To be totally honest, I had no idea what Al-Anon was, assuming it was another nickname for Alcoholics Anonymous. Or "AA," as most people called it. I didn't realize that Al-Anon was a support group for loved ones or family members who have been affected by someone's alcoholism. In fact, Al-Anon was founded in 1951 by the wives of the original Alcoholics Anonymous group that was founded in 1935. Its purpose was to offer emotional support for family members who have struggled with a history of family addiction. So, even though I had decided to completely stop drinking, I didn't realize I still had many unresolved issues from the years of growing up in an abusive, alcoholic home. Even now, I discovered I still have an unresolved, deep-rooted fear of anything to do with alcohol. I had tried to convince myself that I didn't, but I began to recognize that many of my issues had stemmed from my many futile attempts to "fix" my family ... starting in my childhood and all the way into adulthood. And I was still doing it.

I thought that somehow it was up to me to be there to fix my daddy, my mother, and anyone else who I perceived "struggled" with it. And, even worse, the "struggle" was defined by ME, not them ... which is wrong. It had never been up to me to define or control. This was when I first heard the term "codependent," defined by Al-Anon as a person who enables, tolerates, or tries to fix an alcoholic. But I have since learned that it goes way beyond that. I have begun to see that it was an insecurity in me that relied on "needing to be needed." I had to learn to let go and recognize that the only person I could change was myself, and the only One I needed was God.

I'm always on a quest to make better anything in me that is not pleasing to God and to be able to answer honestly that I AM fine, because I know that I am loved and accepted. I want to really be set free. In everything. It's a process, though. I had to decide to adopt the attitude that I cannot change other people. If all of us "fixers", or those who proudly profess we are "control freaks" will realize that we will be unsuccessful in our efforts to fix the world and all of its brokenness, and just look inside ourselves instead, we can be at peace with the knowing that we can only change ourselves. As I stated in a previous chapter, but it bears repeating, do an "I" exam. Let's check our vision and decide which lens of life we want to see others through. I have found that grace and mercy win every time.

21

Nolle Prosequi

No prosecution. Will not prosecute. Case dismissed. Expunged. Free to go. It's a Latin phrase used in a court of law. I had never heard of it. Now, I am quite familiar.

Back to December 2015 ... Judgement Day

I stood before the judge Monday in the Douglas County courthouse. Along with many other inmates, and not just the gals who had become my friends that weekend. It was all of us who had been locked up. There is a difference, you know. It's not simply getting arrested; it's getting your butt locked away. What many people don't know—and I was one of them—is that some people who get arrested can get bonded out or post bail on the same day. They are held for a little while, but as soon as the bond or bail is available, they get to go home. Not everyone "goes in" for more than a few hours, and those of us who do leave with an entirely different attitude. We get to know each other. We bond. (No pun intended. Ok, well, it was kind of intended.) We don't escape the sound of those iron doors slamming shut behind us, not to be opened again until we go stand before the judge. Court day is when we get our sentences.

So, the Monday morning following the Friday night we were all locked up, we all went, in a single file line, shuffling toward the courtroom, wearing those ankle chains and handcuffs. Oddly, by then, it didn't seem to hurt as badly as it had on Friday night. We were both male and female. Some contrite; others kicking and screaming in defiance the whole way, all of us wanting the same thing. To be set free. My friends and I waited our turns, holding hands and praying. Yes, praying out loud. It was surreal. But we knew each other by then. We had become friends in that short time we spent together. None of us cared about the various offenses that had brought us there. We had decided to stand together in solidarity. We all held our breath, waiting to be called.

It was my turn. When I walked up to take my place standing before the judge, I had no idea both Gordon and Cale would be sitting in that courtroom. They had come to support me. There are no adequate words to describe the shame I felt standing there. It wrecked me.

"Mrs. Van Dyke? Do you understand the offense with which you have been charged?" the judge spoke without even looking up. She looked like she was performing a rote, perfunctory duty. This was her job. It was like she didn't fully understand she had the power to change our lives.

"Yes Ma'am."

"The report states that you did, in fact, slap one Gordon Van Dyke, dialed 911 yourself, and asked that a police officer be dispatched to your residence. The report also states that you were intoxicated. How do you plead?" She briefly glanced up to look at me.

"Guilty, Your Honor." I managed to hold my head high but couldn't stop the tears that were quietly streaming down my face, my hands still cuffed. I couldn't imagine how my son must have been feeling, seeing his mother like this. I wanted to be strong, but strength eluded me.

The judge turned to face Gordon and Cale. "If you are here on behalf of this defendant, please state your names and your relationship to her."

"Your Honor … my name is Gordon Van Dyke, and I'm the slap-ee." He said it so matter of fact, and with that strong Scottish accent, both the judge and the bailiffs could barely hold back a smile. I heard my new girlfriends behind me snickering, and even I couldn't believe he said it in such a way. But then again, that was Gordon—he wasn't intending to be funny, but he always was.

"So, you're her husband? The victim in this case?" She cocked her head while waiting for his answer.

"Yeah, I guess you can say that. But, Your Honor, I don't call myself a victim, and I didn't want her to be arrested. My wife tends to be a drama queen, and quite honestly, she often exaggerates things. We both had too much to drink that night, and I fell asleep while we were watching a movie. It made her mad, so she tried to wake me up. When I didn't immediately wake up, she slapped me upside the head and shouted, 'WAKE UP!' She didn't mean any harm, Your Honor." He said this like it was honestly no big deal. Meanwhile, I had to close my eyes, shuddering at the thought. The judge looked at him for a few seconds before responding, "Your wife just plead guilty to this offense. So, what's your point?"

"My point is, I don't hold it against her. I don't want to press charges."

"Sir, that is not your choice. While I appreciate your input, the charges have already been filed by Douglas County, and she was arrested and committed to the Douglas County jail. At this point, it is up to me to decide where she goes from here."

She then turned her attention to Cale.

"And young man—your name?"

"My name is Cale Van Dyke, and she is my mom." Everyone present couldn't help but notice that he did not simply state his name and that he was my son. Instead, he said, "She is my mom," which felt so much more personal for some reason. As if to say that he was not simply a character witness for a criminal standing before a judge, but he was making the point *this is my mother.* I hung my head. I had never felt so small.

"Ok, go on … what would you like to say?" The judge looked briefly from him, to me, then back to him. She leaned in and propped her arm on her desk, resting her chin on the palm of her hand.

"Your Honor, my mom is not a criminal; she's a good person. She made a mistake, I know, but I am here, with my dad, to plead for you to let her go. She has always raised my brother and I to understand that everything we do is a choice, and if I've heard her say it once, she's said it a thousand times; 'make a choice; make a WISE choice, because wise choices bring blessings and unwise choices bring consequences.' She and my dad are not perfect, but they have always taught us to do the right thing. Yes, she made an unwise choice Friday night. But I am here to tell you that she is the best mom ever, and we love her and need her to come back home. Please, Your Honor. Please." His voice cracked, and he turned to look at me. I could clearly hear not only his words, but more than that, I heard his heart. The judge was silent for what seemed like an eternity.

"Thank you, young man." She continued to look at him for a few seconds before turning her attention back to Gordon. "And thank you, Mr. Van Dyke. I will certainly take this into consideration before rendering my verdict." With that, she shuffled some papers on her desk, turned on the bench, and asked the bailiff to call the next person forward. Apparently, I had been holding my breath because I felt myself exhale deeply before my shaking legs took me to the holding area. My heart was still beating at a rate that felt like a thousand beats per minute.

After an hour or two, all my cellmates and I had been through the thing we had dreaded most ... standing before the judge, the one who held the power to set us free or keep us in chains. We were escorted back to our cells and instructed to wait until we were informed that the judge had rendered her decisions.

While we waited, we had time to talk about how we felt about our court appearances. Many felt it had not gone well for them, while others were confident that they had convinced the judge they were ready to be released. None of us knew for sure. We prayed together and sincerely took time to encourage each other. None of us sat in judgement regarding whose "thing" was worse. We weren't in competition. We all wanted the same things: another chance; to be forgiven; to be free.

The kitchen staff had already begun serving our dinner trays before anyone heard a word from the court. I was sitting at the cafeteria table when I heard it.

"Van Dyke! Pack up your rack!!"

I jumped up from the table so fast I knocked my tray off. Heart pounding, I was looking around at my friends, obviously confused.

"What does that mean?!"

They erupted into cheers, and, within seconds, they had converged on me. "It means you're getting outta here!!"

"How do I 'pack up my rack'?" I honestly couldn't even think at that moment. Before I knew it, several of the ladies had run into my cell, laughing, and there was a cacophony of shouts. "Don't worry—we got you! Yay, Mama! Way to go!" and various other things I can barely remember. But the one thing that stands out, the thing I'll never ... ever ... forget. They simultaneously surrounded me and lifted me up, arms holding me and forming this sort of mosh pit as they held me above them. As they were holding me up above their shoulders, they were also walking toward the front of the cell block. I heard the familiar, loud siren sound as those iron doors opened slowly, and I heard the whoosh of the air brakes locking it into place. The jailer was standing there just looking at the sight of us, shaking his head. They gently lowered me back down to the floor so I could regain my footing, and as I stood in that doorway, jailer in the outside hall and my fellow cellmates still within the boundaries the cell, I turned around and faced them. I was literally bawling.

"I don't know what to say…" My voice trailed as I stood with mouth agape. "Is it weird to say that I'm gonna miss y'all?" I wasn't laughing, but of course, they all did. Then, one by one, some of them spoke.

"I'm going to miss you."

"Mama, you don't even know how much you helped me."

"You better keep in touch!"

"You changed my life!"

There were other random comments shouted out as I was gathering myself, as they handed me my "packed-up rack," with many saying varying versions of "It was nice to meet you!" as they waved me off. The jailer released the chains from my ankles, then I heard the click of the handcuffs just before he handed me the release documents. But, before I walked down that corridor to freedom, I paused and looked back at everyone, my eyes still filled with tears. I had one more very important thing to say. My first friend there, the beautiful one with the soft brown eyes and the perfect cornrows, the one who had lifted me up off that floor after I had made my call to Cale during intake, the one who had held me in her strong arms until I could breathe, the one who told me to be strong and not cry … my protector, spoke first, "I'll NEVER forget you, Mama." We embraced and cried for only about three seconds before the jailer shouted, "Alright, Van Dyke, let's go!"

As I pulled away, I looked first into her eyes, then at all the girls standing and crowded around that open jail door, and I said, sincerely, "It was MY HONOR to have met you all … truly, my sincere honor. You have changed the way I see life now. I will NEVER forget any of you." I paused and gave my hero friend one last quick hug before I turned and walked down that corridor, free to move my feet without ankle chains. So thankful for all of them, and especially her. I think we probably all knew that we wouldn't really keep in touch and be friends for life, but there genuinely was a very unique and special relationship that had happened. Funny thing, when you're locked in a cell block with other women who have made mistakes, specifically broken the law, unintentional friendships happen. Even if it was just a few days together. A lot can change in a person in that short amount of time.

It was months before I was truly free, at least by the law's standards. Ironically, I now know I was set free the night I was locked up. I had to be bound in physical chains before I recognized the emotional chains that were wrapped around me, choking my life. And all this time, I had believed I was strong. My personal prison had begun when, as a little child, I had unwittingly decided I would make sure that I would have the perfect family. And yet all these years later, I had gone from being someone whom people looked up to and admired, the one who was always ready to offer prayer and counseling to anyone who was struggling, to a woman whom I perceived that everyone would now look down upon. My eyes had been opened. I could not fix everything. I could not control people or situations. I couldn't even control myself. I had relied so heavily upon the approval of others in my life that I had forgotten to approve of myself.

2016

When I went to the court-ordered family counseling session, specifically domestic violence classes for six months, I had to recognize the irony. So, by golly, I used that time to make sure I remained humble and offered friendship, acceptance, kindness, and zero judgment to all the others in the class with me. I dutifully obeyed the court order week after week, showing up early and staying over if someone needed me, participating in the classes and gleaning from everyone's personal stories. During this time, many of my friends, family, and others who loved me wrote letters on my behalf to the Solicitor General's office. I was humbled and thankful. When I received the official document declaring "Nolle Prosequi," I physically dropped to my knees and cried for an hour, clutching it against my chest like it was a piece of life support equipment. A tool that would resuscitate me, wipe away the memories of the past year ... help me pretend it never even happened.

Then I thought, *Why? I don't want to forget it! I want to be a living, breathing testimony of the faithfulness of God—even when I allowed myself to slide down into a pit ... one that I had mostly been responsible for digging. He was always with me. Loving me, forgiving me, lifting me out.*

My record was clean. No one need ever know. I could've gone on with my life and no one need be wiser. Right? But we lived in a small town, and I knew that it would eventually get out. I initially thought it could be one of those family secrets that none of us would want to talk about, mostly because we would be too ashamed or embarrassed to tell it. Even though my family knew, I assumed it would be a subject we just never talked about again. After all, we had been through a lot, and we were all pretty good at forgiving and moving on. No sense dwelling on the past. But what about my co-workers? My church? I admittedly was very afraid to tell people because I most certainly knew I would be judged.

All these thoughts took me back to four years earlier, back in 2011. I remembered I had been sitting in church on a Wednesday night. For many years, Gordon, the boys, and I attended Wednesday night prayer services faithfully. But for some reason, this night I had gone alone. As I sat on a row near the back, also out of character for me, I remember sitting there observing the service and just thinking about how if we all just "got naked" and took off our "church faces," how much freer we could all be. The pastor was asking any of us who needed prayer, who might be struggling with some things that they were ashamed of, to come forward and receive prayer. I was certainly struggling, but I was hesitant to go forward and tell anyone. I felt I had a reputation to protect, and I dare not tell anyone at church what was really going on. I was afraid of their judgement.

Then it occurred to me that if all of us adopted that attitude, none of us would ever allow ourselves to become raw and confess that we had anything that we needed help with. As usual, I feared good ol' Sister Sally. She might be one of the people who prayed with me, but then she'd surely tell someone about my struggles, all in the name of "Pray for Jackie." I decided not to risk it. As I fought the urge to go forward, I sat in the back of the church, bowed my head, and whispered to myself, *Why can't I just get naked and stop covering up all my fears and insecurities?* But I couldn't. I wasn't ready. Back then, I was still trying to fix things. I had become quite good at it. Until I wasn't.

Conclusion

I Finally Lost My Mind ... And I Highly Recommend It

My mind has always been difficult to manage. From as far back as I can remember, I had a wild imagination that was all over the place. I would use imagery and words to create what I wanted to see and hear. When things were sad, I'd make up a happy story, write it down, then read it aloud to myself. It felt more real if I could hear my voice saying it. Same with pictures. I'd use crayons to draw pretty, little girls with full, pink lips, blue eyes with long lashes, and a sweet smile with straight white teeth. And of course, long full hair that was perfectly coiffed and styled with the biggest hairbow I could imagine. Then my mind would take me back to the reality of a scared, little girl who was certain she was anything but pretty. And who rarely smiled. Her eyes were often sad. And scared.

As I grew older, I'd write the story of the young woman who grew into a well-adjusted, got-it-going-on, smart young lady. I drew pictures of her too. She was thin and confident, excellent at her job, and well-respected by her peers. Fearless. She married Prince Charming, had little prince baby boys—also perfect—and lived the fairytale life. Then the reality would come around of the young woman who had dreamed of all this, but in truth had failed at many things and had never really felt respected and needed. The stories that progressed through the years just became striving, trying to make it happen. Never realizing it hadn't been up to her.

I thought about Mama. A LOT. How she never had that fairytale life. Not even close. But she had raised me, and my sister, Jean, to be stronger. She wanted us to have a better life than the one she had endured. I remember when I had grown up, I would often ask her why she put up with the abuse, both physical and verbal, for all those years.

"Mama ... why did you stay with Daddy? Why didn't you leave him? I know I would have!" I bragged, as if I was the epitome of strength.

"Because of you and Jean. I wouldn't have ever been able to provide y'all with the kind of life you both deserved. I couldn't have afforded it!" She had assumed it was all about money, a roof over our heads, having two parents, stability. How ironic.

"Well, I will *never, ever* need a man to take care of me! I can take care of myself!" I would declare with boldness. The truth was, I had viewed myself as strong and independent, but—just like my mama—I had been codependent. I had "controlled" my life, and everyone in it, right into a state of needing to be needed ... to the point where I had neglected to recognize that I believed my worth came from making sure everything in my life was "good." I would keep my husband happy, my kids happy and well-fed, maintain a good job, and live in a nice house. I believed this until the proverbial "bottom fell out."

The year after my arrest and family domestic violence classes—as my eyes were being opened—Mama's health began to decline. She became very frail and was diagnosed with dementia. Jean and I watched her begin to talk about old memories and were surprised at how she spoke of all the happy times. She seemed to have no memories of all the abuse and dysfunction. We were surprised, yet pleased. We didn't want her to spend her last months of life thinking back to those times that we wanted to forget. She passed away peacefully in 2017, and it was then that I recognized I had become a bit like her in that all I wanted was to create the illusion of a woman who did everything for her husband and kids. I would become just as stubborn as she had been until the day she died. I knew my mind was strong too. Just like my mama's.

Fast forward to now. The woman "of a certain age" who's decided that her mind is not what she needed. Or wanted. Who always thought the expression, "Girl, you have LOST your mind!" was a bad thing. Yep, that's me. It was like admitting I was crazy. I probably was throughout a lot of my life. Crazy enough to think I had all the answers to the barrage of questions that always plagued me.

How can I be so full of laughter and sadness at the same time?

So confident, yet so insecure?

So strong, but still weak and fragile?

So put-together, yet so broken?
So FOUND, but still so lost?

The dichotomies, contradictions that we create inside our own minds, yet would never allow our outward selves to reveal. We want to keep it all buttoned up. Because we're Christians and, God forbid, we ever really allow anyone to see what's going on in our lives. How the truth in our lives might dispute our faith. But isn't even that a contradiction? Faith and truth are supposed to be synonymous. They should be, but the problem is in our own minds, our souls—the part of us that is the mind, the will, the emotions. It's a real battleground. I'm honest enough to just admit it. I KNEW the truth. I had studied and memorized all the scriptures. I could quote them backward and forward all day long. like I thought that could change things. As if I could say it out loud enough and swear to myself I really, really ... down in my heart ... believed it. But I was putting my faith in myself. In my ability to believe it "hard enough," I recall the night that changed everything. I had finally lost my mind.

April 2020

It was almost like a dream. Looking back, it still feels like it could have been, but it wasn't. It was very real. It had been a few years since we'd had any "setbacks" in our family. I wanted to believe we were finally past everything that had happened in the past ... but I had been wrong. And I had decided I was not willing to go through it again.

I dragged myself off my bed and stumbled into the bathroom. With trembling hands placed down, one on each side of the sink in that beautiful, black granite vanity, I dropped my head, not daring to look into the mirror. I was shaking, as I felt my knuckles digging into the hard surface. This was what Gordon and I had believed would be our forever home. Our kids were grown up and married. It was where we had decided to retire and spend the last decades of our lives ... happy and problem-free. We had fallen in love with this house from the moment we saw it. It was near the beach in the low country of South Carolina. The manicured lawn, lush and green, in stark contrast to the sparkling blue pool, a lovely walking trail behind it, and a 200-year-old live oak tree in the front yard, its gnarly branches reaching out like giant arms wrapped around our little piece of paradise.

It took me a few minutes to dare to lift my hanging head and see who might be looking back at me. Would it be the strong version of myself—the one that I preferred—the one who was always there for everyone else? Or was that the person I had contrived in my own mind because that was how I wanted to see myself? The other option might be the pathetic heap of uselessness I felt at the moment. The one who was the most realistic version of myself. The one who'd been lying there crying nonstop for the past two hours, not sure if I should allow the pain to do its work in me, or perhaps I could confess it all away like I had done for years. Declaring the words I had memorized and on which I had repeatedly stood firmly. I wasn't ready to look up to find out. I felt the tears fall out like the first, giant droplets of rain just before the storm came through. I made the choice and began to utter the scriptures ... my voice weak and cracking at first.

"We shall live in peaceful dwelling places, secure and in undisturbed places of rest ...

The rain will fall, the streams will rise, and the winds will blow and beat against the house, but it will not fall because it has its foundation on the rock ... The Lord blesses the home of the righteous..." My voice trailed off. I whispered one last phrase ... the one that mattered, "In Jesus's name."

Then I remembered that I was taught it worked better if I spoke them loudly and with authority. Maybe even shout them. My sister had reminded me that "the righteous are as bold as a lion!" She'd found her voice after all these years. Now she was the strong one.

"Shout it, Jackie! Make sure the devil can HEAR you!"

Apparently, old Beelzebub himself was hard of hearing. He wasn't deaf though. I tried, but the attempt was in vain. I was tired. Really tired. Weary of feeling like I always had to be strong. To not only know the right words but have the "believe it" factor too. Faith, it was called. And without it, it would be impossible to please God. What might happen if I didn't please Him? I honestly didn't care at that moment. Too many things had happened over the years. It seemed when I was "strong enough," it worked. But not always. And I didn't feel like rolling the dice right now. I decided to just stand there and cry. So, what if God's disappointed in me? It wouldn't be the first time. I wasn't even trying to be pleasing today.

After a few minutes, I managed the strength to lift my head and look into that mirror. The reflection looking back at me was sad. Mascara mixed with tears smeared my raccoon-esque eyes. My nose was red and misshapen after lying on the bed, pressing against it with a wad of tissues for two hours. My downturned mouth had evidence of a trail of saliva on the right side. I was a disgusting mess. I *couldn't continue to look. Head back down, barely still standing, only being propped by that vanity, I decided to do it. Speak to God. But maybe not using the scriptures I always had. Maybe I'd just get real with Him. Get naked. Not be afraid to show Him all the hurt and broken pieces.*

"Ok, God ... so I'm just going to say this. If it's okay with You, can I just not do this anymore? Because I don't think I can. I'm not good at it." The words barely came out as a raspy, broken whisper. I decided it was a dumb thing to pray anyway. I shook my head and turned away from the sink and headed back toward my bed. I thought to myself, what a freakin' loser ... I'm not strong enough this time. I felt like I had a rip in my chest that I would never be able to stitch up. And I had lost the desire to even try. I stumbled back onto my bed. My pillow was still soaked. I could barely breathe. I'd done everything I could do. I'd prayed all the prayers; I'd cried all the tears; I'd quoted all the scriptures I could remember. I couldn't fix my life that had, once again, seemed to spin out of control. I quieted down. Listening. Would He answer me? Silence.

After lying there in the fetal position for another half hour or so, I remembered a phone conversation I had with my son just that morning. His words began to resound in my head, words that I wanted to remember. They began to drown out the hateful voices I imagined I heard. His were words of faith.

"You can handle this, Mom! I know you can! You've always been one of the strongest Christians I know!"

What do people mean when they say that? What does a "strong Christian" act like? Aren't we all fallible? Why don't I feel strong right now? I genuinely didn't even give it the effort. Anyway, I was tired of praying and crying all the time. I wanted to shut my mind down. I fumbled for the remote and decided to turn on the television. It happened to be on the music channel. Good. I didn't feel like listening to people talk. I put my head back on my pillow and closed my eyes, taking a deep breath. That's when I heard the voice of Lauren Daigle crooning out a tune from her album, Look Up Child, and the lyrics were immediately louder than the voices in my head. The song was "You Say." These are some of the words (paraphrased),

I had been fighting voices that were telling me that I am not enough–that I had never been enough and never would be. The lies were telling me that I'd never measure up.

But God reminded me that I AM loved, even when I don't feel anything.

That I AM strong, even at my lowest, weakest point.

That I am always held in His hands, even when I feel like I'm falling short and never measuring up.

All the times I had felt that I didn't belong, He reminded me that I belong to HIM.

Rise up, Girl. Declare the truth.

That night, I made a decision. I won't give up. I won't stop declaring the words that have sustained me since that day when I was twelve years old and met "that Guy" at camp.

- 1 Peter 5:10 — He will restore, confirm, strengthen and establish me.

- Psalms 34:18 — He is near to the brokenhearted and saves those who are crushed in spirit.

- James 1:2-4 — The testing of our faith produces perseverance and makes us mature and complete.

- John 3:16 — Because God SO loves us!

- Colossians 3:2 — Set our minds on things above and not on the things of the earth.

- Romans 12:2 — Be transformed by the renewing of our minds.

- 2 Corinthians 10:5 — Bring every thought captive and into obedience to the word. His word.

- Philippians 4:7 — The peace of God will guard our hearts and our minds.

- 1 Corinthians 2:16 — We have the mind of Christ.

- Philippians 2:5 — Let this mind be in you—the same mind that is in Christ Jesus.

These are just a few examples of the scriptures (paraphrased) where God reminds us that He loves us, is for us, and that He has given us the same mind and Spirit that Jesus has! So, YES, I decided to lose my mind; it was causing too much trouble. And of course, even when things still aren't going perfectly for me, I remind myself of one of my all-time favorites…

- Romans 8:28 — For we know that in ALL things, God is working for the good of those who love Him and have been called according to His purpose.

Tackling the "fixer syndrome," then recognizing codependency personality, is a long and difficult journey. And I couldn't do it without my personal relationship with Jesus. He's the ultimate "fixer" ... my Savior.

He is faithful, even when I'm not.

I am loved, and so are you. I am free, and you can be too. Take it one step, one day, at a time. Never give up. All the charges have been dropped.

Nolle Prosequi!

Afterword

Dear Reader:

I hope that, in reading the chapters of this memoir, you have gleaned even just a drop in the ocean of wisdom that is my lovely mother, Jackie Van Dyke. The stories, sentiments, and laugh-out-loud statements contained in these pages speak to the larger-than-life person and woman of God that she is. Simply put, I would not be who I am without her constant nurture, unwavering support, and faith-filled prayers. You are blessed to catch a glimpse of the woman she is, yet I am filled with immense gratitude that I get to see her for the spiritual giant she is.

The message of this book is simple to understand, yet complex in how we apply it. Living as open and as honest as we can before God and each other is what we all strive for, but often come up short of in the chase for recognition, attention, and security as the world defines them. Mom would be the first to tell you (as she has through this book) that God alone knows us deeply and intimately, and therefore He's qualified to write our story and use us in whatever way He sees fit. The story of my mom's life (and quite possibly, yours) is one of hardship, yet triumph. Battles, yet victory. Darkness, yet supernatural light. What makes her so amazing is not her perfection, but her faithfulness. I can only pray that you and I learn to follow God with such tenacity and conviction, knowing the reality of the Scripture: "If God be for us, who can ever be against us?" (Romans 8:31).

This is not just a story, but a testimony to the faithfulness and goodness of God. It's a testimony I've seen lived out for almost 28 years. It's inspired me to love God and people NEKKID-ly (without a mask or cover-up, but with a genuine heart). My mom loves the way I feel Jesus loves us: boldly, kindly, holding nothing back. I am forever grateful to be under the covering of this kind of love. You should be too.

—**Cale Van Dyke**, Next-Gen Pastor, LifeGate Church, Villa Rica

About the Author

Jackie Brewer Van Dyke is a southern gal, born and raised in rural Alabama. She has been a storyteller from way "back in the day." As she grew older, she especially enjoyed writing skits and plays, giving her the chance to dress up, be on stage, and pretend to be someone else—a character. Even as an outgoing little girl, she preferred to keep herself hidden, always wondering if she would be judged as being in a family from "the wrong side of the tracks." Only in the past decade, Jackie decided to just "get nekkid," deciding to strip down and live life uncovered and authentic.

Dogs are her favorite "people," and Wick the Weimaraner is her best friend and loyal follower. Most days Wick lies at Jackie's feet as she crafts words into story while enjoying her two favorite food groups—chocolate and coffee—accompanied by 70's music bouncing off the walls in her writing room.

Currently living west of metro-Atlanta, Jackie is a Jesus-loving wife, mother, and "MJ" to five amazing grandsons. She enjoys thrift-store shopping and refinishing furniture because she relates to the "junk" people throw away, believing that with a little love and a coat of paint, usefulness and beauty can be restored.

Jackie retired from her "real job"—a lifelong career providing eye exams to help people see better. Now she likes to do "I" exams, a careful process of self-discovery that she loves sharing with readers. Yeah, Jackie loves a good metaphor.

Made in the USA
Middletown, DE
21 August 2023

37111936R00137